LONGTERM SAFETY CULTURE IMPLEMENTATION

(make it simple and scientific from workplace to anyplace)

Dr Harbans Lal Kaila

(Behavioural Safety Expert)

2022

Published by

Prints Publications Pvt Ltd
Viraj Tower-2, 4259/3, Ansari Road,
Darya Ganj, New Delhi-110002
Tel. : +91-11-45355555
Fax: +91-11-23275542
E-mail : contact@printspublications.com
Website : www.printspublications.com

ISBN 978-81-927694-6-2

Price : ₹ 995/-

Published and Printed by Mr. Pranav Gupta (Director) on behalf of Prints Publications Pvt Ltd at Mohit Enterprises, Delhi.

Contents

Preface

In India, the employers' pocket size decides the safety size for employees.

Whether employees deserve safety system or culture or no safety is decided by how much profit comes to the company. Care comes second, it is money first, not safety first. That is the bottom line. So the future of businesses is at risk, as without safety, the business does not get sustained.

The at-risk behaviours at site are life threatening to employees and business threatening for employers. Of course, it is preventable with behavioural safety culture. Switch to a BBS approach for sustainable future of your businesses caring employees' safety right. Let's change the OSH scene together.

It is to be realised that at-risk behaviours in industries are unsafe to the citizens in the civil societies, sometimes disabling, injurious, even fatal.

Safety is a moment of spot-correction, Rest is in scope of an incident. Spot-correction is a function of one and all to achieve safety culture.

Sometimes, due to certain contingencies, it is real difficulty for site leaders to convince some people that HSE violations are not acceptable to practice.

There seems to be a bleak future of businesses if companies are not establishing longterm supportive safety culture. Though a large number of companies believe in this, yet they do not appear to be acting accordingly.

Only a few big corporates have implemented proactive safety culture successfully. Others are still thinking or planning for the same. Hence, in this respect, this book can serve as a boon to save both life and business from the incidents and accidents, as every site in India has quite high percentage of at-risk behaviours. One needs to decide fast, choose safety culture or lose.

Acknowledgments

All experts, professionals, institutions, industries, family, friends, publishers, and nearly 5,000 research participants contributed over 2 years to this knowledge base for making societies safer, are thankfully acknowledged for making this publication possible.

Dedication

This publication is dedicated to the entire workforce for their daily contributions in developing supportive safety culture.

Experts' Messages to Industry

Perumal Manoharan
President,
Safety Engineers Association (India)

Traditionally, Engineering controls and Motivation of employees are considered as the prime focus areas in accident prevention and better safety performance. This has not produced desired results and the awareness has come that focus on the behaviour of the people shall be the focus point. Based on this the concept of "Behaviour based safety" has emerged and many companies have significantly improved their safety performance after including Behaviour based safety as a tool in their safety management programme.

In this book. Dr.Kaila has dealt with the need for long term safety culture, its importance and its relevance at this present juncture where the world is working in new norms due to Covid 19.

Narratives in this book on Industrial safety culture, Behavioural bench marking, Role of educational institutions and other subjects are of very much important and relevant.

This book also deals with the challenges in "Making safety as a way of life" in Indian society.

This book will help the safety professionals for developing suitable strategy to elevate the safety performance to the higher level at their work place.

◆◆◆

P.K. Sinha
Ex Executive Director (Safety, Environment management)
NTPC Ltd

It's truly a noble initiative you have taken towards the benefit of industry and people working there. "Organisational antecedents are a kind of prop which works as a support route in weakening the existing safety culture. There should be only a Go or No-Go treatment in behaviour at the workplace. The No-Go gate should bear a penal action depending upon the potential of violations. Leaning on antecedents in explaining an at-risk behaviour allows build up of probabilities for a serious consequences".

◆◆◆

Dr S.P. Garg
Advisor(HSE) & Former Executive Director, GAIL
Co-Chairman FICCI Committee on Disaster Management
Board of Governor, National Safety Council

Developing a good Safety culture in the organization, should be on top of agenda for all forward looking organizations, to ensure long term business sustainability.

I personally keep advocating this requirement, whenever I interact with audience, on the subject. Behaviour based safety is one such component which has large contribution in this direction. Renowned author of the book, Dr Kaila, to whom I know since many years, is very thorough on the subject and has vast knowledge and experience.

This book will enlighten the readers on the very interesting and very apt subject of discussion, these days, i.e. "Safety Culture". He has also put-in all his learnings and experience of Covid-19 period into the book, relating changes observed in human behaviour to certain type of organizational safety performance. Wishing all success to the book."

◆◆◆

R. Shankar

Head – Quality, Safety, Sustainability, Systems & Process Improvements, Sterling & Wilson Solar, Dubai

An organisations' culture is best indicated by the way their workforce behaves when they're away from the workplace.

A shared vision of the people of a Zero Harm future would be the bedrock of a safety culture, reflected by the safety beliefs, values, attitudes and reflecting in everyday behaviour.

◆◆◆

K.K. Sharma
Whole Time Director- EHS,
DCM Shriram Ltd.

In the past 15 months, we all have witnessed direct and indirect pandemic affect jeopardizing many lives with its devastating and painful impacts. It is important to note that Covid appropriate behaviour was a key in controlling the spread of pandemic however due to lack of awareness among majority of the urban and sub-urban communities the spread was uncontrollable beyond anyone's imagination. Unsafe behaviours could be one of the reasons for wide spread of infection even to rural areas during the second wave. This could have been avoided or the extent of damage would have been reduced if people would have behaved responsibly following various Covid appropriate behaviours.

A strong safety culture begins with visible management's commitment and highly engaged & empowered employees at all levels. This result in happy stakeholders due to reduced costs, increased plant reliability and availability, reduced maintenance and better product quality besides other intangible benefits of motivated employees and happy customers making it more sustainable profitable business. I firmly believe BBS is a tool which can be successfully used to mitigate risks arising out of Occupational health and safety as well as process safety.

Furthermore, there is need to extend BBS program to employees families and other key stakeholders of our society especially children and youngsters. This could only be achieved through intervention of Educational institutions and public forums raising awareness on BBS to make it a way of life. One could imagine huge benefits of reducing road accidents; controlling Pandemic and reducing industrial accidents etc. which ultimately would help in creating a happy society.

The prime challenge in implementation of BBS program is the involvement of all employees including contract employees which can only be possible once fear from their minds be removed for carrying out spot correction of at-risk behaviours on the shop floor. In other words, a buy-in by each employee is of paramount for successful BBS implementation. This can be demonstrated by Head of the Departments and other senior leadership team through their visible actions reinforcing safe behaviors and reducing at-risk behaviours. It is pertinent to regularly review the BBS checklist for inclusion of new risks such as Road safety, Covid Appropriate behaviours and Psychological Health etc. in addition to already identified at-risk behaviours. Employees should be encouraged for openly reporting of at-risk behaviours without any fear with 'No Blame-No Fault-No Name' way with prime objective of on the spot fault correction to reduce the risk of accident.

Safety culture is sum of beliefs, attitudes and practices being followed in various activities of business. Hence, positive safety management through BBS program ensures that the businesses are making sustainable profits. A strong safety culture ensures everyone is empowered and feels responsible for safety and pursues it on daily basis by carrying out spot correction of at-risk behaviours without any fear with prime objective of Zero Harm to anyone. When an employee feels valued, listened to and truly cared about, his or her outlook towards the organization is different with high morale and full of positivity in all other aspects too. This puts onus on the senior management to create an environment in which employees feels comfortable speaking up when they see safety hazards or at-risk behaviours. Thus,making Safety a way of life.

I believe creating safety culture through BBS is like a marathon which needs lot of patience, commitment and endurance to reach the finish line for seeing the final results however what matters is the first step taken which is worth it.

The foundation of Behavioural Based Safety (BBS) is positive safety management with focus on caring of people around taking proactive actions to minimize the risk of accidents. Be it work place or outside workplace i.e. in our communities, schools, colleges and other social places, BBS can be applied for all in transforming the culture for creating a safer place of living.

I would like to wish the very best to Dr. H L Kaila for bringing out this book which will be useful for operational team and safety professionals to continuously develop and build on safe practices and to achieve the highest levels of safety excellence. This would play a key role in transforming the behaviours of key stakeholders especially employees and their families and community at large especially our next generation by making safety a way of life building a strong foundation.

◆◆◆

M.K. Rao

Ex-Executive Director, India Glycols

"The book touches upon many topics of today's relevance. I expect it to be a great resource for improving safety culture of organizations and also sustaining the desired culture in the long run"

◆◆◆

G. M. Sivaramakrishna Rao
Ex- Head Safety of Afcons, and Lanco, GMR.

The topics included in the book are very apt and futuristic.

Behavioural benchmarking is one of the most desired inputs for the wellbeing of the workmen. The industry craves for the social wellbeing. Safety is the core value in the industries of the developed nations. There has been dramatic changes in the benchmarking of the safety statistics from all the developed nations. Similarly, environmental standards are implemented as a disciplinary benchmarks. Now due to spread of pandemic COVID-19, health standards and benchmarking have been dramatically improved. but Safety is way beyond the environmental and health benchmarking. It is still starving for the benchmarking. The root cause of every injury caused by incident is behaviour. The fraternity must find metrics to measure the behavioural changes and improvements. This will have cascading effect on environmental and health also.

◆◆◆

Dr Suresh K. Singh
Ex General Manager (HSE), IOCL, Director, Forum of Behavioural Safety, Director, Parbind Petsafety Private Ltd.
Email ID- sksiocl83@gmail.com, parbindpetsafety@gmail.com

Behaviour – a key issue for safety performance: I have been associated with Dr H L Kaila for over ten years as an associate to implement Behavior-Based-Safety in Oil & Gas sector operating unit. The concept which he has chosen is really commendable and highly beneficial to the people & organization as a whole. He has already written number of books on subject related to Behavior-Based-Safety and industries including got advantage of his contributions towards building safe working culture in the organization specially at work place.

He is so much dedicated towards building safety culture through Behavior-Based-Safety concept. He has also given a non-profit organization "Forum of Behavioural Safety" in 2016 and had been organizing various National conferences since then. As a HSE professional, I realized that BBS is only tool to avoid not only accidents even near-miss also.

With this book, he is trying to penetrate into education institution and society through BBS and I am sure each segment shall be benefitted from this book.

I expect him to bring a book for CEO of the organizations with case history so that they will be implementing BBS in their organization.

I wish this book becomes one of the highest selling books in HSE sector.

◆◆◆

Chapter Outline

1. *Organisational Antecedents for Managers' Silence over At-Risk Behaviours*

We do not speak up for others safety as we do not feel connected or we are not sensitised. The world witnessed accidents in almost all sectors killing hundred thousands people and animals across the globe over the decades. Incidents continue in spite of major engineering and technological advancements. The human behaviours matter a lot in this respect. Indian industry managers did not reflect courage, and remained silent to stop at-risk behaviours at sites. As a result, the incidents continue, people lose their lives, get disabled or injured. 342 HSE professionals across Indian locations participating in a qualitative research reflected that the psychological safety embedded in organisational antecedents would improve the relationships with others, employees perceptions of the organisational climate, employees assessment of the safety issue, or characteristics of the job safety, and then in turn, would motivate employees for voicing safety concerns over at-risk behaviours. In overall, managers in most industry sectors were silent over at-risk behaviours.

2. *Case of COVID-19 in view of Behavioural Safety and Health Culture in India*

During the Covid19 scenario, this chapter addresses behavioural safety cultural issues as to why do people take health and safety risks? what are the similarities between Covid19 and behavioral based safety (BBS) management as both interventions drive behavioural change? How to implement BBS post-lockdown in plants? What are the behavioral challenges and solutions to contain Covid19? This article is based on qualitative methods such as interviews, focused group discussions, field surveys. Objective is to review the current scenario and enable people to use this researched information for effective management of behavioural safety culture. Implications are discussed in view of safety cultural context in India.

3. Educational Institutions Need to Focus 'Health and Safety' as COVID-19 reminded

Hundred of thousands students were killed in several incidents at educational institutions in past many years. This research article considers whether 'Health and Safety' in educational settings is need of the hour as Covid19 reminds us. At the same times, other questions also line up. Whether educational settings updated their safety and health practices post-Covid19, and whether would it make them more safety-efficient post-Covid19? Personal in-depth discussions/ focused interviews (with 342 health, safety, environment (HSE), medical, education, management, and mental health professionals across the country) recommended 'health and safety management system' in educational institutions in order to avert and combat the impacts of Covid19-like risks more efficiently. These institutions also updated their HSE management due to onset of Covid19.

4. Why Industry is Losing Faith in Safety Awards?

Heath and safety systems are at the crossroads while in each country hundreds of people are killed while working each year. This paper questions whether the HSE awards failed to recognise or promote best safety practices in organisations.? Safety awards in industry are for business excellence and/or the safety excellence is a critical moot question that needs to probe. For many decades, these awards were so popular in industry, what are the reasons that now people in industry are losing faith in these awards. This article explores the underlying reasons for the same through this qualitative research analysis involving 250 HSE professionals. Ten aspects of these safety awards have come out in the findings of this research, the implications of which are discussed for promoting safety culture. About 80% professionals agreed that the industry is losing interest as HSE awards are merely documents-based, the evaluation criteria are poor, and mostly the commercial awards are being avoided.

5. Contribution of Civil Society toward Industrial Safety Culture

It was the first time ever during the Covid-19 period that the civil society groups participated so actively for their health and safety concerns all over the countries, and the civil society is now emerging stronger year-on-year to represent on worldly issues. This article attempts to explore the civil societies' contributions towards building the safety cultures of industries, and how it may help achieving a safe place to live and work. The journey from a civil society mindset to an industrial culture poses challenges of change and its implementation. This chapter brings forth the positive dynamics between the safety mindsets of civil societies and industries, and a possibility of better relationship between businesses and civil society.

6. Active Humanism in Public Safety Behaviours to Defeat COVID-19 and Restore Economy: Long-term Solution, Not Fire-fighting Approach

The world lost hundred thousands human lives due to Covid19. Could the behavioural safety practices have helped us from covid19 fatalities and also the worsening economy, and how would citizens participation help achieving this objective for future, are the critical questions that concern all of us as citizens for our contribution to creating a safe society by following just safe behaviours. Based on interactions with 252 HSE professionals from diverse backgrounds, this chapter articulates as to what are the disabling or enabling factors towards exploring these questions, and how this objective can be reached in a perspective. It is recommended to incorporate 'Health and Safety Care by each other' by creating awareness among all citizens for 'an observation and spot-correction of any at-risk behaviour from workplace to anyplace daily once'. An individual citizens behaviour whether voting or safety or health behaviour has the power to make a narrative or rule for our country. However, the world is likely to experience many Covid19 waves till the societies learn and adopt proper masking and distancing behaviours. As behavioural changes at national level are gradual, the efforts have to sustain as planned interventions to combat Covid19. Citizens need to understand that Covid19 appropriate behaviours would give nearly 100 percent protection from infection, which is even higher protection than the vaccines could do. A multi-pronged action plan is recommended based on research findings. If India remains in fire-fighting approach and not installing permanent solution, it would affect economy adversely further. Towards success in the Covid19 test, as nations prepare for future, let citizens now focus on safe behaviours.

7. Managing the Difference between Safety Documentations and At-risk Behaviours in Industry

Safety is in behaviour, not in documents. An overemphasis on documentation may underemphasise safety in behaviours. Mismatch of HSE documentations with that of ground behaviours would raise many serious doubts. Of course, there are many reasons as to why the safety documentations and ground realities differ in behaviours among Indian organisations. Probably they do not know how to reduce at-risk behaviours and precisely that is why the incidents do not stop. But there are transformations in the attitudes of management and HSE professionals. This chapter presents the qualitative and quantitative results, discusses the implications and provide experiential conclusions of 243 HSE professionals to improve safety culture as discussed in this article, to save people from injuries and fatalities. The conclusions for the difference between safety documentation and behavioural reality include shocking factors such as missing safety message down the levels, safety documentation to make authorities happy, poor adherence to documentation requirements, compromising risk is a regular practice, no review of unsafe behaviours for corrective action, fast businesses delivering incidents, only behavioural awareness program, not planned intervention, and not focusing on the antecedents of safe/unsafe behaviours. Recommendations are reflected for managing the difference between safety documentations and at-risk behaviours in organisations.

8. Behavioural Benchmarking as a Robust Tool of Total Safety Culture in Industries

People in industry think that if they received awards in business excellence, they are obviously best in safety as well, that is actually not the case. Behaviour based safety (BBS) benchmarking is an approach to comparative assessment of the impact and effectiveness of a BBS program. Most BBS benchmarking compares the successful implementation of BBS in terms of its qualitative and quantitative results. This chapter presents the rich experiential logical conclusions of 171 HSE professionals to compare and contrast peer companies or locations that used BBS approach in similar ways, and within the same industry. Recommendations would help organisations benchmark and improve their safety culture on the basis of a defined criteria as well as the implications of parameters, comparison and safety versus business excellence, as discussed in this chapter.

9. Planned Intervention of Behaviour-based Safety Helps organisations Improve their Safety Time Arithmetic

This chapter describes the value of an intervention of behaviour-based safety (BBS) that can increase the safety time of organizations for collective control of incidents and promote outcomes of positive safety culture as evidenced in research, field based interventions, experiences and practice. The results revealed that safety time arithmetic in organizations can be improved to obtain positive safety culture outcomes to save life and business in companies. The pain of daily fatalities at sites should become a motivational force for committed corporate leaders to achieve zero harm, zero at-risk behaviours, positive safety actions with every effort and cost, and prepare their men and women at sites for daily observation and spot-correction of all at-risk behaviours and other hazards, and continue sharing positive safety actions throughout the organisation.

10. Possibilities and Challenges of Making Safety a 'Way of Life' in Indian Society

How to make safety as a way of life, whether this objective is a myth or reality? This paper provides the results of an exploration study. Enablers and barriers, examples and experiences are discussed related to the possibilities and challenges of making safety a 'Way of Life' in Indian society. It involved 540 Health, Safety and Environment Professionals using focus group discussions/interviews and webinars. From the results implications are drawn toward the research objectives as well as reflections on the existing safety culture and its challenges and solutions.

11. Mission Bharat Bane Surkshit: Safer Corporate India by Behavioural Science Approach

Focusing on the prevention of losses of life and business (in the context of daily incidents like fires and fatalities at sites), this article is based on the industrial settings of Indian corporates, and is an endeavour to address on the possibilities, approach and vision of how an ambitious corporate safety movement namely Bharat Bane Surkshit (BBS) is achievable, through an understanding of a variety of key aspects such as positive outcomes of BBS implementation and key persons in companies who implemented it, BBS culture rating, quality of observations and spot-correction of at-risk behaviours, criteria for selection of BBS observers, dependent safety culture as a risk in safety approach. Other aspects included are the BBS organizational procedure to behaviouralize ISO 45001, focusing on the margins of BBS implementation to optimize it, BBS content design for HODs. adopting site BBS policy, and the recommendations of the 4th BBS national conference of the Forum of Behavioural Safety, 2020.

12. Exploring and Managing Psychosocial Risks in Organisations as per ISO45003

According to ISO 45003:2021: psychosocial risks and hazards are recognised as critical challenges to health, safety, well-being at work and also affecting overall business excellence. ISO 45001 would help manage such risks in the workplaces for enabling employers and employees to address these risks. An objective of this chapter is to focus on exploring these psychosocial risks in organisations, and recommend the doable and practical solutions. One hundred eighty HSE professionals across Indian locations in multiple industrial sectors, reflected their viewpoints. The psychosocial risks across industries are found to be similar irrespective of sectors/locations.

13. Behavioural Economics of Safety Culture Management in Companies

Most companies care for money and profits more than the safety of their human resources. Why companies managements and employers do not decide to spend on safety cultural aspects, as because they are not concerned or less sensitive towards unsafe way of working leading to disaster, incidents, family suffering, impact on new generations, gas leakages, or they are not aware that the benefits of safety implementation in any company, small or big, would definitely outweigh the monetary gains of not implementing it. This article discusses these factors based on observations of 309 HSE and HR professionals, and makes recommendations for HSE policy and planning for safe businesses caring for human cost or losses. While considering the economics of safety management approach, it is important to understand as to why companies stop and refresh their actions for programs leading to longterm safety culture. Though, the slogan seems to have changed, i.e. behaviour first, as we used to say, safety first. However, a large number of Indian companies (90%) are still not able or willing to decide over safety culture management for a variety of reasons as discussed in this chapter.

CHAPTER 1

Organisational Antecedents Responsible for Managers' Silence Over At-Risk Behaviours

Introduction

If you are a safe driver, you could save even a blind puppy provided you have a compassion in your heart and a minute for the other. "If you care, you can save even anyone, and communicate that you care even an animal". My daughter got down from her car to check whether the puppy got hurt as her husband applied brake. She touched puppy and he just felt better and turned a bit, then she saw a token around his neck on which two mobile numbers were written, she called up to check, and the lady said yes, "puppy belonged to her, but he is blind", which my daughter obviously didn't know. Actually she got down from the car because puppy did not move off the road, even car reached near him, as he didn't have an ability to see. So you got to be sensitive to care for one such being also around. Just care (Personal Communication with Sunayna, 2021, June 5).

Speak up if you care. When employees voluntarily do not communicate suggestions, concerns, information about problems, or work-related opinions, and they withhold such input, they are displaying silence and depriving their organization of potentially useful information. There are antecedents and outcomes of such silences of employees

(Morrison, 2014). Employees fear experiencing conflict or controversy, causing both performance and employee morale to suffer. Such fear of speaking up, referred to as 'defensive silence (Jan *et al.*, 2020). Employees stay silent about safety issues based on perceptions of altering relationships with others (relationship-based), perceptions of the organizational climate (climate-based), the assessment of the safety issue (issue-based), or characteristics of the job safety silence is defined as a type of silence when workers do not talk to supervisors about safety issues (Manapragada and Bruk-Lee, 2016).

COVID-19 scenario precipitates that people do not maintain silence when they observe others around not adhering to COVID-19 appropriate behaviours or any at-risk behaviours. "COVID-19 didn't create as many problems as people themselves are doing by their thinking and behavior". "Actually aisa hi hai" (that's what it is), says a Municipal officer Anushree. There were increasing incidents of COVID-19. Everything comes to standstill. Besides there is lockdown announced. Fortunately, industry sites that implemented behavioural safety didn't get as many coronavirus numbers as sites that didn't implement (Kaila, 2020).

Study Objective

The present article is focused to explore the organisational antecedents responsible for managers' silence over at-risk behaviours in multiple industrial sectors, and recommend solutions thereof.

Research Methodology

A total of 342 HSE professionals across Indian locations reflected their viewpoint on what are the organisational antecedents responsible for managers' silence over at-risk behaviours. Multiple industrial sectors such as chemical, oil, petroleum and gas, engineering, manufacturing, power, energy, and construction industries were included in this study. Both primary and secondary data were collected from the study participants with diverse backgrounds of age, experience, designation and education. Open-ended questions based interviews and personal in-depth discussions with HSE professionals were conducted through remote data collection techniques over 3-months (May to July, 2021). Qualitative content and thematic analysis were performed.

Results and Discussion

What are the organisational antecedents responsible for managers' silence over at-risk behaviours? In the context of contemporary India, more organisations are finding that employee voice is critical for developing business intelligence. Yet, organisations often find their employees mostly silent (Subhakaran, 2020).

According to Maheshwaran, a safety professional, "many factors are responsible for managers silence over at-risk behaviours, such as, time schedule of the project, production target, profit, peer pressure, past interventions that fetched bad image to the managers, reactive safety culture, labour unions and their policy, indecisive or unsupportive top management". Management reaction to failure is of shock and disbelief. It should be taken as a learning, and we should move on. It should be accepted as an unintentional deviation (Personal communication with Pavan Rao, HSE Head of a multinational company).

Organisational antecedents responsible for managers' silence over at-risk behaviours:

There are a combination of organisational issues in each of the work sites. As described below, each industrial sector or site has a unique scenario that inhibits or boosts voices of people for safety.

1. Combined factors effect: 84% of HSE professionals reported that many organisational antecedents influence together such as normalisation of deviance, reactive organisational culture, complacency, time/peer pressure, overconfidence. Lack of competency, My two cents. Managers' work performance and good faith against the output is considered every where. Consequences of committee working exist, sometime total silenceness, sometime too much chaos. All these factors combine to work as normalisation of deviance for people at work (Dan, 2021).

2. In engineering and manufacturing industries specifically, 72% of HSE professionals reported that managers keep silence over at-risk behaviours in many situations and it can't be corrected unless there is a change of mindset of managers. High motivation is needed. While the benefits of psychological safety are well established, a new survey suggests how leaders, by developing specific skills, can create a safer and higher-performance safe work environment (McKinsey & Company, 2021).

3. In chemical industries specifically, 78% of HSE professionals reported that it is personal attitude that is above all, if a person feels he cares for anyone and his/her action can risk others including manager, then he will speak-up for sure. In addition, organisation culture and deficiency of resources will act as deterrent or catalyst for manager's action. A study results indicated that safety leadership and attitude factors as well as their interactions predicted safety motivation and knowledge (Basahel, 2021).

4. In oil industries specifically, 76% of HSE professionals reported that the contributing antecedents are weak safety culture, lack of knowledge on HIRA, lack of creating

sensitivity towards safety matters and caring attitude among employees, lack of soft skills among managers to properly counsel the person doing at-risk behaviours etc. The safety culture found itself in the center of interest in order to optimize the impact of corporate culture on the security and safety behavior of employees (Vel'as, 2021).

5. In petroleum and gas industries specifically, 74% of HSE professionals reported that the contributing antecedents are like Ignorance, Poor communication, Non-professionalism, Poor managerial attributes, Overconfidence, Casual approach. Easy going attitude, Target based incentive etc. The oil and gas industry, being potentially one of the most hazardous industry sectors, it's essential for safety managers and supervisors to identify and communicate recommended safety controls and hazards that exist on each work site before work begins (Smith, 2018).

6. In power and energy industries specifically, 69% of HSE professionals reported that pressure approach from company's group top management and lack of intent. Fear of reporting, Enforcing for job completion in schedule time, not having provision of time for safe completion of work. The Economic Times (2021) reported that leave aside ESG, India's bigger problem is EHS.

7. In construction industries, 88% of HSE professionals reported that there are many antecedents for managers' silence as below:

Dependent safety culture: By and large, safety is still considered as the responsibility of safety department, there is no wholehearted involvement from management,

Safety qualification: Safety qualification is not mandatory for managers at entry level. Their understanding and perception always remain at low.

Low perception level: They feel that at risk behaviours despite being present in existing set up are not always leading to injury, hence secondary importance is attached to it. Profit entity: Safety is always considered as a profit entity. Generally it is perceived as something which didn't bring business despite being part of contract.

The construction industry poses unique health and safety challenges for its workers. In fact, about one out of every five workplace deaths in calendar year 2019 were construction-related, according to OSHA. Health and safety processes play a vital role in minimizing risks (Roberts, 2021).

Conclusion

This study participants (93%) agreed that the organisational antecedents that are responsible for managers' silence over at-risk behaviours included a host of factors such as Reactive organisational culture, Personal attitude, Fear of reporting, Target based incentive, Ignorance or Lack of competency, Poor communication, Non-professionalism, Poor managerial attributes, Overconfidence, Deficiency of resources, Pressure approach from company Group's top management, Lack of intent, Casual approach. Easy going attitude, Profit entity, Low perception level, Safety qualification, Dependent safety culture, Enforcing for job completion in scheduled time, weak safety culture (**Box 1**).

In order to resolve the employees silence about safety issues, their relationships with others, their perceptions of the organisational climate, their assessment of the safety issue, or characteristics of the job safety, three critical aspects of the organisational behaviours safety system need a focus by organisations:

1. **Structure:** Steering teams providing continued motivation (HODs), top leadership;
2. **System:** Trained behaviour safety observers to keep all areas safe; and
3. **Approach:** Big brother approach transforms organisational culture.

It is estimated that around 48,000 people in India die every year due to occupational accidents. Due to the lack of safety personnel, it is important for employees to play an active part in increasing their safety. This makes Behaviour Based Safety (BBS) training in India extremely important (British Safety Council, 2021).

If managers value and engage in the employees observations on at-risk behaviours, they in turn feel connected and get encouraged to voice their concerns about safety at sites. Professionals who feel psychologically safe believe it is safe to take interpersonal risks such as voicing

BOX 1: Organisational antecedents for managers' silence over at-risk behaviours.

1. Relationships with others (78% of HSE professionals reported): Fear of reporting, Poor communication, Overconfidence, Easy going Personal attitude, Lack of intent
2. Organisational climate perceptions (86% of HSE professionals reported): Reactive organisational culture, Target based incentive, Non-professionalism, Poor managerial attributes, Deficiency of resources, Pressure approach from company Group's top management, Profit entity, Dependent safety culture, weak safety culture
3. Assessment of the safety issue, or characteristics of the job safety (75% of HSE professionals reported): Ignorance/Lack of competency, Casual approach. Low perception level, Safety qualification, Enforcing for job completion in scheduled time

concerns, asking questions and giving feedback. Psychological safety is an understanding of the influence team leaders, interpersonal relationships and individual characteristics have on individuals' psychological safety and their decisions to engage in voice or silence behaviour. Personal characteristics, past experiences, individual perceptions of being valued, and judged appropriateness of issues/ concerns, are the motivating and inhibiting factors associated with the influence of leadership, interpersonal relationships and individual characteristics on experiences of psychological safety and voice behaviour (O'Donovan *et al.*, 2021). Psychological safety would improve: the relationships with others, employees perceptions of the organisational climate, employees assessment of the safety issue, or characteristics of the job safety, and then also, in turn, would motivate employees for voicing safety concerns. In fact, the concept of psychological safety is embedded in the objective of behavioural safety as big brother approach, that entails compassion, empathy and equality among employees and beyond.

Recommendations

1. Psychological safety need to be demonstrated behaviourally by all people at work to turn into a safety culture. Being psychologically safe with each other organisationally is a wide definition to be applied at workplaces. When employees feel psychologically unsafe, they don't voice for safety. The employees feel psychologically safe, when their voices on safety are appreciated regularly. That's why, the mission of big brother safety (BBS) is emphasised, so that employees feel psychologically safe with each other. If managers value employee's observations, they feel encouraged and continue voicing on at-risk behaviours for spot-corrections. Psychological safety and

behavioural safety are positively correlated. Behavioural safety, if implemented in principle, boosts psychological safety. Hence, the organisational antecedents that are responsible for managers' silence over at-risk behaviours, can very well be changed into employees voices for safety at sites. However, safety voice is an ecological phenomenon which would vary according to individual factors, group (safety-specific transformational leadership), institutions (hierarchical effects), and external environments such as national culture (Mark, 2019).

2. Businesses sustainability would depend upon whether the company employees are regularly being trained to speak up for spot-correction of at-risk behaviours to prevent incidents. Organisational silence is the best enemy of safety (ICSI, 2017). Industry requires a training and implementation model to break managers silence for safety. As a code of business conduct, Everyone at Sembcorp has the implicit responsibility to speak up whenever there is any concern that an action on our part may lead to the violation of the Code (Sembcorp, 2021).

3. Civil society interactions on safety and health: Even when COVID-19 numbers have risen, people remained silent when they observed others in social markets not obeying COVID-19 appropriate behaviours. We need to be contemplating on how to change safety behaviour in civil society. We can do it in our own areas of connects through our actions and sharing the risks and benefits to see the change that we wish to see. We can also do behaviour safety online programs for families of employees in organisations, and also for educational institutions. In a way, families are annually engaged during national safety day or world environment day. However we need to cover everyone making it as biannual or quarterly celebrations (Harbans, 2021).

4. ISO 45003 OHS management includes psychological health and safety at work for managing psychosocial risks such as occupational stress, anxiety, depression, etc. In current uncertainty situation, mental health aspect is grossly neglected. In some countries, there are mental health first aiders specially appointed. In india particularly there is social stigma attached to it. There is always apprehension to discuss about it openly, not only within family support system but at workplace too. This aspect is to be addressed like some companies do as part of implementation of behavioural safety and psychological safety and well-being at work. Psychosocial hazards relate to how work is organised, social factors at work and aspects of the work environment, equipment and hazardous tasks. Psychosocial hazards can be present in all organisations and sectors, and from all kinds of work tasks, equipment, and employment arrangements (ISO 45003, 2021). But this is a huge responsibility on the shoulder of mental health professionals. Industries would need a planned intervention to manage psychosocial risks as per ISO 45003. Industry professionals find that ISO 45003 is relevant. Now it is time for proactive culture and this is need of industry. This is about an organisational plan on employees and their families' psychosocial health and well-being to ensure continuous assessment and care.

5. Building sustainability through data visibility is a puzzle, as because data and behaviours on the ground do not match (Forum of Behavioural Safety, 2021). This is important that managers not only speak up for safety, but they also look for reliability and sustainability between data and safe behaviours. Also, the safety concepts have to be inculcated in the heart of managers. The fact remains that the companies have not enabled their managers sufficiently, and the result is reflected in terms of incidents, accidents, fatalities, loss of property and so on.

6. Quitting reactive safety culture is almost getting ready for adopting psychological safety culture, whereby your people at work begin to feel safe. HSE professionals believed that the psychological safety at workplace enhances ownership and interest of employees towards all activities they do. It helps to enhance productivity as well. Psychological Safety Culture should be implemented all over the industry. Proactive Safety behaviour is an only behaviour which turns the game of Safety. Safety starts with Me, this individual promise will be a game changer (Harbans, 2021, June).

References

Basahel, AM. (2021, Apr 15). Safety Leadership, Safety Attitudes, Safety Knowledge and Motivation toward Safety-Related Behaviors in Electrical Substation Construction Projects. *Int J Environ Res Public Health.* 2021;18(8):4196. doi:10.3390/ijerph18084196.

British Safety Council (2021). The need for BBS training in India. Retrieved on 09 June 2021. https://www.britsafe.in/publications-and-blogs/blogs/read-all-blogs/the-need-for-bbs-training-in-india/

Dan Orr, (2021, March, 16). The Normalization of Deviance (aka "Short Cut Mentality"). Retrieved on 10 June 2021. https://www.divenews wire.com/the-normalization-of-deviance-aka-short-cut-mentality/

Forum of Behavioural Safety (2021). 5th Annual National Conference (virtual)

New Challenges of Behaviour Based Safety (BBS), 24 January, 2021, at Mumbai.

Harbans Lal (2021). HSE Professionals Review the Contribution of Civil Society toward Industrial Safety Culture. *Journal of Psychosocial Research,* Vol. 16, No. 1, 2021, 93-102. DOI No. : https://doi.org/ 10.32381/JPR.2021.16.01.10

Harbans Lal (2021, June). Why the Industry is Losing Faith in HSE Awards? 250 Professionals Rethink*!* *World Safety Journal* (WSJ), Vol. 30, No. 2, 27-36. https://worldsafety.org/wp-content/uploads/ DOI-Incl.-WSJ-2021-FINAL-June-2021.pdf

ICSI (2017). Organizational silence is the best enemy of safety. Retrieved on 07 June 2021. https://www.icsi-eu.org/en/publication/ thought- organizational-silence

ISO 45003 (2021). ISO/DIS 45003(en) Occupational health and safety management — Psychological health and safety at work : managing psychosocial risks — Guidelines. https://www.iso.org/ obp/ ui/#iso:std:iso:45003:dis:ed-1:v1:en

Jan Wynen, Bjorn Kleizen, Koen Verhoest, Per Lægreid & Vidar Rolland (2020) Just keep silent... Defensive silence as a reaction to successive structural reforms, *Public Management Review*, 22:4, 498-526, DOI: 10.1080/14719037.2019.1588358

Kaila Harbans Lal (2020). Challenges of Making Safety a 'Way of Life' in Indian Society. *Indian Journal of Training and Development,* Volume 50, No. 3 July-September, 2020, 26-34.

Manapragada A, Bruk-Lee V. (2016). Staying silent about safety issues: Conceptualizing and measuring safety silence motives. *Accid Anal Prev.* 2016 Jun;91:144-56. doi: 10.1016/j.aap. 2016.02.014. Epub 2016 Mar 11. PMID: 26974031.

Mark C. Noort, Tom W.Reader and Alex Gillespie (2019, August). Speaking up to prevent harm: A systematic review of the safety voice literature. *Safety Science*, Volume 117, Pages 375-387. https://doi.org/10.1016/j.ssci.2019.04.039.

McKinsey & Company (2021, February, 11). Psychological safety and the critical role of leadership development. Retrieved on 11 June 2021. https://www.mckinsey.com/business-functions/organization/ our-insights/psychological-safety-and-the-critical-role-of-leadership-development.

Morrison, Elizabeth. (2014). Employee Voice and Silence. *Annual Review of Organizational Psychology and Organizational Behavior.* 1. 173-197. 10.1146/annurev-orgpsych-031413-091328.

O'Donovan Róisín, Brún Aoife De and McAuliffe Eilish (2021, Feb, 19). Healthcare Professionals Experience of Psychological Safety, Voice, and Silence. *Front Psychol.*, https://doi.org/10.3389/ fpsyg.2021.626689

Roberts, Hewitt (2021, May 26). How to Improve and Promote Safety in Construction. Retrieved on 14 June 2021. https://www.ehstoday. com/construction / article / 21165175/how-to-improve-and5promote-safety-in-construction

Sembcorp (2021). CODE OF BUSINESS CONDUCT. Retrieved on 15 June 2021. https://www.sembcorp.com/en/media/272278/sembcorp-code-of-business-conduct-english.pdf

Smith, Sandy (2018, Jan 04). Safety Practices in the Oil and Gas Industry (Infographic). EHS Today. Retrieved on 12 June 2021. https://www.ehstoday.com/safety/article/21919443/safety-practices-in-the-oil-and-gas-industry-infographic

Subhakaran, Sriji & Dyaram, Lata & Dayaram, Kantha & Ayentimi, Desmond & Khan, Nabila. (2020). Leaders' accounts on employee voice in the Indian context: an exploratory study. *Asia Pacific Journal of Human Resources.* 58. 10.1111/1744-7941.12254.

The Economic Times (2021, June 10). Leave aside ESG, India's bigger problem is EHS. Retrieved on 14 June 2021. https://economictimes.indiatimes.com/markets/stocks / news / leave-aside-esg-indias-bigger-problem-is-ehs/articleshow/82394008.cms

Vel'as, A., Andrej Veas, Martin Halaj, Ladislav Hofreiter, Katarína Kampová, Zuzana Zvaková & Richard Jankura (2021). Research of security and safety culture within an organization. The case study within the Slovak Republic. *Secur J* https://doi.org/10.1057/s41284-021-00291-5.

If all managers at site constantly say no to the unsafe and support safe behaviours, then longterm safety culture is possible in favour of safe business operations.

CHAPTER 2

Case of COVID-19 in View of Behavioural Safety and Health Culture in India

Introduction

COVID-19 impacted all countries, this article is about India's behavioural safety and health culture among its huge population. Behaviour based safety is a culture of caring (Janis, 2020) for people around to ensure "0" harm. Whereas, safety is not in our behaviors in our cultural context, and don't even think that due to COVID-19, safety would stay in our behaviors. Until it is emphasized on continuous basis, these COVID-19 at-risk behaviors would re-emerge, and it would threat the human resources and economy of our country again. According to **WHO** (2020), the most critical element of reducing this virus transmission is behaviour of people. During this scenario, to combat COVID-19 permanently, the governments (alongwith public private partnerships in all states) are trying harder to engage citizens and corporates of the country toward health and safety behaviors and mindsets. What is most compelling today is to engaging human mind with the work post-lockdowns. The government, the workforce and managements are finding ways in this direction through brainstorming discussions so that the economy can come back on track in all countries (**ILO**, 2020).

COVID-19 outbreak changed our approach toward workplace (HSE) health, safety and environment (EU-OSHA, 2020). Although, robust plant design, engineering controls, SOPs, organizational safety structure are essentiasl but are ineffective without behavioural safety aspects of HSE systems. Also it should be understood that in present scenarios, the businesses that are going to survive are those whose HSE systems are behavior-based, and are not merely reflected in documentation. The business leaders must underline this that further the business journey is focused on safe behaviours involving people from top to bottom. The leaders must see through these changes in ways that gain and maintain the trust of their people (Accenture, 2020). COVID-19 posed a major challenge that people are finding harder to adjust and internalize new behaviors expected during lockdown. Human minds are hard-wired. Imbibing new behaviors such as distancing etc. takes much time for most people, as because behaviors are rooted in cultures. BBS as an application of behavioural science indicate precautions that any unsafe/at-risk behaviour at any place by anyone would certainly lead to incidents and illnesses.

Objectives

Behavioural safety approach is a training methodology to emotionally sensitize all including top leaders towards inculcating an interdependent safety culture. In India, BBS is also referred as Bharat Bane Surkshit (Nation becomes safe), of which the responsibility lies on the shoulders of all corporates and citizens by implementing BBS and saving human life from incidents/illnesses.

- Objectives of this article are to review the current scenarios of COVID-19 for effective management of behavioural safety intervention and enable people to access this researched information; and

- Using arguments and the logic underlying to help develop some key areas for interdependent behavioural safety culture advancement.

Method

Participants

For this research paper, a total of about 1000 persons were approached through remote data collection techniques. The research participants had already implemented behavioral safety at their sites. The participants included, the CEO, directors, managers, heads of departments, safety professionals from public and private industrial sectors such as chemicals, construction, gas, power, and steel across Indian locations.

Measure, Procedure

This paper, is based on the qualitative methods using personal interviews, focused group discussions, and field surveys. This study is part of an ongoing interdisciplinary intervention of behavioural science, management and industrial safety disciplines, which is national longitudinal action survey in India.

Statistical Analysis

Their responses to the COVID-19 related questions were collated and thematic data analysis was used to reflect the findings. Interestingly, as part of this action survey, the participating organizations started implementing COVID-19 related new behaviors at sites.

Results and Findings

Safety is a matter of culture of caring, a very strong tool, which can be developed by leaders and their teams down the levels till the last person by inculcating BBS procedure at sites to practice daily. This research explored the following critical behavioural safety cultural aspects of COVID-19.

Research Statement 1: Why do people take risks?

It is time to reflect on our safety cultural values (Berman and Thurkow, 2020). Psychologically, people don't change with a change in safety definitions, which introduces risk into their life. Also people define safety differently for others from themselves, and gap remains narrow between compliance and compromise at work, road or work situations. Risk-taking behaviors vary among people, cultures and countries. Risk perception of COVID-19 is based on risk consequences being felt as immediately visible, which is not. Hence people keep taking risk. Also the risk perceptions depend upon the antecedents, the social realm and cultural backgrounds of people (Jens, 2019). According to Susan Michie (2020), given differences in behaviours and their contexts, the factors maintaining them differ as do the ways of changing them. As a citizen, when we don't follow safety practices in general on daily basis, our risk perception remains low. Moreover, we don't conduct new safe behaviours (social/physical distancing, wearing face mask, hands hygiene etc.) as they are not in our cultural background. As soon as, the lockdown enforcement is relaxed, we come back to our old behavioural patterns, possibilities of COVID-19 spread exist and our risk-taking behaviors remain high. In order to prevent or circumvent this, we need to spread safety messages through multiple ways such as media, government, motivational speeches on continuous basis. Behavior based approaches are long term interventions to contain HSE risks. The lockdown enforcement, political thought process etc. are temporary and short-term responses to these pandemics. Hence the managements ought to prepare accordingly.

A critical question remains, would lockdown exit mean that we exit the risk of COVID-19? Post-lockdown is more critical period when people are less alert about the risk exposure. The answer lies within everyone that how we handle post-lockdown risks around, when we go out, whom do we meet etc. Thus being alert or not, would render everyone safe or unsafe. According to Cloete (2020), much of the expected impact originate from behaviour and lifestyle changes. Lockdown essentially introduces a slowdown in everyone's life. Hence adjusting to slower life conditions as compared to the faster life styles would take time.

Another vital at-risk behavior is why certain groups of people did not cooperating in fighting COVID-19 despite government's support and resources being made available. Is it because they have not internalized safe behaviours yet, or not understood the consequences of this disease. That's one reason that the chain of COVID-19 is not broken yet. How to achieve over this behavioral aspect is critical. Is it because the crisis have increased in personal, professional and economic life of vulnerable section of society? Cricket stars urged that the country can be successful in its fight against COVID-19 only if people cooperate (India Today, 2020). It seems that these people are still following the pre-COVID-19 unsafe behaviors as existed in their cultural practices. Un-risking the present context would require sustainable and focused efforts alongwith COVID-19 implications and impact on human lives. Hence, COVID-19 fatalities would continue till people adopt a required culture of safe behaviours.

Research Statement 2: What are the similarities between COVID-19 and behavioral safety culture?

People take a couple of months to understand and adapt to the new behavioural changes expected in a new environment such as lockdown in the context of large public of a nation. Some deviations to these new behaviors appear and reappear till people adjust and self-control, irrespective of a place/country, and we deal with the implications thereof, and keep innovating new solutions. We come across similar deviations while implementing behavior based safety at industry sites.

A question arises, when could we say that we have achieved COVID-19-free situation? What are the likely problems and solutions. It would depend, not only on lockdown enforcement, planned lockdown exit, mass education and awareness, physical distancing, motivational speeches, economic relief packages but also on continuous identification of cases through testing, re-testing, quarantining, monitoring, treatment, innovation etc. as a long-term perspective. Any such country-wide or global multilevel socio-medico-economic-behavioral intervention requires rigorous follow ups over the years, failing which the chances of relapse/reoccurrence are equally high. We need to be ready for its long-time implications and solutions of any such pandemic social health issue. In brief, such interventions have to become a part of the existing HSE management style in order to avoid relapse and achieve zero-coronavirus patients or zero at-risk behavior at sites.

COVID-19 and BBS management, both drive behavioural change approach. Negligence of both can cause havoc. Both COVID-19 and BBS can lead to high severity if not corrected by taking adequate precautions in terms of behaviour (self as well as others), everyone's safety is interdependent. Another similarity is both are observable, measurable, implementable and curable. But, on the contrary, as seen in past few decades, the safety enforcement in industry as well as community is poor by <30%. That is why, precisely, the behavioural implementation is recommended (Kaila, 2019). To save humanity, we need to focus on our behaviour which alone will ensure our victory in this hour of peril. BBS and COVID-19 management are similar. For COVID-19: 1. Make an individual aware about COVID-19; 2. Educate him why precautions are necessary; 3. Tell him what is the risk; 4. Ask him what is missing; 5. Take promise that he will follow throughout; 6. Thank him.

BBS management is nurtured through harmonious and cohesive way, whereas COVID-19 pandemic is working through fear-based approach which is opposite to BBS. According to a former executive director of India Glycols, an application of BBS is the need of the hour. Wearing PPEs and physical distancing are very much the desired behavioural aspects. During COVID-19, the Police have become the observers and they also need BBS training. Of course, there are exceptions with some police people trying to counsel the public in a positive way. In many cases, they are not polite and many among the public also don't understand being polite, despite advices from leaders, celebrities and media. Patience and politeness are keys of any behavioral change intervention. Moreover, control by oneself (self-observation of social distancing, face mask) in community sites is very crucial for one's own health and safety.

The types/levels of safety culture are: 1. Reactive safety; 2. Dependent safety; 3. Independent safety; 4. Interdependent safety. In COVID-19, we are almost operating at level 1 & 2. We have reacted to the situation proactively and now dependent on the governments actions for our citizen's safety. Example, till the time, we are dependent on parents, we keep committing mistakes, as soon as we become independent, our behavioural alertness is increased/multiplied. If we wish to go to level 3 & 4, then we need to open/

exit lockdowns, everyone is supposed to manage the personal risk on his/her own. We need to understand here that our behavioural alertness is highest; when risk is known/well-defined. For example, we are at high risk during daily morning/evening's city peak traffic time, and we are highly alert at that time for road driving behaviors knowing the risks involved. Presently, in COVID-19, we reached a situation when everyone is aware and alert of risks. However, in levels 3 & 4 of safety culture, an enforcement for face masks and physical distancing is not relaxed. It is considered a violation if people don't wear PPE or maintain physical distance at all places etc. Companies also thought of a new better safety idea during this lockdown time that would be practiced in the times ahead at sites. They reported that we are maintaining 100% social distancing on daily basis. We started temperatures scanning from 12th February 2020.

Research Statement 3: How to implement BBS post-Lockdown in plants?

"Safety" whose responsibility, is a million dollars question that remains unresolved, therefore causing a global concern. If safety is everyone's responsibility, then why it is not being done. That means something is lacking in the learning, awareness, values, culture of the person which needs attention and reinforcement by focusing on which can save us million dollars and lives of people as well.

HSE Vice President of Dorf Ketal company said, "we made the COVID-19 related behavioural changes and advised all BBS observers at sites to do observations/spot corrections accordingly". This indicates the role of leadership guidance/ thrust all over in organizations. A safety head said, "power plant being essential services is continuously in operation and uninterrupted electricity is provided while ensuring all required safety precaution to prevent COVID-19".

An organization must provide feedback to employees using multiple communication channels to keep them informed about the company's response to the crisis (Cooper, 2020). According to a director of DCM Shriram, these are the thoughts and actions in order to change the post-COVID behaviours to prevent further spread and resuming operations safely. Above all, this is the high time that each citizen/employee play the role of safety catalyst in promoting interdependent safety culture everywhere. Governments alone cannot achieve zero number of people having COVID-19. Sooner the better for society that the public and each person understands this significant role in critical times in favour of human race by contributing safe behaviours. Be an active observer.

A focused group discussion came up with concerns/ insights as follows:

1. Managing plant safety with 1/3 of limited manpower is challenging;
2. Migrant labourers have gone back, taking work from new workmen is a challenge;
3. People at plant are much more conscious of safety due to COVID-19;
4. Unknowingly, organizations have started practicing interdependent safety culture which created positive vibrations. People are extra-cautious if someone is behaving unsafe;
5. Managements are saying to employees, instead of creating panic, develop extra-cautions;
6. Let the workmen develop immunity by giving them nutritional foods, so that they can fight with infection;
7. Employees shouldn't feel that their safety depends upon management, rather they should care for each other;

8. COVID-19 would encourage plants to manage safety more by automation, design and engineering controls to manage physical distancing;
9. Behavioural safety is a top down policy emphasis, and bottom-up reinforcement and practicing of safe behaviours is key to success of BBS;
10. Migrant labourers' fear of coronavirus rendered them move to their native places. But nearly 2 months of joblessness rendered them living without appropriate food which would have caused them reduced immunity. So it is a management concern to increase their immunity levels when they are engaged;
11. Middle managements are also challenged to implement safety procedures to their workers;
12. When physical distancing is difficult, facemask/face-shield is compulsory to reduce exposure to infection;
13. Trust of workers has to be revoked and communicated for their job security and safety;

Research Statement 4: What are the Behavioural Challenges and Solutions?

COVID-19 is long tunnel, may be endemic. Act early and get prepared. Initiate the change and see that it gets larger and sustain. Everyone is aware and unaware of his as well as other's safe/unsafe behaviors. Moreover, everyone needs correction as well as can contribute towards behavioural changes in others. According to Betsch, *et al.* (2020), behavioural insights for COVID-19 are of critical importance. Behavior remains a challenge for safety implementations. Hence regulated training, retraining, monitoring, measurement, rewarding, should continue by respective area-incharges.

Some challenges are:

1. **Fear and Stress:** Everyone is feeling low these days with COVID-19. Keep listening and talking to people. Keep environment positive. Personal/group counselling is right approach that would keep organizational morale up.

2. **How to mobilize people to be safe:** Continuously engaging people mentally through mass-communications helps to mobilize them for behaving safe. For example, in Mumbai local trains, people travelled on rooftops of electric trains due to overcrowding. Everyday a couple of persons would die. Then the Railways decided to communicate in every local train every 3 minute through public address system, that "the overhead wires are flowing with 20,000 volts, traveling on rooftop of trains is deadly". This communication went on for year by year. Today we don't see such fatalities in Mumbai public trains.

3. Maintaining peace of mind during free nonwork times has become real difficult for most people. Some people are mature enough to maintain their emotional balance by engaging in yoga, meditation, new learning, pursuing hobbies, writing, reconnecting with old friends etc.

4. **How to be creatively joyful during nonwork times:** Unroutine your activities, unknot your daily practice, do what you don't do, engage in new thoughts and actions, but all this within COVID-19 laid down rules. This would re-energize yourself and remove boredom in nonwork situations.

5. **What challenges further are:** Because of unavailability of sufficient testing kit (resources), only limited

testing per day is possible in Gujarat, our media should give a positive news who came out from COVID-19 (praise is more required to motivate and courage for others), and still people take it easy due to lack of knowledge and not sincere and serious.

6. How to get difficult persons engage in safe behaviours is a major challenge. Peer-based approach in respective areas seems workable as people are known and acceptable to each other, and the local leaders (Panchayats) are influential to facilitate safe behaviours in present times of COVID-19 which was initiated on video conferencing on 24th April, 2020 by Mr. Narendra Modi, our great PM.

Human safety is a pure service of humanity to save human lives. Some Indian companies organized COVID-19 behaviors awareness drive, involving all HODs, Section Incharge, EHS Leader, Task Force Team Members, COVID-19 Audit Team, Safety Team and Security Team; and began an awareness drive (**Fig. 1**) on the BBS theme "Roko, Toko aur Sudharo" for following points:

- Proper PPEs
- Social Distancing
- Face Cover
- Spitting on Ground
- Use of Mobile Phone
- Road Safety
- Tobacco Chewing and Smoking in Plant
- Hand Sanitization

BBS = Baar Baar Samajao

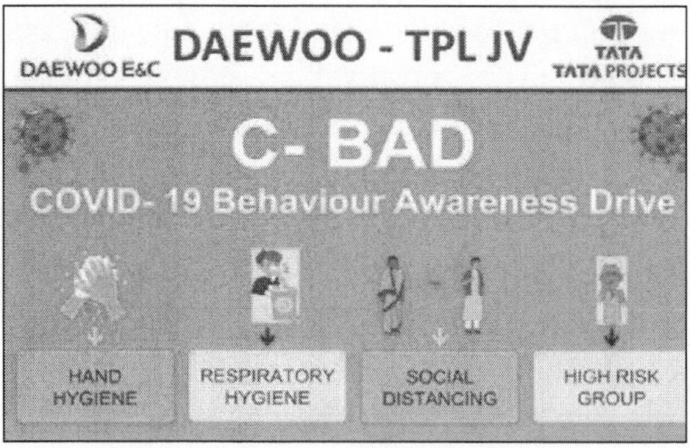

FIG. 1: COVID-19 Behavioral Awareness Drive (C-BAD).

A safety group experts expressed that the plants should thoroughly examine their facilities, carry out pre-start up safety checks and ensure availability of emergency resources, before restarting facilities after long shut down. The questions still that need to be answered are: How can Technology and Artificial Intelligence help in improving safe behaviour at workplace? What is the COVID-19 policy? Another challenge in legal compliance - it may go in back burners? How to remove fear from workmen during working at workplace? How to maintain social distancing during construction? What is practical immunity improvement method?

Research Statement 5: How do we break COVID-19 spreading chain?

COVID-19 chain begins knowingly or unknowingly, from one to another, and one to many, and hence logically, this chain is behavioural in nature. As in BBS implementation, we train and involve many observers to spot-correct at-risk behaviors, similarly we need to create a chain of behavioural safety active observers/mentors (such as social and community workers) in each area and location who will keep an observation like a targeted missile to fight its objectives.

Observers need appreciation of HODs to continue doing observation/spot-correction. This is to be followed across the nation. This dedicated chain of observers would break the chain of COVID-19 spreading in communities by observing and spot-correction of COVID-19 related risks. It is a people-driven support framework like a tested behavioural science BBS approach. COVID-19 pandemic can be brought under control by massive and rapid behaviour change. To achieve this we need to systematically monitor how different individuals perceive risk and what prompts them to act upon it (Betsch, 2020).

According to a senior manager at Tata projects, "prevention by physical distancing is the only solution". A safety professional of GAIL stated that there is an immediate need of developing local contingency plan in small pockets. Like all societies, muhallas (old settings) should prepare contingency plan and which should be led by one expert. As per opinion of a HSE Manager of Dorf Ketal, "spreading chain is more due to behaviours and reasons such as overconfidence, lack of awareness about consequences, inadequate precautions, improper communication, and lack of resources in terms of adequacy and accuracy of testing".

It is an environment that makes people perform, management empowers them to perform, and BBS implementation drives the behavioural culture/environment. COVID-19 is indeed a behavioral issue. The administration/police need to be trained on this matter. Also, media, celebrities and prominent personalities to constantly address the public. Politicians may not be doing enough. According to a CEO of chemical plants, more symptomatic testing by Government is needed, asymptomatic private testing to be made mandatory for running establishments, post-lockdown only alternate is 50% attendance allowance to ensure physical distancing, and for Red & Hot Zones, the restrictions should continue as COVID-19 persons increased.

Implications for Social Policy and Planning

Ironically, a safety expert admitted that COVID-19 is a natural course of pandemic in the sense that the water, noise, air pollutions were found much lower than before during lockdowns. With COVID-19, BBS intervention spreads from industry to country, and people became more safety-minded than before. But unexpectedly, the state government's low concern for life safety of large numbers of contractual labour is reflected during lockdown for transportation to their hometowns, and they were forced to walk hundreds of miles. An ex-executive director of India Glycols stated that the steps mentioned below would have helped or lack of them was the cause of spread of COVID-19 in India.

1. We were a bit late in anticipating what was coming. Lockdown should have been announced in the first week of March 2020.
2. Monitoring activities and prompt actions (This could have avoided Nijamuddin episode).
3. Applying BBS, especially by police/admin, for a better public response.
4. Creating more hospitals through makeshift arrangements (say, by converting gymnasiums, convention halls into hospitals).
5. Promptly procuring/distributing PPEs and testing kits for identification and containing the spread.
6. Allowing vendors to deliver essential items at door steps while closely monitoring the health of these distributors. Inviting volunteers and poor people (on payment basis) facilitate this distribution. This would have avoided more people rushing to shops.

7. Overall monitoring of people movement through more drones.
8. Donations were prominently by Centre only (through PM Cares) and not by States. There was perhaps more potential for contributions from willing public to help this cause.

Certain implications are described below for consideration.

- COVID-19 is behavior based management, there are specific behaviors that will reduce the risk of viral exposure for ourselves, our co-workers, and our communities. Decades of research show the power of behavioral science in increasing the consistency of safe behaviors. The spread of COVID-19 serves as an important reminder of what organizations can gain by incorporating a behavioral component into a comprehensive exposure-reduction process. The behavioural science principles and an approach toward change implementation drive is almost similar for both community and organizations.
- Behaviors are rooted and wired in cultures. We, in India, have not emphasized safety behaviors in our culture and many a times, unsafe behaviors are justified. That's the prime reason that it's becoming so hard to break the COVID-19 spreading. All countries witness today that how difficult it is to sell the value of safety to its own citizens. In this regard, behavioural reinforcements are the major factor to ensure that people are adopting new behaviors related to COVID-19. People will take shortcuts and violate. Active observers will not fail to spot-correct such at-risk behaviors, be it anywhere, at workplace or public place, or residence. A safety manager said, "we at Agrocel company, started spot-correction and

employees are spreading the message to each other to follow COVID-19 precautions. Companies develop a faith in behavioral safety programs and gradually, it becomes their corporate value and culture.

- Currently no much improvement in many States of India, COVID-19 numbers are increasing. Remote areas are not affected by COVID-19 as untouched by crowded population. At Factory site: social/physical distance is maintained. Handwash every hour. Work from home for majority of people who are not needed at site. Nose mask is compulsory for all. It is important to let people know that post-lockdown when factories operations are being managed at less workforce, the employees need to be doubly cautious as many fatal incidents occurred at sites in Maharashtra, Delhi, Gujarat, Tamil Nadu in India.
- According to a senior safety professional from DCM Shriram, some reasons that actually increased the number of people who have COVID-19 included: lack of risk anticipation due to COVID-19, "If it had not happened to me till date it will never happen to me as I am immune, false sense of mental immunity. Its similar to typical safety mindset. I am working here in this plant for last 25 years, never ever got injured nor see any hazard here which poses high risk. Do not see others carrying corona/suspected patients as risk. Till COVID-19, wearing of face mask and social/physical distancing is included in BBS checklist". He added further, "This is purely behaviour of maintaining safe physical distancing in true sense and just not for name sake. I know many essential services/industries are being operated without distancing compliance that makes entire effort futile. This is similar to at-risk behaviours at work place which can cause serious accidents if not corrected".

- Our speed of decision-making based on accurate data as well as actions determine what we achieve in managing the risks and their consequences. In India, we lacked in speed of decision making, and timely management of actionable points. Moreover, Tablighi Jamaat participants spreaded COVID-19 in Indian States (Sharma, 2020). There were attacks on people, police, media and medical personnel during COVID-19 times, which posed a greater and scary challenge to government, corporates and everyone else. Also, in India, people normally need many reminders to change for safe behaviours as compared to New Zealand or Australian countries. That's the prime reason, breaking the chain of COVID-19 spreading becomes so difficult. At personal levels, we all need to gradually develop our will and determination to stay with our safe behaviours which would balance our lives from at-risk behaviors and environments.
- This is a period of change/challenge for human race. Stress, anxiety, irritability, fear are experiences of adjusting to new behaviors during COVID-19 (Hoof, 2020). People would explore new definitions of their own behavioral safety. People have to deal with their own cognitive confusions. It would be surely a long-term affair. Employees would need to brainstorm for new work formats in order to avoid COVID-19. According to chairman, Maruti Suzuki, the key for us is to prepare workers with many health and safety measures that are here to stay (Business Standard, 2020). COVID-19 pushed corporates to implement HSE measures more seriously than before.
- According to safety practitioners, we have to live with this now like other diseases, early we accept, better it

would be. Probably, the human beings would learn to live with certain viruses with more safety precautions as we progress to deal with or without COVID-19. Behaviour and attitude are the reasons for increasing COVID-19 numbers across the globe. Hope post-COVID-19 mindset of people would be positively different in terms of their spiritual insights, re-balancing person-environment-fit, compassion, tolerance, adjustment, understanding, patience, and so on. Pray, All be safe. Don't get scared, rather resolve it. Share motivational positive messages of strong determination to fight and break COVID-19 spreading chain (WHO, 2020). A senior psychologist said, "develop immunity system by right lifestyle and keep high quality hygiene in regular behaviour".

- Human life is more valuable than the business or economy. So, let the countries understand clearly that lockdown exits in particular places are logical only when the number of COVID-19 persons have significantly decreased. Till then, let the businesses be allowed with minimum workforce, online, work from home or another innovative formats. In India especially, the spread of COVID-19 persons has taken a complicated political, religious, socio-cultural, communal base (Mufsin and Muhsin, 2020). Some opposition parties made it difficult instead of being a support in this human cause. For various reasons, people have been hiding that they have COVID-19 which increased the incidence of this problem multifold. As a result of which, the COVID-19 spreading chain could not be broken. Hence, most strict measures are needed to be enforced by our central/state governments as soon as possible failing which the problem is likely to get further intensified.

- COVID-19 challenged everyone for re-survival, and we are challenged for, what we can achieve! A plant manager said, "for survival, boost your immunity through, positive thinking, take care of hygiene, healthy diet, listen good music, pray to god". According to a HSE general manager, "It will teach us: how to survive in worse situation, get closer to your family, importance of PPE, learnings from our Honourable Prime Minister's leadership action/ reaction/calmness and the way he handles each of us".
- Certain indirect implications of COVID-19 are also likely to emerge. For example, hugging (as against physical distancing, reflection of human bonding that people use in many cultures across the globe), it seems COVID-19 would take that away from human race, or people would be afraid of. Similarly, handshaking - an expression of human touch may become a thing of the past. Globally, COVID-19 has also become the reason for cold war between China and many countries that are severely affected by Chinese virus as it is called by the American President. Most affected countries are against China as COVID-19 cropped up there and spreaded in globe (Awasthi, 2020).
- Behavioural revolution is a requirement which means a change into a set of safe behaviours to contain COVID-19 and break its chain from spreading further. How to revolutionize safe behaviors to combat COVID-19 before losing more lives? COVID-19 made people, industry and the nation more alert and safe than before. People are taking care of each other, the rich of the poor, the strong of the weaker, and the educated of not-so-educated. People across the globe

would have better sense of their personal HSE due to COVID-19 experiences that came with lots of pain and hurt. Business leaders would be more alert for HSE systems in their organizations. Hence this behavioral revolution would thrive nations economically safer and stronger than before (Biswal, 2020). Sadly, COVID-19 is the hardest way of teaching safety to the mankind. In the present scenario, safe behaviours are well defined, only option is to follow them or get badly hurt which stands true for companies or communities across the globe. The governments have set safety procedures and also reinforcing them. Unfortunately, people would surely face consequences if these are not followed. An individual safety is personal responsibility. Moreover, countries/corporates would not give up till the safety culture is evolved and followed by people.

- Another challenge of COVID-19 is that people are not able to maintain physical distancing as because it has never been part of their culture (**Fig. 2**). Culture drives the behaviors. They need observers to correct them on-the-spot repeatedly. Many of us, subconsciously are not maintaining physical distancing, be it media persons, doctors, police. Everyone is getting affected. Same behaviors would repeat at work sites as well. We can't observe ourselves, but we can observe others. Hence make it a point of spot-correction for everyone daily. Announce it every hour on public address system whether people are observing their co-workers around and correcting on-the-spot. One observation a day, keep the risk away. Make safety observations a part of an individual performance at sites. Observations help save lives. Leaders need to get focused on it for safety of their human resources and business, as because safety is compromised when safety is under pressures of production and profit by seniors. Safety culture is a function of leadership initiatives and employees/workmen/everyone involvement on continuing basis. Also, it boils down to the family safety cultures which vary across cities, districts, etc. Some families are more safety conscious than others. Moreover, people have taken COVID-19 non-seriously. In India, people are roaming around in spite of the lockdowns being extended. Safety seems far away from their actions. That's why COVID-19 positive numbers have increased. People don't understand safety being idle without working. Especially, in a cosmopolitan nature of city Mumbai, people understand safety while working. People get driven by predominant work motives.

FIG. 2: Lack of physical distancing behaviors during lockdown.

- Largely people, right upto the villages, are much aware about the risks associated with COVID-19. Now people are supposed to maintain physical distancing etc., which they didn't do earlier. The difficulty is balancing between old and new behaviors of following physical distancing, wearing mask, handwashing. Hence, when they maintain these behaviors, they will sometimes go back to original behaviors, which would pose greater risk to everyone around. It is not easy for people to adopt new behaviors, they do what they see around most of times. Monkeys see, monkeys do. Thus, *imbibing new behaviors is a gradual process,* which essentially requires continuous monitoring and handholding by corporates and communities. People intend to remain non-compliant toward a new set of behaviors as they perceive it to be a temporary phenomenon. More importantly, people need to be alerted repeatedly by observers around whenever they engage in any such at-risk behaviors. It all depends upon how an aware person or observer effectively conveys the risk to the less aware for his/her safe behaviour and spot-correction, which is called a risk based conversation (RBC). Citizens ought to observe and save each other, this is an essence of behaviour safety approach. Because, this is the time when the governments have taken lots of measures and COVID-19 numbers are still rising. Public cooperation is low as rising COVID-19 numbers lead us to say that the people are violating safe behavior rules. Hence, public can no longer depend upon governments for their safety. Public has to help themselves as per COVID-19 rules laid down by their governments, failing which we would surely witness more fatalities taking place in near future. This behavioral shift is very critical, till the public adopted independent safety culture, COVID-19 fatalities would most likely continue. Public cooperation needs to be strengthened through NGOs, religious/community groups, corporate social responsibility. CSR funds can be spent on activities related to addressing COVID-19 impact (Financial Express (2020). Companies integrate social and environmental concerns in their business operations and interactions with their stakeholders. There are nearly 10,000 CSR projects in India. Moreover, India has more than 3.2 million registered non-government organisations (NGOs). These resource groups and expertise are capable to mobilize social policy and programs into achievable results. These initiatives would take us further from reactive and dependent safety cultures to independent and interdependent safety cultures for saving human lives.

- The behavioural changes in a safety culture are achievable subject to certain presuppositions and preconditions as discussed. Safe person is considered to be the one who is alert, and observes and spot-corrects unsafe behaviour of others. Further, it is high time to focus on economic activity, as the number of people who are violating safe behavior rules are very small as compared to those following. The economic slap is harsher than the disease itself. Economy and employment falls are serious implications to manage in the years to come for many countries. So focusing on economy with safety measures would normalize the situation with positive energies. People should not get scared if COVID-19 numbers rise, rather be bold enough to be a part of the economic activity. Those who violate SOPs/get affected by COVID-19 would be managed by the governments' health systems. It is crucial to understand that nearly 99.9% of India population are obeying safe behaviors for hoping that if they continue safe behaviours, then only they can thrive economy forward. However, it is crucial to realize and underline that the intervention effects of behavioural safety changes (Nilsen, 2006) at the national level in India would be gradual and long-term in nature especially when the existing safety culture is poor, reactive and dependent. This would help the concerned agencies remain focused towards policies and programs requiring large financial investments.

- Best medicine to defeat COVID-19 is safe behaviour, everyone has to take it sooner or later for safety of his/her life. Countries expect only safe behaviour (from citizens) which is the strength of economies. Countries would have better economies that have safe behaviours from their citizens. According to Director-EHS, "till yesterday, no case in my housing society, now with one zee employee infected, all are scared. Till yesterday, all thought we were safe. Hope our prayers work which works when everything fails". A safety veteran said, "we don't have any visible cure in hand. Only prevention using our safe behaviour is the solution". Best safety plans failed as we didn't continue them. We need to continue focusing and reinforcing on safe behaviours till we succeed. Since the population is large, it would take time, numbers of COVID-19 would increase or decrease. We can't afford to dishearten, but continue to win over COVID-19 and finally defeat it for humanity.
- The entire world and everyone else around us overreacted at this juncture of fear, stress, helplessness and anxiety due to COVID-19. At this time, each one of us has to try consciously to calm down during the post-lockdown periods and be rational to self as well as others around. It is testing times for all. COVID-19 has rendered everyone feel helpless but persevere. Nevertheless, there are many positive implications/impacts of behavioural control or otherwise during lockdowns (Springer, 2020) as gained by safety professionals across the country as follows. "my positives of lockdown: I reduced 5 kg in 2 months with warm water and one meal off. Feeling much healthier". "I have learned to run 5–7 km in my

flat and maintain physically and mentally fit. I am a great cook now making many dishes for family. Lastly started singing some bhajans (religious) and filmi songs too. Connected socially with all knowns whom I had not called in last 2–3 years time especially sr. Citizens. Great fun of life explored!". "As working lady, I am with my angels, twin daughters". "I am lucky one who is working in factory when millions are at home. My subordinate could not come back after leave who have already gone before lockdown". "I too reduced by 5 kg and also developed a leaner physique with lots of exercise at home". "Yoga, full exercise and running 40 minutes kept my body fit in lockdown. No reduction in food. I increased physical activity". "I have also reduced. I walked around 15 km a day during lockdown but within premises and by maintaining social distancing". "I also reduced but will check my weight. I could work on my hobby and did lot of introspection". "I learned online training. Use of Zoom and Cisco Webex. ONGC is trying online training". "Have reduced 8 kg in last 4 months, due to nutritional diets". "I too tried and lost 2.5 kg and will keep it forever". "Got time for my Sitar riyaz (musical instrument practice)". "being in essential service, doing 12 hours duty per day, lots of hardships, makes me feel engaged during lockdown, felt like serving nation".

A recent focused-group-discussion with safety experts brought out the following:

- Consider yourself as asymptomatic carrier of COVID-19 and rigorous self-discipline would help; Ten thousand observations of employees helped to sustain social distancing, facemask wearing, hand washing but also revealed that 15% deviations existed for COVID-19 related behaviors; Keep plan B ready when someone is infected with virus; BBS works best with other safety systems, but systems alone wouldn't ensure plant safety; Sanitize every material that is brought from outside, sanitize your hands if you touch it; Employees interact with their family, family interacts with society, hence virus exposure can come from anywhere; Encourage employees for voluntary declaration of their health conditions that can put others into unsafe conditions; Behavior is dynamic in nature, people are behaving safe as if new COVID-19 behaviors are being imposed, as the relaxation is provided, cities open after lockdown, people would come back to old original behaviors that would increase virus exposure; A Corona positive person was found and quarantined, and further contact tracking was done by site engineers.

- India most likely, because of reactive and dependent safety cultural background, would be seeing an upward trend of incidents in industry and society at large due to COVID-19 scenario. This would surely, directly or indirectly, impact our national economy, until and unless, there is an all-out seamless ongoing effort to build/inculcate the independent and interdependent safety culture. Personal capacities of each leader matters most in order to achieve this and mobilize further to sustain these cultures and lead respective administrations and departments as it is much needed. Ones who compromise with safety knowingly/unknowingly would invite incidents/ COVID-19.
- Now, everyone has to take oath that he/she will keep observation and care that at least one person next to him/her is saved from COVID-19. He/she will do

everything possible to fulfill this promise. This way, entire nation will be saved from deadly virus. This is true vaccine and safest behaviour. In fact, behavioural as well as medical vaccines are used in combination. In overall, the COVID-19 related behavioural management is all about change management (Human Capital, 2020). It is pleasant to be change-friendly, or you would be pushed into change process. Professionals and everyone else has to keep mobilizing the change management process, be the media, health, governments, corporates, the citizens, police, etc. Let the changes be top-initiated and change be absorbed by one and all as necessary. Sustaining behavioural change is a natural gradual process for large public, and change leaders and catalysts don't ever get disheartened. COVID-19 related safe behaviors can be achieved by everyone whom the change matters. Every small/big change in a corporate or country would have proportionate direct/indirect implications which complicate the change management process and one has to deal with strategically. Behavioural safety is a buzzword in today's scenario, it is easy to understand but complicated in adopting for nations where safety culture is already in nascent stage. We have to be on it to succeed. "To me it is forced perseverance and might have transformed few. I was surprised yesterday when saw people rushing/overtaking/ honking while I was on road to meet my parents after almost 3 months. Saw many flouting directions by not wearing masks and maintaining SD as they feel 'Hame kuchh nahee hua naa hoga' (nothing will happen to me)". There are a mixed of both good and examples of behavioural safety application during COVID-19.

A case: "In my society, there was no COVID-19 positive person so far due to restrictions imposed on walking and movement out of society and also no outsider came inside the society since 24th March, 2020. One person was found positive, as he went to office due to essential services. However, his entire family was tested negative. Now mindset of people is that we should be allowed to move out as their family is negative and person is under treatment in hospital, so we all are not infected. Do you think this is right?" We need to be aware of asymptomatic situations, its tricky, caution, remind people daily to be "Mindful" as virus may be around, as COVID-19 numbers are rising.

References

Accenture, (2020). COVID-19: Managing the human and business impact of coronavirus. APRIL 30, 2020. https://www.accenture.com/in-en/about/company/coronavirus-business-economic-impact

Awasthi, P. (2020). Covid-19 virus accidentally leaked by an intern in China: Fox News report, April 18, 2020. https://www.thehindu businessline.com / news / world / covid-19-virus-accidentally-leaked-by-an-intern-in-china-fox-news-report-claims/article31373917.ece

Berman, M. and Thurkow, T. (2020). Covid-19 Creates a Moment of Truth for Corporate Culture, April 01, 2020. https://www.bain.com/insights/covid-19-creates-a-moment-of-truth-for-corporate-culture/

Betsch, C. (2020). How behavioural science data helps mitigate the COVID-19 crisis. *Nat Hum Behav* 27 March 2020. https://doi.org/10.1038/s41562-020-0866-1.

Betsch, C., Lothar, H.W. and Katrine, H. (2020). Monitoring behavioural insights related to COVID-19. The Lancet, 25 April 2020, Volume 395, Issue 10233. https://www.thelancet.com/journals/lancet/home

Biswal, N. D. (2020). India has opportunity to build a more resilient and diverse economy after COVID-19 pandemic: USIBC. PTI, Apr 14,

2020. https://m.economictimes.com/news / economy / finance / india-has-opportunity-to-build-a-more-resilient - and - diverse - economy - after-covid-19-pandemic-usibc/articleshow/75139553.cms

Business Standard (2020). What lessons has India Inc learnt as it prepares for life after lockdown by Surajeet Das Gupta, April 06 2020. https://www.businessstandard.com / article / companies / challenges - await - firms - after - covid-19 - work - from - home -may-become-permanent-120040500935_1.html

Cloete, S. (2020). Behaviour Change: Covid-19 lockdown kicks open the door to a net-zero pathway, Energy Post, April 14, 2020. https://energypost.eu / behaviour-change-covid-19-lockdown-kicks-open-the-door-to-a-net-zero-pathway/

Cooper, D. (2020). Faces of EHS: Talks Behavioral Safety and Managing COVID-19. EHS Daily Advisor, Mar 27, 2020. https://ehsdailyadvisor.blr.com / 2020 / 03 / faces-of-ehs-dominic-cooper-talks-behavioral-psychology-and-managing-covid-19/

EU-OSHA (2020). Coronavirus disease (COVID-19) outbreak and work-place safety and health, 16.04.2020. https://osha.europa.eu/en/highlights/coronavirus-disease-covld-19-outbreak-and-workplace-safety-and-health

Financial Express (2020). Covid-19 & CSR: Time for India Inc to step up, April 2, 2020. https://www.financialexpress.com/opinion/covid-19-csr-time-for-india-inc-to-step-up/1916628/

Hoof, E.V. (2020). Lockdown is the world's biggest psychological experiment - and we will pay the price. World Economic Forum, 09 Apr 2020. https://www.weforum.org/

Human Capital (2020). Combating COVID-19 with an agile change management approach. https://www2.deloitte.com / in / en / pages / human-capital/articles/in-hc-combating-covid-with-an-agile-change-management-approach.html#

ILO (2020). COVID-19: stimulating the economy and employment. ILO Press release, 07 April 2020. https://www.ilo.org/global/about-the ilo/newsroom/news/WCMS_740893/lang--en/index.htm

India Today, (2020). Noticing people not following Covid-19 lockdown guidelines, moving in groups: Virat Kohli, March 27, 2020. https://www.indiatoday.in / sports / cricket / story / virat-kohli-warns-people-coronavirus-india-lockdown-government-guidelines-1660430-2020-03-27

Janis, J. *et al.* (2020). Workplace Safety, Enablers and Barriers. *WSJ*, Vol. 29, No. 2, 1–23.

Jens, O. Z. (2019) The meaning of risk-taking – key concepts and dimensions, *Journal of Risk Research*, 22:(1)1-15, DOI: 10.1080/13669877.2017.1351465

Kaila, H. L. (2019). Behaviour Based Safety for Corporates: A Shift toward an Interdependent Safety Culture, *WSO World Safety Journal*, 2019. https://worldsafety.org/wso-world-safety-journal/

Mufsin, P. P. and Muhsin, P. P. (2020). Sociocultural and Religious Factors Complicate India's COVID-19 Response. The Diplomat, March 25, 2020. https://thediplomat.com/2020/03/sociocultural-and-religious-factors-complicate-indias-covid-19-response/

Nilsen, P. (2006). The theory of community based health and safety programs: a critical examination. *Inj Prev.* 12(3)140-145. https://www.ncbi.nlm.nih.gov/pmc/articles/PMC2563514/#__ffn_sec title

Sharma, N. (2020). Cases doubling in 4.1 days; without Jamaat, it would've been in 7.4 days. ET Bureau, Apr 05, 2020. https://m.economictimes.com / news / politics-and-nation / rate-of-doubling - of-covid - 19 - cases - 4 - 1 - days - without - tablighi-jamaat-incident-it-would-have-been-7-4-government/articleshow/74994181.cms

Springer, S.H. (2020). The Psychological Impact of COVID-19: Key points we are missing as a society. Psychology Today, Mar 24, 2020. https://www.psychologytoday.com/us/experts/shauna-h-springer-phd

Susan, M. (2020). Behavioural strategies for reducing COVID-19 transmission in the general population. *BMJ*, March 3, 2020.

https://blogs.bmj.com/bmj / 2020 / 03/03 / behavioural-strategies-for-reducing-covid-19-transmission-in-the-general-population/

WHO (2020). Mental health and psychosocial considerations during the COVID-19 outbreak. WHO reference number: WHO/2019-nCoV/MentalHealth/2020.1. 18 March 2020.

WHO (2020). WHO tool for behavioural insights on COVID-19. http://www.euro.who.int / en / health-topics / health-emergencies / coronavirus - covid-19 / novel-coronavirus - 2019 - ncov - technical-guidance/who-tool-for-behavioural-insights-on-covid-19

Longterm safety culture is merely an outcome of daily safe behaviours of our people at sites, there's no shortcut.

CHAPTER 3

Educational Institutions Need to Focus 'Health and Safety' as COVID-19 Reminded

Introduction

The death of a student due to a snakebite raised questions on child safety in schools, and how to prevent such incidents further (Alex, 2019). Nothing is as important as creating safe learning environment for our children. The children deaths due to building collapse, fire accidents make it necessary for us to be continually vigilant to ensure safety of students/staff in schools. An incident of fire that killed 93 children reiterate the need to have school emergency preparedness and response plans, schedule practice drills to respond efficiently to occurrences that might be encountered (Government of India, 2004, p8). Hindustan Times (2017) reported 50 deaths in two months revealing coaching centres driving students to suicide, and the HRD ministry in November 2015 proposed setting up a regulatory mechanism.

Devastating incidents elevated concerns about the safety culture in academia. The safety culture of an institution is a reflection of the attitudes, and behaviours of its members concerning safety, an organisation's collective commitment (American Chemical Society, 2012). In another fire incident, 24 students and teachers were perished in a religious school in Kuala Lumpur. Malaysian local media reported that since

2015, there have been more than 200 fires at such schools (Pais, 2017). The recent changing scenarios necessitates the workplace HSE review.

During 2018–2019, there were 66 school shootings with casualties at public and private elementary and secondary schools (NCES, 2020). The National Crime Records Bureau, for the year 2016, reported 11,812 deaths in India due to road crashes near educational institutions. One reason attributed for these fatalities in this age group is their lack of experience; they are prone to bad judgments, i.e. risk-taking, thus getting involved in road traffic crashes (Baskar, 2020).

Recently, there is an increased emphasis on HSE in educational settings across the globe, due to COVID-19. "Health and Safety" need to be on the syllabus in all education levels as a reinforcement constantly from school to university to employment to retirement. Life-long learning helps to achieve such global perspective to save human lives. This mission is possible when it begins with family, school and social values and a long-term orientation.

Research Question/Objective Statement

To explore the perceptions, if "Health and Safety" education was introduced as a subject at schools way back, India would not have seen such a huge impact of COVID-19 on its citizens, as it is now. Secondly, whether educational settings updated their safety and health practices post-COVID-19, and the need is felt to integrate HSE as an integral part of educational institutional management?

Methodology

Participants, Measures, Procedure, Analysis

Open-ended questions based interviews and personal in-depth discussions with 342 HSE, medical, education, management, mental health professionals were conducted through remote data collection techniques over 3-month (June-August, 2020) in India from diverse locations and organisations. The responses of these professionals are presented in the following themes.

Findings

Responses of HSE, Medical, Education, Management, Mental Health Professionals

If "Health and Safety" education was introduced as a subject at schools way back, India would not have seen such a huge impact of COVID-19 on its citizens, as it is now. In this regard, the responses of the HSE, medical, education, management, mental health professionals are in affirmative and the broad themes emerging from these specific responses are as follows:

(*a*) The need for Health and Safety education (99%)

(*b*) Introduce Health and Safety as a subject (98%)

(*c*) Role of Government and Institutional leadership (95%)

(*d*) Preparedness and Implementation (94%)

(*e*) Infrastructure like safe design of educational sites (80%)

(*f*) Priorities and Values (70%)

(*g*) Risk is a part of our daily life, but accidents need not be (99%)

(a) *The need for Health and Safety education*

Safety education should be a part of the school curriculum (Azad, 2018). The tragic death of 14 and injury of more than 45 pupils of Kakamega Primary School is yet another reminder that our children are not safe in schools.

Unless the country rises as one to boost the safety of school children, more mass deaths will continue to be reported countrywide (PDonline, 2020). The professionals (99%) in India who participated in this research agreed for the need for Health and Safety in educational settings. They expressed that with COVID-19 storming the world and humanity at large, Children and Students are the roots of development. Schools, colleges are the best places to water the habit of Health and Safety. Health and Safety education is important. That is why India is behind the Western world as such practical topics are not part of curriculum in schools. Health and Safety is lacking in our basic education. It must include in education. Because then we are educated to be disciplined and follow the standard procedure of safety, which is required to be healthy and safe in present pandemic situation. I would say cleanliness also. In India, we are not a clean city or nation as such. The condition today is due to lack of awareness among the citizens. This is an excellent idea of health and safety in all schools. This would have helped lot. Young generation is future, hence need to mould in safety and health culture. Behaviour has to be developed at sapling stage rather than at a fully developed tree. If we have to choose between the three: Home safety, Workplace safety, Behavioural safety, Which one we chose? Research suggests that social distancing techniques, along with careful hygiene, cleaning, and use of quarantine, can reduce the spread of disease in schools, and protect the health and safety of students, staff, and families (Melnick, *et al.*, 2020).

(b) *Introduce Health and Safety as a subject*

The New Education Policy (NEP, 2020) is restructuring the Indian education system after 34 years, and would possibly include HSE subject in all educational levels (Nanjappa, 2020). The professionals (98%) who participated in this research recommended to introduce Health and Safety as a subject in educational settings. There are many incidents where it was understood that people (well educated/ qualified) were not aware about emergency measures to be taken. It was observed in recent fire incidents in few of the hotels in Mumbai, then in Surat commercial complex where 22 casualties of students took place from coaching classes (Mehta, 2020). Health and Safety must be introduced as subject in school. One view is that already we had health and safety in subject in school age but they are in bits and pieces. For example we are taught about road safety and it's consequences, but if we are not having good behaviour, there are no consequences written in book. About environment enough is taught at school time. So there must be a separate subject with pros and cons as well as their impact. HSE is a valuable addition to our education. In the old times Indian educational system, Ayurveda was one of the compulsory subject. Health and Safety must include Ayurveda, Allopathy, and various other disciplines. Indeed this is a very valuable suggestion. As per Citation (2020), in schools, there are environments that are considered low risk, such as classrooms, but the risks in labs, toilets, play grounds, etc. need to be evaluated and controlled. These hazards need to be assessed and controls ought to be put in place in order to reduce the harm.

(c) *Role of Government and Institutional leadership*

Even now it is not late, some solid proposal in this regard is needed to the governments. Government of India did something on environment front but for safety particularly, for General Safety, Fire safety, Road Safety, Electrical safety should be included in school level. The professionals (95%) in India who participated in this research agreed for the Role of Government and local leadership to implement health and safety in educational settings. The integration of occupational safety and health into the educational settings is an important aspect of the risk prevention culture. This allows everybody, teachers and students alike, to find out the ways to live and engage in a secure and healthy environment. The educational staff must become aware of the risk factors in their working environment (Gilda, *et al.*, 2013).

The Supreme Court of India had listed detailed guide-lines and ordered that all government and private schools in the country to follow the safety measures prescribed by the National Building Code of India 2005. But till 2017, out of 500 educational institutions with the Greater Hyderabad Municipal Corporation limits, only 29 adhered to the fire safety standards prescribed by the government. A huge number of 471 schools failed to get the No Objection Certificate from the District Fire Officer, which ensures that the school building is well equipped with all safety measures, as prescribed by the Education department, puttinz the lives of children at risk, appears to be no great matter of concern (Government of India, 2004, p7). The National Association of Secondary School Principals (2018) strongly emphasised to build a culture of safety. School safety issues, especially after the shooting at Marjory Stoneman Douglas High School in Florida, energized students, 650 school students participated in a walkout with the support of the school administration.

(d) *Preparedness and Implementation*

The Ministry of Human Resources Development (MHRD) in India issued detailed guidelines on school safety in 2014, but the implementations and safety mindset are lacking. The murder of a Class 2 student in Ryan International School raised uncomfortable questions, despite the large body of regulations, implementation is sloppy (Roy Chowdhury, 2017). What matters most is our mindset. Health and Safety aspects were taught in the school as environmental science. COVID problem in India is because we are not following guidelines. The moral science and ethics have taken back seat, which needs reinforcement. For effective implementation of HSE, the educational institute must deploy the structures such as annual risk assessments, planned walk-through inspections, training events, meetings, replacing sub-standard infrastructure, introducing new equipment, refurbishing key locations (Rapid Global, 2020). The professionals (94%) in India who participated in this research stressed for the preparedness and implementation for health and safety in educational settings. Critically, a school counsellor settled in USA expressed that question is attitude. Even now when the COVID-19 problem is at the doorstep, some state governments are playing politics rather than focusing on the problem.

It's all about building a culture, fixing the foundation, best to shape the pandemic preparedness. Certainly, if we have certain guidelines from very beginning in school, we would be more safe from any epidemic. There are some very basic things also people can't follow for health and safety because there is no orientation, hence they don't understand the importance. Broadly, there are three phases of preparing organisations for health and safety culture as follows: orientation and awareness to all, rollout action plan and implement it, monitoring and sustaining. GRENADA ELEMENTARY SCHOOL (2018) has a School Safety Plan which includes a comprehensive emergency management plan by which families are encouraged to establish major emergency family protection plans.

(e) *Infrastructure like safe design of educational sites*

Whether education alone would make people safe? Some say that infrastructure matters. Parents and teachers called for stringent safety measures in school buses, following a 7-year-old school boy being run over by his own school bus while crossing the road (Iyer, 2019). The professionals (80%) in India who participated in this research emphasised for infrastructure like safe design of educational sites, the school building and buses etc. The educational institutions should install a fire safety system under which mechanisms for the detection of a fire, the warning resulting from a fire and standard operating procedures for the control of fire are evolved. This may include sprinkler systems or other fire extinguishing systems, fire detection devices, stand-alone smoke alarms, devices that alert one to the presence of a fire, smoke-control and reduction mechanisms and fire doors and walls that reduce the spread of a fire. Students and staff should be trained within the effective operation of firefighting devices. Mock drills for fire situation should be undertaken at least once in a semester (UNIVERSITY GRANTS COMMISSION, 2020).

(f) ***Priorities and Values***

Statistics from the National Crime Records Bureau shows that nearly 43 children die in road accidents across the country every day. In 2015 alone, more than 400 school children were killed in bus related incidents. Total of 15,633 children were killed in road accidents across India in 2015 (Bhatia, 2017). Our traditional basic priorities are still "Roti, Kapda aur Makan" (food, dress, house) and our education system is also laid down on our basic priorities. This needs a change. The professionals (70%) in India who participated in this research emphasised for priorities and values of the educational institutions. The safety and health concept has to emerge as an organisational value and priority. Critically speaking, the school education on HSE alone, may not have brought the COVID-19 numbers to Zero, but definitely would have reduced. In addition, other concerns are like safety consciousness, poor knowledge, poor health infrastructure, over population etc. A behavioural change among people can be stimulated by (*a*) Ideal behaviour has to be modelled and brought to light by social proof and (*b*) Change and adaptation has to be made easy. As per Department of Education (2020), ensuring health and safety in schools is an essential part of any school manager's responsibility and to do this successfully, an effective health and safety management system needs to be in place.

(g) *Risk is a part of our daily life, but accidents need not be*

For accidents not to happen, the inevitable risks need to be reduced to manageable level. Almost 99% of the professionals who participated in this research believed that the risk is a part of our daily life, but accidents need not be. Always we take some calculated risk in our life to see some achievement. Whereas, on some times, there are some unknown risk we are not calculating and taking into consideration all the times, that makes us into the trouble. If we could be able to do some analysis on the unknown risks, accidents could be avoided. Some of the natural disasters we cannot make into the account. Risk is part of daily life, it can be minimised to reduce accident. Risk involves uncertainty about the effects/implications of an activity with reference to something that humans value (such as health, well-being, wealth, property or the environment), often reflecting on negative, undesirable consequences. Accidents can be controlled only if we mitigate risk. An accident is result of risk overlooked or underestimated. As we can prevent and minimise the risk impact through our action, an action exhibited through behaviour which is driven by mindset. We must prevent accidents by all means and measures.

Risk is an inevitable part of our whole life. Accidents are, either we invite due to our unsafe act or unsafe conditions.

Risk is involved in every activity but we always take action to eliminate it or reduce at reasonably low to acceptable level and accident shouldn't be happen. Believing that risk is part of our daily life but accidents need not be, so while schools need to make sure that staff, pupils and visitors are safe, they also need to make sure that, as the citizens of tomorrow, pupils are helped to become risk-aware without becoming unnecessarily risk-averse. In this sense 'teaching safely' and 'teaching safety' need to go hand in hand (RoSPA, 2020, p3).

Conclusion, Recommendations and Implications for Social Policy and Planning

The research objectives that were pursued are, whether educational settings updated their safety and health practices post-COVID-19, and whether would it make people more safety conscious post-COVID-19, and the need is felt to integrate HSE as an integral part of educational institutional managements?

Conclusion

Hundred thousands students were killed in incidents at educational institutions as reports revealed. The concept of safety and health culture challenged the institutions once again due to COVID-19. The findings reviewed 'Health and Safety in educational settings' by way of seven areas of concern, such as the felt need and importance of health and safety education, introducing it as a subject, role of government and leadership, preparedness and implementation, infrastructure like safe design of educational sites, priorities and values for educational institutions to focus on it in a systemic way, and the risk is a part of our daily life, but accidents need not be.

The educational institutions acquired gains in HSE domains due to onset of COVID-19. They are more safety conscious than before which needs to be sustained and become an integral part of their management system. It is necessary for them to manage the safety and security in order to prevent accidents/incidents, creating an environment for physical, emotional and social well-being. These institutions promote safety, only to meet regulations, without any sensitivity and commitment. It is necessary to mainstream safety processes integrated in school management, involving all the educational community (Vicario, 2017). The fire incident took place at Delhi University's College; two classrooms were charred, even as all universities and schools were shut across the country due to the coronavirus pandemic (Bhandari, 2020). It is time for educational institutions to learn to manage health and safety more efficiently. The current situation requires institutions to consider and implement all possible solutions to ensure the safety of students, their parents and our staff (Awasthi, 2020). In Mumbai, the Early Childhood Association and Association for Primary Education and Research updated guidelines as well as each school to have a safety coordinator to assure the implementation of safety procedures and these guidelines (Borwankar, 2020).

If "Health and Safety" education was introduced as a topic at schools way back, India wouldn't have seen such an enormous impact of COVID-19 on its citizens, as it is now. In this regard, a safety veteran said, "I endorse, support and advocate this since the day I opted to become a professional safety man" (Chakarborty, 2020, p1). A school Principal having 30 years of experience in education, Jose Kurian reiterated that no doubts about implementing health and safety in schools. Moreover, there are so many other very important value orientations like sense of cleanliness, social responsibility, respect for public property, respect for others and their belongings and many more. COVID-19 scenario is a reminder for all this, people need such orientation and reinforcements. However, the educational institutions needed experts guidance on implementation of health and safety standards and procedures.

Importantly, the HSE professionals highlighted on HSE value as belief that if one firmly believed that all accidents could be avoided, then only one can avoid it. Otherwise, they will keep happening. A recent plane crash on 8th August 2020 at Calicut, India was avoidable too. The airport was given notice 9 months back for many deficiencies, nobody bothered. Why was it necessary to land the plane under heavy rains? Flight could have been diverted. That's where behavioural interventions matter. All accidents are preventable. Fate, bad time, ill luck are myth only. But, it is two categories, within our hands and beyond our control. Fate of passengers is beyond their control. But may be within the hands of the pilot, knowing it is a table-top runway and skidding chance exists due to heavy rain and plane landing is not frequent due to pandemic situation, and the report warned that this airport was not safe for landings (Saxena, 2020).

Recommendations and Implications for Social Policy and Planning

UNESCO (2020) is engaged in empowering schools and their communities in the identification of the hazards and risks they are exposed to, their vulnerabilities and their capacity to manage them. The goals of this Comprehensive School Safety framework are: to protect children and education workers from death and injury in schools; to plan for educational continuity in the face of expected hazards; to strengthen a disaster resilient citizenry through education;

and to safeguard education sector investment. All professionals, participants of this study agreed that if "Health and Safety" was introduced as a subject at schools way back, India would not have seen such a huge impact of COVID-19 on its citizens, as it is now. They recommended for all educational institutions to prioritise and value the same. Hence to avert and combat any health and safety risk and its impact (such as COVID-19) more efficiently for the country's citizens, the main recommendations are in the areas that need to focus the attention of decision makers in education/HRD sectors that there is a strong need for health and safety education to be emphasised by the Governments and the concerned stakeholders, introduction and implementation of health and safety as a subject to be prioritised and valued, and also emphasise upon the infrastructure/safe design of educational sites.

Health, safety and environment (HSE) aspects in educational settings got sidelined due to an over-emphasis on performance and meritocracy which led to hundred thousand fatalities of children and young people across the globe. The state education department and the fire and rescue services department ordered an inquiry on educational institutions, including coaching centres, across Tamil Nadu, India that operate without safety precautions. Every classroom that can seat more than 45 students must have two exits and the fire drills should be conducted once in 6 months. Heads of such centres must conduct fire audits (Aditi, 2019). Like industry, HSE systems in educational institutions brings results when they are implemented successfully along with safe design of educational sites, safe infrastructure and procedures as well as regular behavioural reinforcements. For example, an activity-based HSE resource was developed for New Brunswick schools, to make it as a way of life for children.

This is the high time to introduce safety and health in schools syllabus. Some of the HSE basics, need to be added in our syllabus according to the level, like for kinder-garden students, how to handle sharp needle pencil and how to wash their hands for own hygiene. Similarly for the engineering or science students, an environmental and safety subject should be included once it becomes the practice on their day to day activities, culture can be established. It would help removing the industrial accidents directly from the field. A safety professional said, "we should incorporate the inputs at an early level of the educational system. If we focus now on the generation who are going to take charge of society in coming years, then it will give results". HSE is an important part of all educational institutions to carry out risk assessments for buildings as well as school buses to foresee and minimise risk to students, staff and other stakeholders (Borneo Bulletin, 2020). The educational institutions that don't implement HSE system for caring the human assets of their nations need to be warned for closure/banned as they misuse public money due to the losses in the incidents and fatalities that take place, and then they claim the funds from insurance companies. Its a double loss of human life and public properties.

Besides, educational institutions, HSE systems also need to be further strengthened in all health care facilities, as very recently, two COVID-19 hospitals at Andhra Pradesh and Gujarat in India got fire in the month of August 2020 killing several patients, indicating a lack of safety culture. Risk is inevitable part of our life, they need to be evaluated and optimised with layers of protection before it is resulting into accident. It is imperative to note that in case, the HSE systems are not implemented more systematically in educational and health care institutions, then there are larger implications in terms of incidents and fatalities as observed in this article.

References

Aditi, R. (2019, May, 28). Educational institutions flouting fire safety norms under scanner. Retrieved on 23 July 2020. https://timesof india.indiatimes.com / city/chennai / educational-institutions-flouting-fire-safety-norms-under-scanner/articleshow/69529061.cms

Alex, Ashish (2019, December, 26). Child safety in schools: Whose responsibility is it? Retrieved on 24 July 2020. https://www.thenewsminute.com/article/child-safety-schools-whose-responsibility -it-114795

American Chemical Society (2012). Creating safety cultures in academic institutions. WAShington, DC. Retrieved on 22 July 2020. academic-safety-culture-report.pdf

Awasthi, Ashwani (2020, April, 18). Higher Education Institutions Are Ensuring Students' Safety During COVID-19 Pandemic. Retrieved on 25 July 2020. http://bweducation.businessworld.in/article/Higher-Education-Institutions-Are-Ensuring-Students-Safety-During-COVID -19-Pandemic-/18-04-2020-189510/

Azad, Yashovardhan (2018, April, 19). Safety education should be a-part-of-the-school curriculum. Retrieved on 26 July 2020. https://www.hindustantimes.com/analysis / safety-education-should-be - a - part - of - the - school - curriculum / story-DfW8d9jwqlVSCKsSs 7FYDP.html

Baskar, Harish (2020, February, 15). The unsafe roads near schools. Retrieved on 22 July 2020. https://www.cag.org.in/blogs/unsafe-roads-near-schools

Bhandari, Ankita (2020, June, 08).Fire breaks out at Delhi University's Ram Lal Anand College; 2 classrooms charred. Retrieved on 27 July 2020. https://zeenews.india.com/india/fire-breaks-out-at-delhi-universitys - ram-lal-anand-college-2-classrooms-charred-2288780. html

Bhatia, Anisha (2017, December, 11). Road to Safety. Retrieved on 22 July 2020. https://sites.ndtv.com/roadsafety/43-children-die-road-accidents-india-every-day-2546/

Borneo Bulletin (2020, April, 7). HSE crucial in educational institutions. Retrieved on 22 July 2020. https://borneobulletin.com.bn

Borwankar, Vinamrata (2020, May, 18). Association gives post-covid-19 guidelines for school. Retrieved on 24 July 2020. https://m.timesofindia.com/home/education/news/association-gives-post-covid-19-guidelines-for-school/amp_articleshow/75796668.cms

Chakarborty, Bhaskar (2020, July, 18). Personal communication on safety and health in educational settings. Mumbai, India.

Citation (2020). How is health and safety for schools implemented? Retrieved on 19 July 2020. https://www.citation.co.uk/industries/education/how-is-health-and-safety-implemented-in-schools/

Department of Education (2020). Managing health and safety in schools. Retrieved on 20 July 2020. https://www.education-ni.gov.uk/articles/managing-health-and-safety-schools

Gilda Rusu-Zagar *et al.* (2013). Procedia - Social and Behavioral Sciences, 92 (2013), 832 – 837.

Grenada Elementary School (2018, April, 11). Safety & Disaster Preparedness. Retrieved on 22 July 2020. https://ge-gesd-ca.schoolloop.com/safety

Government of India (2004). Ministry of Home Affairs, National Disaster Management Division. A Handbook for Administrators, Education Officers, Emergency Officials, School Principals & Teachers. New Delhi.

Hindustan Times (2017, Oct., 22). 50 deaths in 60 days: Are coaching centres driving students to suicide? Retrieved on 26 July 2020. https://www.hindustantimes.com / editorials / 50-deaths-in-60-days-are-coaching-centres-driving-students-to-suicide / story-eVmULTa YCUDi4Gdbry4MSI.html

Iyer, Swathy R. (2019, June, 19). Bengaluru: 7-year-old boy's death shocks parents; teachers emphasise safety measures. Retrieved on 22 July 2020. https://timesofindia.indiatimes.com/city/bengaluru/7- year-old-boys-death-shocks-parents-teachers-emphasise-safety-measures/articleshow/69848679.cms

Mehta, Dipen (2020, January, 02). Preparing for fires. Retrieved on 23 July 2020. https://www.thehindu.com/opinion/op-ed/preparing-for-fires/article30453391.ece

Melnick, H., & Darling-Hammond, L. (with Leung, M., Yun, C., Schachner, A., Plasencia, S., & Ondrasek, N.). (2020). Reopening schools in-the-context of COVID-19: Health and safety guidelines from other countries (policy brief). Palo Alto, CA: Learning Policy Institute.

Nanjappa, Vicky (2020, July, 29). Union Cabinet approves new education policy: What-is-NEP 2020? Retrieved on 29 July 2020.https://www.oneindia.com/india / union-cabinet-approves-new-education-policy-what-is-nep-2020-3126712.html

National Association of Secondary School Principals (2018, September). Principal Leadership: School Safety. Retrieved on 22 July 2020. https://www.nassp.org/2018/09/01/school-safety-a-principal-concern/

NCES (2020). Violent Deaths at-School-and-Away-From-School-and-School-Shootings. Retrieved on 20 July 2020. https://nces.ed.gov/programs/crimeindicators/index.asp

New Brunswick Department of Education Instructional Resources Branch. (2000). Health & Safety Choices for Life. Audio Visual, 2000 Media Catalogue. Fredericton, New Brunswick.

Pais, Nichola (2017, September, 14). A burning question - are our kids fire safe at school? Retrieved on 24 July 2020. https://www.scoonews.com/news/fire-alarm-schools-need-to-wake-up-now-1932

PDonline (2020, February, 6). Enforce safety rules to stop school deaths. Retrieved on 22 July 2020. https://www.pd.co.ke/opinion/editorials/enforce-safety-rules-to-stop-school-deaths-23514/

Rapid Global (2020). Health & Safety principals in educational institutions. Retrieved on 20 July 2020. https://rapidglobal.co.za/health_-safety-principals-in-educational-institutions/

RoSPA (2020). Managing Safety In Schools & Colleges. Retrieved on 17 July 2020. https://www.rospa.com/rospaweb/docs/advice-services / school-college-safety/managing-safety-schools-colleges.pdf

Roy Chowdhury, Shreya (2017, September, 11). Why are children not safe in India's schools? (Hint: the problem is not lack of laws). Retrieved on 26 July 2020. https://scroll.in/article/850255/why-are-children-not-safe-in-india-s-schools-hint-the-problem-is-not-lack-of-laws

Saxena Sparshita (2020, August, 08). Kozhikode plane crash not an accident but murder. Retrieved on 08 August 2020. https://www.

hindustantimes.com / india-news / kozhikode-plane-crash-not-an-accident - but - murder - air-safety-expert-capt-mohan-ranganathan / story-FmzwXnfwCFbUYgFQm7ySwJ.html

UNESCO (2020). School Safety. Retrieved on 21 July 2020. http://www.unesco.org / new/en / natural-sciences / special-themes/ disaster-risk-reduction/school-safety/

University Grants Commission (2020). UGC Guidelines on Safety of Students on and off Campuses of Higher-Educational Institutions. Retrieved on 21 July 2020. https://www.ugc.ac.in/pdfnews/ 4006064_Safety-of-Students-Guidelines.pdf

Vicario, Anna. (2017). Practices that promote comprehensive school safety. New Trends and Issues Proceedings on Humanities and Social Sciences. 3. 304-312. 10.18844/gjhss.v3i1.1779.

Institutions that don't prepare safety leaders, don't build longterm safety culture.

CHAPTER 4

Why Industry is Losing Faith in Safety Awards?

Introduction and Literature Review

Rewards give false value to a company, a business head of a MNC emphasised. Why do we need the awards at the very first place other than the recognition or bench-marking, when the safety systems are functional, being implemented and total employee participation is fully active in risk-correction at all work areas of the site or plant. Possibly, these awards get into the organisations when all these safety systems are in place but not fully functional for enabling the total interdependent safety culture. Secondly, the safety awards in industry are used to balancing between the business excellence and the safety excellence, more so for promoting the business excellence and less for the safety excellence. This divided focus of the managements is a prime reason behind the people being killed at every work site despite these HSE awards (ILO, 2020).

Every year we invite you to our most prestigious awards, celebrating health and safety excellence across all industries in more than 50 countries worldwide (British Safety Council, 2020). The Confederation of Indian Industry's SHE Award is to evaluate an Organization's interest towards the well being of its employees through adequate measures, not only for the Regulatory requirements, but also as a part of the Management's Commitment towards ensuring that the workforce is adequately protected through effective Safety, Health & Environment measures (Confederation of Indian Industry, 2020). ICC National Occupational Health & Safety Awards recognize best practices in OHS (Indian Chamber of Commerce, 2020). The National Safety Council awards are given annually to individuals and organizations that have demonstrated leadership in keeping people safe at workplaces (National Safety Council of India, 2020). Federation of Indian Chambers of Commerce and Industry emphasises safety systems excellence awards every year or Industry (FICCI, 2020). The Government of India instituted National Safety Awards (NSA) in the year 1965, to recognise safety performance of Industries to maintain the interest of both the managements and the workers in accident prevention, (DGFASLI, 2020). The National Safety Council is America's leading nonprofit safety advocate, to focus on eliminating the leading causes of preventable injuries and deaths. The Council offers the variety of individual, team and corporate awards. Employers providing exemplary off-the-job safety and health programs are eligible for the Community Safety Award (NSC, 2020). The safety awards programs provide companies, a means to gauge their program against the industry it does business in.

Critically speaking, there are huge number of at-risk behaviours at every site and the companies still receive safety awards, this highlights doubts about the validity of such awards (Kaila, 2011, p2135). Industry achieve awards every year in HSE despite the fact they practice at-risk behaviours daily violating procedures which lead to incidents on regular basis. There are gaps in practices, manuals and standards. At the same time, there is also a mushrooming of awards agencies around. There is a need and scope to explore the lacuna and improve further.

Research Question/Objective Statement

To explore the perceptions and reasons, whether the people in industry are losing faith in HSE awards, and to suggest the scope for improving various aspects of HSE awards management.

Methods and Analysis

Open-ended questions based interviews and personal in-depth discussions with 250 HSE, medical, education, management, mental health professionals were conducted through remote data collection techniques over 3-month (July-September 2020) in India from diverse locations and organisations. Their responses related to questions on HSE awards were collated and thematic data analysis was used to reflect and analyse the results. The responses of these professionals are presented in the following 10 themes as tabulated.

Results and Discussion

In overall, 80% of the study participants agreed that they are losing interest or lost interest as the HSE awards are only documents-based, and also it would depend on the type of National or International, private or government agencies providing these awards, and their evaluation criteria, but the commercial awards are being avoided.

Ten insightful aspects of HSE awards have come out in research findings as below.

Tabulation of results of themes analysis

1. Awards are Ornamental with no much value: (80%)
2. Rationale of Awards is not clear: (84%)
3. Criteria, fee and assessment are important: (100%)
4. Much scope of improvement in being fair: (84%)
5. Reputed Awarding Agencies matter: (54%)
6. Authentic Awards do value: (51%)
7. Management perspective: (75%)
8. Self-realisation is the key: (69%)
9. Seeking awards for Safety Culture: (52%)
10. Awarded sites also met serious incidents: (50%)

1. Awards are Ornamental with no much value

The value of safety awards is being questioned as being only ornamental for organisations. The responses received from 80% of the HSE professionals indicate that there is not much value in the HSE awards. They have become ornaments to showcase. According to a safety head, "I have all and sundry associations giving safety awards without doing any review. I do know, where just after fatal incident, the organisations showcase safety awards from Delhi association". An objective and thorough methodology of assessment are needed to bring in faith for these awards. The safety awards to Massey Energy and Transocean were questioned after the coal and oil disasters (The Rural Blog, 2020). The value addition of awards schemes that exist in the Occupational Health and Safety area is very limited (Health and Safety Laboratory, 2020). These schemes can result in safety behaviours, if they are focused, well implemented, evaluated.

2. Rationale of Awards

ILO updates seem to question the logic or the genuineness of these awards while there is an increase of accidents corresponding to over 6,000 deaths every single day and increased ill health despite all HSE efforts, then why awards for the companies (ILO, 2020). Organisations are not only losing faith in safety awards, they are generally worried about so many useless awards (about 84% all types of awards), being pushed for commercial purposes these days. Majority corporates are choosy and don't even apply in many such awards. Many organisations lack in sincere, honest, ethical approach in filling-up the awards application. Even, the awarding agencies are interested in nothing more than the commercial aspects.

3. Criteria, fee and assessment are important

Nearly 100% of HSE professionals emphasised that the safety awards should be provided to organisations and the people who really demonstrate safety at field. If mechanism of giving safety award is not sound, then one can face above problem of losing faith in safety Awards. People are losing faith, now a days safety awards are linked with entry fees. In some awards, even assessment processes are also not up to the mark. But yes, some awards are really worth due to their assessment process.

Some agencies are following assessment based on an application. No data verification and site assessment. Second type assessment based on application and data verification.

Third assessment has steps below which are quite comprehensive.

1. Application assessment & data verification
2. Site assessment by independent bodies
3. Final presentation by organisation for best practices

The University of Iowa (2020) suggested the review criteria to include annual safety reviews, implementation of corrective actions, departments not to be penalised for reporting incidents, engagement to improve safety culture, and innovations in safety practices.

4. Much scope of improvement in being fair

Much uncertainty exists regarding the effectiveness of safety awards (Goodrum & Gangwar, 2010). A safety head stated, "recent days, there are some open biases, and also some real achievers are recognised. I see it from my own experience. We got to be non-judgemental in evaluating the contributions". Nearly 84% HSE professionals agreed that there is a huge scope of improvement in this area. It is crucial to guide organisations to provide fair information about safety performance even if it is not favourable (WorkSafe, 2020).

5. Reputed Awarding Agencies matter

Nearly 54% of the HSE professionals expressed that the people believe in grabbing reputed organisation awards like CII, FICCI, NSC, BSC which can bring laurels to their organisation. The award can be a big motivational tool. The main goal of the NSC awards is to support the broader mission to save lives and prevent injuries, from the workplace to anyplace (Safety and health magazine, 2020).

6. Authentic Awards do value

Is Indian industry losing faith in the safety awards? "I don't think so", says an EHS vice president of Dorf Ketal. "I am going to introduce one new award". If people are guided correctly they are keen to work upon exact requirements in safety improvement and can achieve these awards (Personal communication, 2020). About 51% of the HSE professionals expressed that the authentic and quality awards like that of NSC, OISD, Ministry are always welcoming. Rewards are a recognition towards demonstrated commitment to safety of an organisation ensuring that the workforce is adequately protected through effective HSE measures (Confederation of Indian Industry, 2020).

7. Management perspective

People still have faith in safety award. Such awards boost morale of employees. Also it marginally increases faith of employees in their own safety systems. However sometimes, the management takes it in a different perspective. About 75% of the HSE professionals expressed that nowadays management is mostly sales focused, believing in statistics to answer to the board. They believed that big companies like L&T and Tata, the awards can be purchased based on providing rosy information. Management think that awards for safety would help build safety culture and keep workers working safely but it disinterests everyone except the award winner as management perspective is to use awards for sales promotions (Burns, 2020).

8. Self-realisation is the key

Over the years, the awards have motivated companies for adopting best safety practices and systems in their sector benchmarked with the best in the industry (FICCI, 2020). But, one has to be very critical if these best practices are only document-based. According to a veteran EHS Director, "It depends on which safety award we strive for, getting 5-star BSC rating is also easy, as it has become more of business than an endeavour to improve industrial safety. Most of the safety awards are data-based which is not the correct picture of the safety performance". Nearly 69% of the HSE professionals expressed that the self-realisation and purpose behind safety drive itself is an award for industry, if each milestone achieved is celebrated, as safety is a journey, as achieving every milestone brings self-satisfaction and self-appreciation to keep us motivated for safe practices.

9. Seeking awards for Safety Culture

Make 'working safely' on continuous manner will set a standard. Whereas this will make a benchmark for the organisation in a period of time. Then that will become the culture for the organisation. So setting standard and establishing the system will give you the guidelines to work more safely, continuously working in a safe manner will be leading to the better culture, by following others to follow and adhere the same. Many (52%) corporate professionals opined that they are promoting safety culture in their sites across Indian locations so that they could apply and achieve National Safety Awards. So they are working hard to strategically plan and approach these awards. It is like planning forward, implementation backwards. Toronto Construction Association's (2020) Outstanding Safety Culture Award, recognizes a company that treats safety protocols with a genuine sense of urgency and is innovative and rigorous about ensuring workplace safety is paramount.

10. Awarded sites also met serious incidents

Nearly 50% of the HSE professionals agreed that there are many serious incidents that happened in the sites across the globe that were certified and awarded by the national and international agencies. This implicates several aspects, that the awards are possibly limited to feel-good factor or appreciation, or whether the sites get complacent after receiving these awards. The major fire at Indian Oil Corporation's (IOC) Jaipur terminal was caused by the non-observance of normal safety procedures (Business Standard,

2013), whereas this site had achieved all national and international laurels and certifications.

Conclusion, Recommendations and Implications

Conclusion

1. There exists a large number of HSE awards in order to recognise the work places with safety excellence, nevertheless incidents and fatalities keep increasing. Whether, these awards deliver what they stand for, is a million dollar question. Each country has hundreds of work-related fatalities each year. For example, 110 Australian workers were killed at work in 2020 till 10 September. In 2019, 182 Australian workers were fatally injured while working. Whereas, 3,751 workers were fatally injured while working from 2003 to 2018 (Safe Work Australia, 2020). Hence, we need to go beyond than just the face value of these safety awards which are actually meant to add a huge value to a work place for 'peoples safety'.

2. As high as the 80% of HSE professionals perceived that the industry is losing interest/have lost interest in safety awards, for many reasons, that need to be pondered over, which include that the: awards are ornamental, useless awards, rationale, criteria, fee and assessment are important, much scope of improvement in being fair while providing information, reputed awarding agencies matter, authentic awards do value, management perspective, self-realisation, seeking awards for safety culture, and the awarded sites also met serious incidents. The International Stainless Steel Forum introduced a Safety Award Programme which invited members to submit good ideas from their Safety Programmes, which are circulated among members, following the principle that people would learn from the accidents of others (Core Sector Communique, 2020).

3. Whether industry is losing faith in the Safety Awards? The mixed perspective is that whereas the people who are working in the developing organisations are being benefited. Because for applying of any new tenders, company wants to use the accreditation for their order bookings. Secondly, whereas the developed organisations are concerned, some times, they are not believing the awards, they look for results on their own HSE implementations. They mainly focus on ISO kind of certifications to enhance their systems and implementation. The DuPont Safety and Sustainability Awards invite organisations that successfully implemented innovative ways of safeguarding employees, communities and the environment, while also contributing to the economic and social health of society (DuPont Sustainable Solutions, 2020).

4. The management focus is clearly to achieving business rather safety by bringing in the national and international HSE awards and accolades. Every corporate has these awards in their cupboards, nevertheless the fatalities did not stop. Beside awards, we have so many experts everywhere, then why so many accidents are happening regularly. Hence, one view is clear and crystal that awards are not meant to say that the organisations have achieved safety excellence by availing these awards. Preventing workplace fatalities is a necessary goal of safety management system, but quite often, the employers fail in their leadership roles and approach towards fatality prevention and the unthinkable happens and some-one dies at the work (Walter, 2020).

Recommendations and Implications

1. SRC & Johnston (2019) observed that the safety culture was more than just working safely, it was about celebrating our successes and continuously improving. The critical question is that when organisations on an average have

almost 30% at-risk behaviours, which obviously means they lack in the safety culture, how they could be considered for safety awards. On the other hand, awards agencies ought to consider the behavioural aspects of safety, behaviour that is the root cause of almost all incidents (Kaila, 2020). In this regard, if the accounting of at-risk behaviours are not part of awards criteria, then these awards are not valid, and incidents would surely occur, even after receiving the best safety awards. Unsafe practices/at-risk behaviours are the early warning signs of a potentially serious incident and the zero initiative ought to include steps like: Targeting zero injuries, Empowering individuals, Creating a positive reporting culture, Reporting of near misses, Managing workplace incidents, Commitment to sustaining a safe workplace, Communicating openly, Influencing long-term change (Webcke, 2020).

2. Moreover, most of the safety awards defy the fundamentals of the occupational safety and health (OSH) which is generally defined by the ILO as the science of the anticipation, recognition, evaluation and control of hazards arising in or from the workplace that could impair the health and well-being of workers, taking into account the possible impact on the surrounding communities and the general environment (Alli, 2008). In principle, a safety award based on well-rounded evaluation is needed to determine the extent to which it is intended to capacitate workers to be safe and productive at workplace (Wegman & McGee, 2004). Safety awards criteria must include the field-level increase of safety awareness till the last person at work areas for enhancing more robust safety systems for everyone at site (Yumpu, 2020).

3. The awards lack much in application value, ethical standards, value for life etc. Most progressive companies

affirmed that their business excellence is almost 100%, however, the HSE excellence is nearly 70–80%, but they received all kind of awards, which is questionable in view of value for human life and zero-harm focus. It is clear that the safety awards and safety culture do not seem to fit together. We need to understand the safety awards in the pretext of existing safety culture in the industry which poses a critical question as to the purpose that awards serve. Safety policies and procedures differ so much in practices in every plant. According to a veteran Vice President (HSE) of an MNC, "Bent for profits of the managements over-writes safety culture, 'safety first' even becomes 2nd/3rd, it is ok, but safety takes last seat in favour of business". Many safety culture awards are available with a well defined criteria (SAFE Work Manitoba, 2020) but incidents keep happening on regularly which does not support the rationale/ effectiveness of the HSE awards. The safety awarded workplaces need to be simply safe with zero incidents at all times for all persons reporting for work daily.

4. The work sites are not totally safe, how come they get awarded, as most companies revealed their safety culture management score is around 80% on the basis of following ten points criteria measurement (Kaila, 2020).

- There is a strong belief in BBS (behaviour based safety) concepts of all employees and management. BBS is rolled out among all employees at the site/plant.
- BBS is adopted as corporate policy/value and in employee performance management.
- BBS is being practiced on daily basis by all employees and associates.
- Online observations reporting in each department including contractors.

- Each department has got rid of the reactive and dependent safety cultures.
- Motivational rewarding for best observers and department every month.
- People at site don't bypass unsafe behaviour, rather spot-correct it.
- Departments are aware of the Hot Spots
- Departments have action plan to address the Hot Spots
- HOD is motivating employees and associates for BBS

To reach a score of 100, certain improvements action plan are needed especially for contractors staff to move from dependent safety culture to independent and interdependent safety cultures. Also a new action plan to make safety culture as way of life, there is a need to linking BBS to CSR, communities and colonies around as well as homes. Building a Safe System is a holistic, long-term exercise, and is based on shared responsibility (ITF, 2016).

According to a HSE Strategist, the HSE awards need to consider the following:

- Vision Zero can be achieved only if the BBS processes are meticulously followed.
- BBS: A Key element needs to include in HSE as the Key element in all industries.
- HSE guidelines need to be redefined in light of this global pandemic with BBS playing key role.
- BBS influencing HIRA strategies inculcating responsible behaviour in the minds of workers.
- BBS trainings shall be mandatory in the training calendar of every Industry.

According to AFCONS company: Gopalpur Port Project, the Winner in CII (Confederation of Indian Industry) eastern region Safety, Health & Environment Award 2019-2020 beating 9 Construction companies, "if you follow BBS guidelines, you can win every platform". A senior professor of the National Institute of Industrial Engineering (NITIE) stated, "BBS reinforces the traditional safety systems aiming towards zero incidences in the workplace".

5. Also, it needs to be noted that there is low concern for safety for the contractors staff. The absence of workplace protections reflects on the efforts to undermine worker safety (Leibenluft and Olinsky, 2020). Most organisations admitted that they are able to develop safety culture for their employees but failed to do so for contractors' workmen. Then how they receive the awards when the benefit of safety culture has not reached unto the last person in the premises of the company. Hence, there needs to be a planned intervention to step up safety awareness among the low-paid contractual persons.

6. Practically, the corporates are not ready for safety awards, as they have not established safety culture at sites for which they are awarded. There are a widespread failure to take the safety regulations seriously (DORRELL, 2020). Also the awarding agencies take this opportunity to award them for vested commercial interests. Proactively, either the companies must achieve the safe workplaces and then go for awards, and/or the awarding agencies must enable, support and develop the safety cultures and then award these aspiring applicants for awards. Many corporates stopped taking interest in these awards rather are trying hard to remain focused on developing safe workplaces for their workforce as nobody likes to get even a first-aid injury.

7. Finally, the serious implications of the findings of this research can be imagined in terms of fake awards based on

rosy information of safety leading to incidents of fire or fatalities sounding very critical in nature. While this scenario endangers lives of people to the unmitigated risks that the employees and contract staff are exposed to. The role of the HSE is questioned in preventing accidents at work which would lead to more injuries and possibly lost lives (PFM, 2020). Also, with these fake/so-called HSE awards being received based on mere documentation leading to better image of the company for more sales promotions, and insurance coverages for being awarded/certified sites, are some complications and violations of business ethos.

8. The benefits that the effective Board level ethics, organisational vision, leadership and direction of occupational health and safety can bring in terms of health and safety of people and the overall business performance, are inseparable. Then why is it that the business excellence is far ahead, and, the HSE excellence is far behind which puts the lives of employees at greater risks killing people each year. The organisations aspiring for awards and the HSE awards agencies need to revisit this imbalance seriously in terms of ground realities of safe practices (Health and Safety Executive, 2020).

9. Remember, you may be taking a somebody's life by awarding an unsafe organisation. Thus, it is recommendable in view of the above proceedings of this paper that a company (which does not have a safe culture or has a past record of incidents and fatalities) should not be awardable, and awarding such an entity should be unlawful and to be avoided by the awarding agencies. It is hoped that these implications shall be interpreted positively as a piece of research information towards a scope of improvement in HSE awards for corporate safety and human life.

10. In view of the above discussions, there is strong need felt for local governments' control over the wrongful selection

criteria on the safety awards, and installing corrective action on agencies awarding companies with unsafe HSE cultures, in the larger interest of the society for developing safe systems based on innovation and excellence (Australian Government, 2020) and finally, to probe a vital question as to why so routinely the ethics of human safety are being sandwiched and bypassed between business profits and safety excellence, and someone gets killed.

References

Alli, B. O. (2008). Fundamental principles of occupational health and safety. Geneva: International Labour Office.

Australian Government (2020). Excellence in Road Safety Award. Retrieved on 16 Sept. 2020. https://www.regional.gov.au/local /awards/2013/fs-excellence-in-road-safety.aspx

British Safety Council (2020). international safety awards 2020. Retrieved on 26 August 2020. https://www.britsafe.org/awards-and-events/awards/international-safety-awards/

Burns, Kevin (2020). 5 Reasons To Stop Annual Safety Awards. Retrieved on 31 August 2020. https://www.kevburns.com/blog/bid/ 401563/5-Reasons-To-Stop-Annual-Safety-Awards

Business Standard (2013, January 21). IOC Jaipur fire due to lack of safety measures: Probe. Retrieved on 12 Sept. 2020. https://www.business-standard.com/article/companies / ioc-jaipur-fire-due-to-lack-of-safety-measures-probe-110020300031_1.html

Confederation of Indian Industry (2020). Safety Health & Environment Award (SHE). Retrieved on 26 August 2020. https://www.cii.in/AwardsDetail.aspx?

Core Sector Communique (2020). ISSF announces winners of Safety and Sustainability Awards. May 25, 2019. Retrieved on 12 Sept. 2020. https://www.corecommunique.com/issf-announces-winners-of-safety-and-sustainability-awards/

DGFASLI (2020). Vishwakarma Rashtriya Puraskar (VRP). Retrieved on 31 August 2020. http://14.143.90.243/dgfasli/awards/ vishwakarma-rashtriya-puraskarvrp

DORRELL, E. D. (2020). HSE to clamp down on practices that flout CDM safety regulations. The Architects' Journal. (2003, May, 1). Retrieved on 14 Sept. 2020. https://www.architects journal.co.uk/archive/hse-to-clamp-down-on-practices-that-flout-cdm-safety-regulations

DuPont Sustainable Solutions (2020). The 2020 DuPont Safety & Sustainability Awards. Retrieved on 15 Sept. 2020. https://www.consultdss.com/dssa-2020/

FICCI (2020). Handbook for FICCI safety Systems Excellence Awards for Industry. Retrieved on 27 August 2020. http://www.ficci.in/study-page.asp?spid = 23037&sectorid = 27#

Goodrum, Paul and Gangwar, Manish. (2010). Safety Incentives A study of their effectiveness in construction. *Professional Safety.* 49.

Health and Safety Executive (2020). Case studies that identify and exemplify Boards of Directors who provide leadership and direction on occupational health and safety. RESEARCH REPORT 499, 2006, p6. Retrieved on 13 Sept. 2020. https://www.hse. gov.uk/research/rrpdf/rr499.pdf

Health and Safety Laboratory (2020). An Evaluation of Reward and Recognition Schemes in the area of Occupational Health and Safety, HSL/2006/17. Retrieved on 13 Sept. 2020. https://www.hse.gov.uk/research/hsl_pdf/2006/hsl0617.pdf

ILO (2020). World Statistic. Retrieved on 7 Sept. 2020. https://www.ilo.org/moscow/areas-of-work/occupational-safety-and-health/WCMS_249278/lang--en/index.htm

Indian Chamber of Commerce (2020). ICC National Occupational Health & Safety Awards 2020. Retrieved on 26 August 2020. https://www.indianchamber.org/icc_events/icc-national - occupa - tional-health-safety-awards-2020/

ITF (2016), Zero Road Deaths and Serious Injuries: Leading a Paradigm Shift to a Safe System, OECD Publishing, Paris.

Kaila, Harbans Lal (2020). Planned Intervention of Behaviour-Based Safety (BBS) Helps Organisations Improve their Safety Time Arithmetic. *World Safety Journal*, WSJ-Vol-29, No-3, 34–41.

Kaila, H. (2011). Organizational cases on behaviour-based safety (BBS) in India. *International Journal of Human Resource Management*, 22: 2135-2146. 10.1080/09585192.2011.580180.

Leibenluft Jacob and Olinsky Ben (2020, June, 11). Protecting Worker Safety and Economic Security During the COVID-19 Reopening. https://www.americanprogress.org/issues/economy/news/2020/06/11/486146/protecting-worker-safety-economic-security-covid-19-reopening/

National Safety Council of India (2020). NSCI Safety Awards. Retrieved on 26 August 2020. https://nsc.org.in/2019/03/06/nsci-safety-awards-2019-applications-invited/

NSC (2020). NSC Safety Awards and Recognition. Retrieved on 30 August 2020. https://www.nsc.org/work-safety/get-involved/safety-awards

Personal Communication (2020, August, 25). EHS Vice President of Dorf Ketal. Safety Awards.

PFM (2020). Role of HSE questioned by trade union. (2016, September, 20). Retrieved on 14 Sept. 2020. https://www.pfmonthenet.net/article/124065/~/article/146582/products.aspx

SAFE Work Manitoba (2020). SAFEty Culture Award. Retrieved on 10 Sept. 2020. https://www.safemanitoba.com/safetyculture/pages/safety-culture-awards.aspx

Safe Work Australia (2020). Fatality statistics. Retrieved on 15 Sept. 2020. https://www.safeworkaustralia.gov.au/statistics-and-research/ statistics/fatalities/fatality-statistics

Safety and Health Magazine (2020). Celebrating impact: 2020 Green Cross for Safety awards. Retrieved on 10 Sept. 2020. https://www.safetyandhealthmagazine.com/articles/20226-celebrating-impact-2020-green-cross-for-safety-awards

SRC Communications and Johnston Suzanne (2019 May, 08) FROM IDEA TO LAUNCH - DEVELOPING A SUCCESSFUL SAFETY AWARDS PROGRAM. Retrieved on 14 Sept. 2020. https://www.src.sk.ca/blog/idea-launch-developing-successful-safety-awards-program

The Rural Blog (2020). Safety awards to Massey and Transocean questioned after recent coal and oil disasters (2010, November, 12). Retrieved on 13 Sept. 2020. https://irjci.blogspot.com/2010/11/workplace-safety-awards-questioned.html

The University of Iowa (2020). Rewards and Recognition Program. Retrieved on 31 August 2020. https://ehs.research.uiowa.edu/lab-safety/rewards-and-recognition-program

Toronto Construction Association (2020). Outstanding Safety Culture Award. Retrieved on 1 Sept. 2020. http://archive.tcaconnect.com/Outstanding_Safety_Performance_Award.html

Walter Laura (2020). Facing the Unthinkable: Fatality Prevention in the Workplace. Dec 31, 2007. Retrieved on 15 Sept. 2020. https://www.ehstoday.com / safety / article / 21904194 / facing-the-unthinkable-fatality-prevention-in-the-workplace

Wegman D.H. and McGee J.P. (2004). National Research Council (US) and Institute of Medicine (US) Committee on the Health and Safety Needs of Older Workers; Washington (DC): National Academies Press (US). Retrieved on 31 August 2020. https://www.ncbi.nlm.nih.gov/books/NBK207711/

Webcke Shane (2020). Safe Work and Return to Work Awards 2017. Retrieved on 3 Sept. 2020. https://www.worksafe.qld.gov.au/__data/assets/pdf_file/0009/98685/Category-4-Example-entry.pdf

WorkSafe (2020). SAFETY STAR AWARDS CRITERIA. Retrieved on 31 August 2020. https://www.worksafenb.ca/media/59260/safetyawardnominationcriteria.pdf

Yumpu (2020). Safety Awards Criteria. Retrieved on 3 Sept. 2020. https://www.yumpu.com / en / document / view / 42329664 / safety-awards-criteria-examples

Longterm Safety is a Degree of freedom from Harm and Risk.

CHAPTER 5

Contribution of Civil Society toward Industrial Safety Culture

Introduction, Rationale, Context

Any industrial safety incident or disaster precedes with a series of observations made by the civil society, employees, or others, which are generally ignored and compromised. The civil society is emerging stronger year-on-year to represent on all worldly issues (The World Economic Forum, 2013). To understand the context further, the research throws light here further. The Fukushima nuclear accident raised critical questions concerning the role of civil society prior to the accident, civil society's reactions to the accident, and the impact civil society had on nuclear policies following the accident (Hasegawa, 2014). The civil society can and has actually contributed to safety of industrial activities. Safety as a public concept and the concept of public safety need to be well informed (Mutadis, 2015). On the 8th anniversary of the Baldia factory fire in Pakistan, which left 260 workers dead, civil society and aggrieved families of the deceased demanded of the government to implement the Joint Action Plan devised after the incident to improve health and safety conditions at work places (The Express Tribune, 2020). The studies indicate that civil society participation in safety scenario has resulted mostly only after the incidents, which is obviously not a planned or proactive measure to prevent incidents. SAF€RA (2020) studied the contribution of civil society and local representatives to industrial safety culture, to the quality of decisions and to the resilience of organisations as regards safety.

The role of safety culture and leadership are highlighted in every incident, because when leaders are not focused, the slippages are possible. Indirect cost of accidents is too high. Fire and explosions in chemical industry has gone up in last 3 months. Conducting safety implementation guidance series would help industry to look within as to how this can improve their safety culture. According to a DuPont consultant, "the scale of losses have increased, though the number of incidents are reduced, this is a global trend" (Personal Communication, 2020). Zero-incident companies can also have incident any time, as risk is prevailing every time. Hence safety observations must also prevail every time to spot-correct it by the safety observers. Any delay in spot-correction is very risky. So develop spot-correction teams across all work areas for achieving total safety culture. Interdependent safety culture helps to move from compliance mindset to competitive edge. Co-creating safer place to live and work is an ambition to achieve with better safety governance through civil society dispositions of good citizenship (White, 2006).

Research Objective

A premise that civil society contribution is of paramount relevance to make this world a safer place to live and work, this article attempts to explore the possible contribution of the civil societies to the safety cultures of industries, and recommends certain actions for the same.

Methodology

A total of 270 HSE professionals were requested to reflect their viewpoints on contribution of the civil societies to the safety cultures of industries, and to provide recommendations on how the civil societies should be more influential to the corporate safety implementation. Both primary and secondary data were collected from diverse organisations during October to December 2020.

Research Findings

Some of the research response patterns that emerged to a study question as how does civil society contribute to the industrial safety culture, are described below.

Industrial safety is not in isolation from civil society but the fact remains that the civic safety is a neglected part in India. Safety is not an organisational SOP combined with casual mindset of legal authorities in controlling the impacts of risk, resulting into corporate behaviours that the civil societies contributions are ignored, hence impact remains limited to the safety culture of industries.

1. *The industrial safety is not in isolation*: The environmental advocacy group Earthworks, and affected communities and civil society groups around the world are marking the first anniversary of one of the world's deadliest mine waste disasters by highlighting the dangerous practices of the mining industry, and calling for stricter oversight (Business Wire, 2020). This exactly shows that the industrial safety is not in isolation. Safety is cultivated and improved by people, in other words, civil society. An industrial worker is also a father, a son, a brother (of course, we may also say, a mother, a daughter, a sister). Behaviour of a worker is crucial, especially in industrial safety, where he is in constant exposure to various types of potential workplace hazards. Family plays a crucial role in modifying one's at-risk behaviour into a safe behaviour. For example, we see advertisements on TV and in news papers. A school-going daughter reminding her father to take and wear his helmet (as he rides a two-wheeler), a college-going son sitting in the passenger seat of a four-wheeler urging his father to wear his seat belt who is about to start the vehicle. Now-a-days, most of the latest cars are coming with in-built mechanisms, giving an indication to the driver and other car users to wear seat-belts, and in some good models, unless the driver and the persons sitting in the front seat wear their seat-belts, the car won't move. A very popular advertisement is about the use of helmet (choice is yours). Such examples are many. Mother, wife, son, daughter, friend, the list is only representative, can contribute a lot to inculcate safety awareness in an industrial worker. So is the case, with a Supervisor, a Manger, an Executive – all can contribute to enhance safety awareness among workers significantly. This is in addition to the other well-known and widely followed methods in the industry - through appropriate and adequate training and close supervision.

2. ***Civic safety is a neglected part in India*:** In the last two decades, the NGOs, labour leaders, media agencies, investor institutions, religious leaders and other civil society representatives have played a critical and diverse set of roles in societal development. In India, industrial safety does not exist in the agenda of civil societies. They address civic rights and responsibilities, keeping our neighbourhood clean and green is citizen's responsibility. So civic safety is a neglected part in India. Developed countries teach safety in schools and communities. There rewards and penalties are huge. In India, as there is a factory inspector, but is he there to check and report compliance? So all the laws are applicable to industrial sector, not for public. Just now, how dangerous and hazardous is COVID-19? It's a disaster but who cares? The only control is by police. So we need a lot of discipline, control, awareness training and compliance.

3. *Safety is not an organisational SOP*: Caring and compassion for everyone around selflessly are necessary to reap the benefits in the present and for all future generations for achieving sustainable culture of interdependent safety culture. But unfortunately, the killing of 1,244 people and 2,500 injured among the worst industrial accidents awoke the world to the poor labour conditions faced by workers in the ready-made garment sector in Bangladesh (ILO, 2020). Industrial managements have a duty to make safety an organisational behaviour. Some organisations just conduct safety training, it does not help unless it is practiced as an organisational SOP. According to a vice president of AM/NS, "if you don't have safety in your behaviour, its difficult to take your life ahead". People kill themselves with their unsafe behaviour (Personal Communications, 2020).

4. *Casual mindset of legal authorities in controlling the impacts of risk*: There are direct and indirect impacts of risk and hazards of industry on the civil society. First when employees and contract workmen are directly exposed by working at plants or sites. Contractors workmen represent almost 70% of civil society who work on temporary work periods and imbibe safety cultures from organisations. Secondly, when there is a potential threat of industrial units being situated within civil society limits and jurisdictions. Bhopal gas tragedy impacted 3,000 deaths and 30,000 cases of injury in civil society in 1984, yet not much has been done to control the impact of industrial hazards that exist. The civil society groups are intensely committed and driven by the injustice and lack of action, laws were changed but not followed (Narain and Bhushan, 2015).

5. *Civil societies contributions are ignored, hence impact is limited*: A non-profit organisation, Forum of Behavioural Safety (2020) promoted safety culture by organising five national conferences in India including 900 public and private

multi-national companies. **Box 1** depicts that both the civil society groups and corporates/industry interact and impact safety culture among people. Civil society organisations' top leaders/activists' participation and of the industries influence the safety culture for zero harm and to what an extent would people behave safe on daily basis. Using feedback from local residents surrounding industries is necessary for evolving safety culture. But, under apartheid government, civil society had limited or no power to advocate local concerns against a risk society on the environmental and pollution problems that affected them (Leonard & Pelling, 2010).

The 90% of HSE professionals in this study are of the view that the civil society organisations and representatives do contribute to the industrial safety culture. But there are certain critical risk issues that are still not dealt with, like how do civil societies get affected due to industrial presence within cities, and how would citizens groups raise their voices when there are fire explosion or gas leakages. It is found that nearly 40% of the small and major industrial units do not follow the prescribed safety and maintenance norms (The Times of India, 2020).

BOX 1: Both civil society and industry interact and impact safety behaviour culture among people

1. Civil society organisations (CSO) leaders/activists' effective participation in decision making on how safe is industry to public and property
2. Industries leaders' top participation with civil societies to control risk exposure and develop safer place to work and live
3. Outcome: Safety culture assuring zero-harm to public and property, and the extent to which would people behave safe.
4. Limitations: Public feedback is ignored by government authorities and/or industries, and therefore the CSO impact may be limited.

Shockingly, it was observed that the civil society voices are ignored for their safety. In an explosion in a chemical factory in Maharashtra that killed 13 persons and 72 injured, the local residents had complained to district authorities about foul fumes coming from the plant weeks before the incident, but they were ignored (The Indian Express, 2019). The World Economic Forum (2019) observed that though the civil society organisations and leaders have become global initiatives for social protection, there is inevitably a lag between the emergence of a social challenge and a systemic response supported by the enforced law and investment by businesses. In most countries, the contribution of civil society to the safety culture of industrial have not been recognised. Secondly, most industries do not have safety programme for their corporate social responsibility projects. That is one reasons for low civil society participation in industrial safety programmes. Moreover, the alerts given by civil society are ignored by legal authorities, the recommendations of the audit committees are compromised, and companies delay the corrections of observations made by employees. As a result of ignoring and compromising practices, the incidents keep on happening.

Conclusion versus Recommendations

The negligence on part of the CSOs, industries, authorities to sync on the objectivity of their core safety issues, run the risk of achieving the desired result for making society a safer place to live and work. Though the HSE professionals view that the industrial safety is not in isolation from civil society, this study results revealed how difficult and complex it becomes for civil society to remain focused in managing and controlling the impacts of risk. In this regard, certain recommendations of this research may help serve a better tool to strike balance between the mindsets of variety of responsible civil society institutions, industries etc.

These conclusions-cum-recommendations are: reinforcing safety as an organisational SOP, increasing sense of civic safety and recognising contribution of civil society institutions, legal enforcements to control the impacts of risk, including safety syllabus in school level, making civil society interventions more effective, and co-creating proactive safety scenarios.

1. ***Reinforce Safety as an organisational SOP in small and major industries***: Safety culture has its roots in organisational behaviour, and safety systems are its branches. Hence, safety culture is to be nurtured on daily basis by everyone, from top to bottom, failing which incidents keep happening. Federation of Indian Chambers of Commerce and Industry (FICCI, 2020) envisaged to promote safety culture in consultation with industry experts and civil society organisations. It needs to be remembered that the organisational behaviour safety is not merely a 'series of training' as some companies do. It is to be practiced as an organisational SOP by all sites/plants for achieving best ROI. Every bit of lethargy on part of safety observers gives way to incidents, and when this happens, the entire safety system comes into questioning as to what went wrong. The organisational leaders have to be alert that once the safety observers are trained, they need to be engaged in daily sharing of even minor observations.

2. ***Increase sense of civic safety and recognise contribution of civil society***: All industries must have safety programme for their corporate social responsibility projects for increasing civil society participation in the industrial safety programmes. Understanding safety by the civil society and the lay people is as important as for safety officers in an

industry. Hence, each industry has an obligation to serve this cause for neighbourhood industry units. The exchange between the civil and industrial societies would make perfect safety culture. It is recommended that no alerts and observations made by the civil society organisations should be ignored and taken for immediate correction for developing a culture which is safe for all stake holders. There are always reactions of the civil society and village authorities with regard to their safety concerns arising from the operations of the industrial units surrounding them. Most of the times, these safety voices are ignored by industrial units. One good example was set by a public sector company, i.e. GAIL that introduced structured community safety programme inviting participation of heads of village panchayats and discussing with them any safety hazards they perceived from the industries around. The company safety officers also visited the villages around and clarified of any safety and health risk and its impact on their life or on their crops (Harbans, 2020). It is recommended that such initiatives with the partnership of civil and industrial societies make best safety culture. The Confederation of Indian Industry (CII, 2020) works to create and sustain a safe environment conducive to the development of India, partnering industry, government, and civil society.

3. ***Legal enforcements to control the impacts of risk***: In India and elsewhere, many industrial plants exist within civil society residential limits. It is noticed that the risk of chemical pollution and industrial incidents cannot be ignored, especially when such industries are not regulated or don't follow the law (Hydrocarbon Processing, 2020). Hence in the interest of public, the industries must not be situated within a residential areas. There is a need to provide a set of tools (such as funding, trust, technology, citizen engagement) to enable civil society leaders to drill down and address the questions of most importance and relevance to their local context, community or organisation (The World Economic Forum, 2013).

4. ***Safety syllabus in school level is must*:** Civil society has long way to reach safety consciousness of industrial safety. We should start teaching safety syllabus in school during development/growth from child to industry employee, communication by teachers and education patterns as well as learnings by involvement in public incident/accident of near and dear ones.

5. ***Making civil society interventions more effective*:** There are limitations when the appropriate CSOs, the government and the industry are not agreeable on certain issues, there are battles of dialogues, and the issues get complicated or unresolved (Down to Earth, 2020). It is good to realise that due to COVID-19, many local, national and international CSOs came together to discuss many issues toward a common goal of making this world a better place to live and work. Hopefully, the spirit of objectivity prevails for larger social good. Also, there are innumerable CSOs exist whose social impact is huge, invisible and unmeasurable. Hence, the contributions of civil society are to be acknowledged. The success that civil society has had working with businesses on climate change, shows that improved commitments from businesses on civil liberties and human rights would bring obvious benefits to civil society, and businesses could also benefit (The World Economic Forum, 2017). Civil society interventions can be more effective by using policy engagement approaches such as avoiding adverse political contexts, adequate use of evidence, working together with other organisations (Overseas Development Institute, 2020).

6. *Co-creating proactive safety scenarios*: This study results indicate that there are positive dynamics between the safety cultures of civil societies and industries. Thus, a strong need emerges for robust HSE education at both ends. Civil society movement needs to be a tool to put a stop to the industrial incidents killing people. The civil society organisations intervene to correcting wrong-doing/compromising safety laws. The government support is essential for civil societies to fight for the cause of safety matters in the interest of public. Moreover, the civil society participation in safety scenario should not be just an incident-based, but a planned or proactive intervention of both industry and the governments to prevent impact of incidents. The community safety committees should review and regulate the progress of such interventions. An example is of the International Centre for Chemical Safety and Security (ICCSS, 2020) that seek their implementation locally, nationally, regionally and globally to reduce chemical threats and enhance public security, environmental protection and sustainable chemistry, in partnership with governments, industries, international organisations, science and academia, local authorities and media.

7. *Framework for better relationship between businesses and civil society towards safer culture*

BOX 2: Action plan/roadmap to implement civil society-industry partnership towards safer culture

1. Reinforcing safety as an organisational SOP in small and major industries,
2. Increasing sense of civic safety and recognising contribution of civil society institutions,
3. Legal enforcements to control the impacts of risk,
4. Including safety syllabus in school level among civil society areas,
5. Making civil society interventions more effective, and
6. Co-creating proactive safety scenarios.

Box 2 provides an action plan/roadmap to implement civil society-industry partnership in developing a sustainable safety culture to prevent losses due to incidents. This 6-points framework can be used which is recommended by the HSE professionals of this research study. The civil society-industry partnership steering team can be formed to implement, review and report its progress by training and developing teams from civil society and industries associations. There are many such local, regional, national, international associations that already exist, need to be strengthened further on above suggested agenda to promote safety cultures in all countries. In fact, the civil society as a whole is not separated from industrial society, as they are integrated internally. Hence, it becomes absolutely essential that all societies are in empowering processes together for living and working in a safer world. The civil society and industrial society are sides of a same coin. It requires a continuous process and journey of leaderships and coordination across organisations. COVID-19 management is one learning of planning such intervention for HSE culture across nations.

References

Business Wire (2020). Communities & Civil Society Call for Action to Prevent More Mine Waste Disasters on First Anniversary of Deadly Brazilian Spill - Earthworks. Retrieved on 13 Dec 2020. https://www.businesswire.com/news/home/20200123005885/en/Communities - Civil - Society - Call-for-Action-to-Prevent-More-Mine-Waste - Disasters - on - First-Anniversary-of-Deadly-Brazilian-Spill-Earthworks

CII (2020). About CII. Retrieved on 15 Dec 2020. https://www.cii.in/

Down to Earth (2020, July, 13). Civil society praises Centre's draft order banning 27 pesticides. https://www.downtoearth.org.in/news / pollution / civil-society-praises-centre-s-draft-order-banning-27-pesticides-72259

FICCI (2020, Nov. 27). Online Training Programme on Industrial Safety: Planning and Management. https://nidm.gov.in/pdf/trgReports/2020/November/trg_25-27November2020akg.pdf

Forum of Behavioural Safety (2020). Souvenir of 4th National BBS Conference held at Scope complex, New Delhi on 17th January 2020. www.besafe.org.in

Harbans Lal (2020, December). Possibilities and Challenges of Making Safety a 'Way of Life' in Indian Society. *world safety journal*, Vol. 29, No. 2: 51-61.

Hasegawa Koichi (2014, June, 20). Japan's civil society: Context, reactions, and policy impacts. Retrieved on 03 Dec 2020. https://doi.org/10.1177/0268580914536413.

Hydrocarbon Processing (2020, Nov. 20). Engen blast triggers questions about industrial safety in SA. Retrieved on 14 Dec 2020. https://www.hydrocarbonprocessing.com/news/2020/12/engen- blast-triggers-questions-about-industrial-safety-in-sa

International Centre for Chemical Safety and Security (2020). ICCSS News. Retrieved on 15 Dec 2020. https://www.iccss.eu/

ILO (2020). The Rana Plaza Accident and its aftermath. Retrieved on 13 Dec 2020. https://www.ilo.org/global/topics/geip/WCMS_614394/lang--en/index.htm

Leonard, Llewellyn and Pelling, Mark (2010). Civil society response to industrial contamination of groundwater in Durban, South Africa. Environment and Urbanization - ENVIRON URBAN. 22: 579-595. 10.1177/0956247810380181

Mutadis (2015). Contribution of civil society to industrial safety and safety culture : lessons from the ECCSSafe European research project. Retrieved on 03 Dec 2020. http://www.mutadis.org/projects/governance-risk-activities/eccssafe- project/

Narain, Sunita and Bhushan, Chandra (2015 July, 08). 30 years of Bhopal gas tragedy: a continuing disaster. https://www.downtoearth.org.in / coverage / environmen t/ 30-years-of-bhopal-gas-tragedy-a-continuing-disaster-47634

Overseas Development Institute (2020). Policy Engagement: How Civil Society Can be More Effective. Retrieved on 13 Dec 2020. https://www.odi.org / sites/odi.org.uk/files / odi-assets/publications-opinion-files/200.pdf

Personal Communications (2020, Dec, 03, 11). safety cultures and civil societies.

SAF□RA (2020). Exploring contributions of civil society to safety - ECCSSafe. Retrieved on 11 Dec 2020. https://projects.safera.eu/project/1

The Express Tribune (2020, September, 12) Civil society demands better safety at work places. Retrieved on 09 Dec 2020. https://tribune.com.pk/story/2263655/civil-society-demands-better-safety-at-work-places

The Indian Express (2019, September 1). Maharashtra: 13 dead, 72 injured in blast at chemical factory. Retrieved on 15 Dec 2020. https://indianexpress.com/article/india/dead-72-injured-in-blast-at-maharashtra-chemical-factory-5955146/

The Times of India (2020, Dec. 12). How seriously do we take industrial safety? Retrieved on 14 Dec 2020. https://timesofindia.indiatimes.com/india/timestopten/ msid-75602715,card-75607280.cms

The World Economic Forum (2013). The Future Role of Civil Society. Retrieved on 12 Dec 2020. http://www3.weforum.org/docs/WEF_FutureRoleCivilSociety_Report_2013.pdf

The World Economic Forum (2017). Big business and activists finally agree. On this one issue at least. Retrieved on 14 Dec 2020. https://www.weforum.org / agenda / 2017/06 / activism-civil-society-good-for-business/

The World Economic Forum (2019, January). Civil Society in the Fourth Industrial Revolution: Preparation and Response. Retrieved on 12 Dec 2020. http://www3.weforum.org/docs/WEF_Civil_Society_in_the_Fourth_Industrial_Revolution_Response_and_Innovation.pdf

White, Melanie (2006, November, 21). The dispositions of 'Good' citizenship: Character, symbolic power and disinterest. Pages 111-122. https://doi.org/10.1080/17448680600905882

Leadership, strategies, constant hard work are required for longterm safety culture.

CHAPTER 6

Active Humanism in Public Safety Behaviours to Defeat COVID-19 and Restore Economy: Long-term Solution, Not Fire-fighting Approach

Introduction

Containing COVID-19 and restoring our economies require not just good policy decisions and medical advice; it also needs continued compliance with the recommended behavioural changes that in many ways go against social and cultural conventions (Srikanth, 2020) as India topped 200,000 dead as virus surge broke health system (Nzherald.co.nz, 2021).

Governments are forced or impelled to choose lockdowns or curfew as public fail to conduct safe behaviours. Police, enforcement agencies show minimum tokenism and fail in the social change process as there is no humanism. They do not touch the hearts of public at large. They are reactive in approach. Also people at large, are driven by the social ritual and beliefs, hence the huge religious gatherings precipitated COVID-19 crisis. The election rallies by political parties add to such medical emergencies. Safe behaviour is yet not a social belief in India, and people normally don't obey civic safety rules or regulations. All this situation of citizens irresponsible behaviour has given rise to the COVID-19 bushfire. With so much about society at stake, there may be an opening for the human sciences to be more humane in their aims and ambitions (Nelson, 2020) and maximize humanism in the care of COVID-19 patients during this crisis and focus on staff-patient communication and expression of compassion (Sonis, *et al.*, 2020).

The outbreak of COVID-19 brought social and economic life to a standstill.There is an opportunity to participate in global supply chains, as multinationals are losing trust in China. To 'Make in India', some reforms are needed, labour reforms being one of them (Chaudhary, *et al.*, 2020). Government of India is taking several steps to ensure that we are well prepared to face the challenges posed by COVID-19 by building Atmanirbhar Bharat (National Portal of India, 2021).

Though, the experts recommended COVID-19 appropriate safe behaviours (CASB), yet people failed to understand as to why individuals don't practice these safe behaviours as part of their cultural backdrop. Also it needs to be considered that the behavioural change across the nation is an often long-term activity, hence the effects of COVID-19 infections may be seen for many years as long as people don't change their socially responsible safe behaviours. Also, it needs a clarification that there is a difference between safety and safe behaviour of people. Safety is taken as if someone would look after my safety, whereas safe behaviour is a personal responsibility. No one is safe until we are all safe. Hence, we need to continue emphasising CASB (McKinsey, 2021).

Country leadership failed in humanism. There is a death of humanism. Political leaders backed out on humanism as they chose power over humanity, terrorism over nationalism, corruption over compassion and care. The powerful and the rich started hoarding resources such as Oxygen, Remdesivir etc. that they might need in future, and the poors suffered. Hence the civil leadership has to awaken, or let people die from incidents and infections. In the battle against coronavirus, humanity lacked leadership (YUVAL, 2020).

Objective

The present article is focused to explore an action plan to promote active humanism in public safety behaviours to manage COVID-19 and restore economies.

Methodology

Since the behavioural safety interventions are implemented in many countries, it will be good idea to explore these learnings and good practices for COVID-19 scenarios. A total of 252 HSE professionals were requested to reflect their viewpoint on the Humanistic Behaviourism in Public Safety During COVID-19, to restore economy. Both primary and secondary data were collected during January to April 2021. Themes were identified to describe research findings. The behavioural safety method, being a generic one, can be adopted to assess present safety behaviours and find in what respect it has to improve safety culture in community (Beriha, Patnaik and Mahapatra, 2011).

Results and Findings

Nation is going through 'Health Behaviours Crisis, not simply health or medical crisis. Hence, the crisis need to be fixed with holistic behaviour based interventions as permanent solution. All other interventions look short-lived ones, so the relapses of COVID-19 waves are happening. The research participants response themes revealed very significant aspects as follows to combat the impacts of COVID-19 and to restore economy as a long-term solution:

1. COVID-19 appropriate behaviours: Nearly 90% of the study participants believed that COVID-19 appropriate behaviours is the only solution of the problem at this junction. It is about safety behaviour, people are deliberately careless. Is it due to unconsciousness, misinformation or a devil may care attitude? It is the behaviour which is taking the toll. Indiscipline is the root cause. Obviously everyone must adhere safe behaviour and follow corona discipline. In India 2nd wave of corona exploded due to risky behaviour of Indians which is integral part in DNA of Indians so until we follow safe behaviour and discipline of COVID-19 guidelines, Indians would be in trouble. Another part of COVID-19 spread is casual approach of Indian leadership, Election commission who does not have safety mindset, due to that, lacking in anticipating disastrous scenario and it's preparedness by Government at large. WHO emphasised that adopting COVID-19 appropriate behaviour is the best way to stop transmission of coronavirus, its variants: (The Hindu, 2021).

2. Safety Culture: Almost 88% of the study participants emphasised that we need to develop a safety culture and not just a safety climate. Safety climate merely looks at enforcing rules and regulations in a land of people that tend to not follow those. However, by developing a safety culture we will be able to achieve greater results, in order to do so we need to target a persons behaviour. Assimilate safe practices within a persons lifestyle. That is use of masks and sanitisers, because at the moment that is all we can do to bring about a change. All organisations can facilitate employees' deep compliance with safety and health procedures (Xiaowen, *et al.*, 2021).

3. Indian Context and Settings: 75% of the study participants stated that the behavioural changes need to happen from the top, whether it is in an industry or at the national level. We Indians are notorious at breaking rules and we always need someone to monitor us. With a varied demography, holding different dogmas and from multiple cultures, it is a huge challenge. Ethics, honesty, morality and discipline are attributes to be imbibed at the kindergarten level in schools. It is much easier to mould a young and innocent mind. The electronic media can play a major in bringing about behavioural changes among the masses. India's massive COVID surge puzzled the scientists as virus spread through unrestricted social interactions, and low vaccine coverage (Nature, 2021).

4. Media is responsible. As many as 66% of the study participants felt that Govt must try to focus on the media telecast and stop the frequency of corona news. Also social media be used for positive behaviour development towards fear and stress. Public must try to change spreading negative messages. People from education sector, cinema, drama, safety to come forward for behaviour changes in this epidemic to work together for Nation to solve this issue. The Indian government needs to address the fear of vaccines before implementing the process of mass vaccination, as the attitude of Indian citizens towards COVID-19 vaccine is not very positive (Praveen *et al.*, 2021).

6. Crisis management: Fire fighting. Unfortunately that is regular feature in our many (almost all) crises, hence mostly temporary, short-lived solutions. 84% of the study participants stated this, which demonstrates the attitude of the governments towards management of crisis in the country. Experts criticised a lack of planning and flexibility in the COVID-19 response (Bhuyan, 2021). If India is still fire-fighting and not installing permanent solution, it would affect economy adversely.

7. Personal Immunity: 90% of the study participants opined that reality intervention is developing immunity at the first place to fight the virus and maintain good health through healthy behaviour as part of lifestyle. People are loosing lives. Nothing is important than life of the person. One has to do whatever possible to save someone's life. The practice of daily yoga, exercise are prescribed to remain fit to fight infections. Yoga has been part of Indian culture for years and is accepted around the world for its health and wellness (Shukla, 2020).

8. Positive Reinforcements: It's about how people elevate themselves to at-risk behaviours. The probability of getting infected is high. It's only behaviours at end of the day. Yet the interventions taken are negative reinforcements by authorities. 68% of the study participants believed that a proactive culture should have been built on positive reinforcements too. More you try to tie up people, more they will resist. It's a training issue again. Some schemes looking at rewarding and awarding correct behaviours, should also have been built up with the level of education. while talking about vaccines and the power of positive reinforcement, the experts found that the people are more willing to get the Covid-19 vaccine when told how popular it is, and the fraction of people reluctant to get the vaccine dropped by 5 percent (Dizikes, 2021).

9. How to motivate public to change behaviour: 87% of the study participants emphasised to have an action group and think tank in this direction to evolve national action plan. The expert doctors views on TV, their common opinions about Covid treatment are not converging (except precautions) probably due to non clarity/varying of corona-virus effects. But the national safe behaviours on safety precautions to some extent are happening partly which only can save people as rightly suggested. This would contribute in fighting the prevailing situation in the country. Only behaviour modification works. Everyone need to deliver responsibility for our Nation. The Indian industry added COVID Appropriate Behaviour as a category in their Behavioural safety Programme a year ago for timely intervention. That is how the precautions for Covid-19 can be adopted as habit/culture for day to day routine and will have to develop courage for intervention at public life.

10. Influence of Environment: Foreigners who are safety conscious when visit places like Goa, are found doing unsafe acts while riding motor bikes without Crash Helmets. This is mainly attributed to the environment that influences them to follow unsafe practices. So besides attitude, environment does play an important role in behavioural safety 65% of the study participants stated that. The large COVID-19 numbers being reported, demonstrates the unsafe practices are still on among people of India, impacting the economic activity in the country. Although a few positive impacts of COVID-19 on the environment were seen, these were the short-term effects induced largely by nation-wide lockdown. Indeed, the pandemic is expected to pose long-term adverse effects on the environment in future for proper management of plastic and chemical waste, and also mental stress of children who had been forced to live in locked conditions in homes (Ankit, *et al.*, 2021).

11. Behavioural Safety Technique: In COVID-19 pandemic many human lives we have lost, how behavioural safety would have prevented this loss? 80% of the study participants stated that behavioural safety programme is very dynamic. In March 2021, Sembcorp included "Social Distancing and Personal Hygiene" as the 11th Behaviour to our behavioural safety programme. They are 1st Power Plant to do a Capital Overhaul where they got 1250 Associates from all of the India, done 1800 Covid Tests and successfully completed 53 days Shutdown. Managed 35 Covid Positive Associates and few employees by successfully isolating (Kaila, 2020).

12. Long-term Effort and Effect: 77% of the study participants admitted that behavioural safety requires a long time for organisations to establish a simple principle of caring for each other's safety (an interdependent safety culture) but its worth, ask families who lost their earning members. Why do organisations take long time on this aspect of safety management. Manager (EHS) confirmed that BBS monthly observations played a vital role in how have achieved 5 star from BSC at Torrent power limited, Surat, Dahej and Ahmedabad plants, and now we are planning for BSC 5 star in Environment (Personal Communication, 2021).

13. Complacency: 2nd wave is no different than the 1st. 86% of the study participants expressed that people have become complacent over last 9-10 months due to lack of risk anticipation. Individual pledge of caution and care is the only way and may be we need to take pledge of Covid Appropriate behaviour for our own self/family so at least we don't add to the problem. Self-Discipline, patience and care for others is key to the success of winning over this pandemic. Really feel sorry for the state of affairs around as demand for beds or treatment has surpassed supply. Let us do a bit in this war for good times ahead. The goal is to not let one citizen become imperilled to COVID-19 due to complacency (health.mil, 2020).

14. Risk Anticipation: 89% of the study participants said that everything depends on risk anticipation, a caring person will never allow any near-miss opportunity to mitigate the root cause while others will ignore with 'chalta hai' attitude carried in their mind as part of upbringing and environment in which they are. Present COVID-19 is a real life example, where organisations are taking due care for employees by allowing Work-From-Home but this is being misused by a few. Mulraj (2018) emphasised to dump 'chalta hai' attitude, and usher in better governance.

Conclusion, Implications and Recommendations

Humanistic safety means someone touches your heart to convey the risk so that it does not appear again. It encompasses many aspects such as empathy, interpersonal caring, patience, communication sensitivity, engagement savviness, connectivity, human touch, and so on. It essentially means to develop an organisational SOP on these behaviours for safety culture management involving everyone at workplaces.

Behavioural safety approach is a continuous social education intervention even beyond your circles of influence. if any vendor in the market is not wearing mask, please don't buy anything from him. In our society market this has ben reinforced. Resident remind shopkeepers whenever they falter. Behavioural reinforcement is necessary for change process.

The recommendations are presented in 4 categories as below:

1. Action plan strategy to focus on
2. Containing COVID-19 and restoring economies
3. Implementing the Model of Humanistic change Management
4. Antecedents (A), Behaviours (B), Consequences (C) of COVID-19

1. Action plan strategy to focus on: The 18 sub-themes that emerged from the data are as follows to develop an action plan towards a host of lagging and leading factors for public/citizen behavioural change strategy which seems a multi-pronged approach to be used as a long term strategy to combat COVID-19 and restore economy. These 18 factors would often interplay and impact each other to get the best output.

1. Individual citizen to deliver responsibility
2. Developing personal Immunity
3. Behavioural safety planned intervention from the top by industry and government
4. Philosophy of doing whatever, save lives
5. Training safe behaviours in education
6. Courage for intervention at public life
7. Develop safety culture as permanent strategic solution
8. Social media to play major role for positive attitudes of masses
9. Nurture Positive thinking of all players
10. Unrestricted Awareness creation
11. Government to coordinate media news on Corona
12. Devil's attitude, political negativity
13. Unsafe behaviours taking toll on lives
14. How to motivate public to change behaviour.
15. Don't panic/rush on the health system
16. COVID-19 behaviours not being followed
17. News media is scary and sensational
18. Firefighting is not Crisis management.

The post-epidemic stage will see the emergence of a new human being, whose daily behaviour and thinking will differ from what it was before the COVID-19 outbreak. Humankind is going through a humanitarian revolution, the kind that has occurred only thrice before: first, after the discovery of fire;

second, with the advent of agriculture; and third, following the industrial revolution. The most prominent sign of this 'fourth revolution' is the predominance of new technology (ORF, 2020).

Safety and health is not reflected in the senses or sentiments of the modern Indian culture, and so is true in behaviour of the public resulting into incidents and accidents on road or industry. The surge in COVID-19 cases during 2nd wave is the result of Indian cultural context. COVID-19 is changing human attitudes and behaviors today and also forcing organizations to respond. However, the need to respond won't end when the virus's immediate threat eventually recedes. The permanent solution lies in behavioural change (Accenture, 2020).

How can we prevent future new variants of the COVID-19 virus? According to WHO (2021), stopping the spread at the source remains key. Current measures to reduce transmission - including frequent hand washing, wearing a mask, physical distancing, good ventilation and avoiding crowded places or closed settings - continue to work against new variants by reducing the amount of viral transmission and therefore also reducing opportunities for the virus to mutate.

The social economy actors have assisted the recovery from the crisis by providing innovative solutions that are aimed at strengthening public services to complement government action. In the long term, social economy organisations can help reshape the post-crisis economy by promoting inclusive and sustainable economic models (OECD, 2020). It is recommended that all institutions private or public shall implement behavioural safety as per COVID-19 appropriate behaviours (CAB) checklist below to combat unsafe health behaviours:

2. Containing COVID-19 and restoring economies along with maximising active humanism at all levels need behavioural changes as follows (as defined by Pavan K Rao, HSE Head of a Singapore based multinational company: personal communication, 2021):

- All who are not required at Workplace, can work from home.
- Hybrid Working will become norm.
- Spilt team working with 12 hours shift 4 days work and 4 days off
- No leaves. If emergency, in return quarantine for 7 days and test on 8th day
- Double masks and social distancing at Workplace, travel and canteen
- RT-PCR test at slightest symptoms and 7th day CT Scan.

Behavioural safety/BBS is a journey, its a decision making for people and organisations to behave safe for self and others. Observer is the core implementer and driver of BBS system. everyone in an organisation is a trained observer. The success of the program depends on observers. So how he/she interacts with people, how he/she responds, matters. Behavioural safety observers are the backbone of safety culture, it is necessary to reorient them through the following test (Kaila, 2020).

Behavioural safety observers checklist to facilitate COVID-19 observations:

- Is an observer trained or not?
- Is he/she doing observations daily?
- Is he observing barriers in safety?
- Is he sharing observations in tool box talk (TBT) daily?

- Is he conducting behavioural safety mass-communication weekly?
- Is he filling in behavioural safety checklist daily?
- Is he also correcting own at-risk behaviours?
- Is he observing outside workplace also?
- Has he been recognised by his department?
- Is he reactive or friendly, proactive?

This rapid test would help retraining the observers. Organisations need a month to an year to orient all observers for observations and feedback process.

3. Implementing the Model of Humanistic change Management of Behaviour-Based-Safety (BBS) requires many inputs such as:

- Safety comes in seconds, not minutes;
- Behaviour is either totally safe or totally unsafe
- Economy excellence comes with safety excellence;
- Safety excellence is not in documents but in maximising safe behaviours across locations;
- Behavioural safety is an application of behavioural science;
- Behavioural safety comes with humanistic behaviourism;
- Behavioural safety implementation is a planned intervention;
- All health workers, employees are trained as observers;
- Behavioural safety brings cultural change;
- This Change is measured and monitored.
- Behavioural safety implementation is an observation and communication of risk;
- Behavioural safety implementation is possibly sustainable with one top leader;

- Behaviour is definable, observable, correctable, measurable, impenetrable;
- Behavioural safety Observers are the backbone of interdependent safety culture:
- Behavioural safety is to implement caring not scaring as a corporate value;
- Behavioural safety is a corporate decision making not a journey;
- Behavioural safety is an approach, not a name and blame or fault finding process;
- Behavioural safety is part of KPA;
- Behavioural safety Steering team meeting is important every month to review/reward the sites;
- Finally, its also an ISO45001 Compliance, and the incidents reduction is possible on a sustained basis to save life and economy.

Shankar Rajagopalan, a senior HSE expert said," its a blend of the Head, the Heart and the Guts that would get us safely out of the pandemic". The reality is that the leaders, numbers of corona positives and the public are deceiving the COVID-19, Most leaders never talked about the socially appropriate behaviours on the media, the public still is not convinced about the effects of COVID-19. The numbers must be double or triple to what is being reflected. Hence COVID-19 is going out of control in India.

Human spirit, humanistic behaviourism, Calculated optimism, and awakening efforts of the like-minded are the dynamic forces of our country. National behavioural changes take time. Positive thinking and planned interventions of our leadership need not be underestimated. Every positive and active person contributes bit by bit to the national cause to come back with better synergy levels To fix the present health crisis, the behaviour based interventions with cultural penetration by local level health volunteers all across the board using humanistic approach would be useful as a long-term strategy, all other interventions even the medical, or administrative ones are short-lived approaches. The people need the external stimuli or behavioural reinforcements for cultural change. It needs to be understood that short-term temporary interventions would delay or increase the health crisis. Nation is going through 'health behaviours crisis', Not simply health or medical crisis. Hence the crisis need to be fixed with holistic behaviour based interventions as permanent solution. All other interventions look temporary or short lived ones. Hence, the relapses are also happening.

Indian Public changed their COVID-19 appropriate behaviours temporarily in 1st wave, as a result of which we witnessed the worst 2nd wave in India. If we need to save lives further, we must adopt COVID-19 appropriate behaviours permanently. How can we do that as a planned intervention? Business Line (2021) emphasised mass vaccination to handle the crisis, along with the enforcement of appropriate behaviours and continuous communication from doctors, political leaders and administration. Public active participation is the right answer. We each one of us, need to speak up for safety of each other. Imagine if we daily do it once and all do it consciously, there would be a national level behavioural change. Simply we need to observe daily around us, if there is any one not practicing COVID-19 appropriate behaviours, we look at the person twice to alert him or her, and if need be, also request the person politely to observe safe behaviours for self and others safety. This simple intervention at citizens level in the whole country helps resolve the current crisis to a greater extent. Humanistic care is a priceless gift, one can afford to give to anyone, never delay it, connect as a big brother/sister and save life.

4. Antecedents (A), Behaviours (B), Consequences (C) of COVID-19: ABC perspective of COVID-19 needs to be understood in terms of antecedents (A), behaviours (B), consequences (C) as below. B is a function of A and C.

Antecedents (A)	Behaviours (B)	Consequences (C)
1. Government Policies 2. All level Leadership 3. Awareness on all Media 4. Enforcement regularity 5. Resources availability 6. Volunteer Organisations 7. Citizens participation 8. Seeking International help	COVID-19 Behaviours (safe or unsafe) are influenced by the antecedents as well as consequences. Non-compliance, Non-adherence to regulations etc.	Risk perception of consequences by citizens decide the severity and frequency of incidents like infections, fatalities. Low risk perception leads to higher number of non-adherence and vice-versa

We need to strengthen these antecedents and improve the risk perception to lower and minimise the unsafe behaviours to reach zero COVID-19 positives. Larger is the population size, more is the time needed to correct COVID-19 inappropriate behaviours, or enlarge the antecedents to reduce the time.

Promote COVID-19 safe behaviours on social media by leaders touching hearts of public, as every leader is connected to hundreds, thousands of citizens. Leaders at all levels (such as union leaders, religious leaders, school and college principals, university professors and institutes directors and vice chancellors. doctors, all professionals) serve as social change catalysts. Their humanistic messages and call for safe behaviours and safety of each other can save people from health behaviours crisis (United Nations, 2020). In order to achieve adherence to health regulations, elaboration on possible consequences improves individuals' health-preserving attitudes, and should be used during the resumption of social and economic activities under COVID-19 pandemic, as lasting adherence should rely on personal attitudes and behaviours (Ilan, *et al.*, 2020). This is what the world needs and we are just a perspective away from the total safety culture. Strictly following COVID-19 five appropriate behaviours guarantees almost 100 percent protection from coronavirus which no vaccination would do. Both are necessary for everyone. Value humanity, restore economy. According to Indian philosophy, service to human beings' health and safety is considered equivalent serving to the Almighty which refers to Nar Seva, Narayan Seva (PARASHAR and SINGH, 2021). Finally, better economies would bounce back as human determinations would surely defeat corona.

References

Accenture (2020, April, 3). COVID-19: 5 new human truths that experiences need to address: How organizations should respond to the never normal. Retrieved on 19 April 2021. https://www.accenture.com / in-en / about / company / coronavirus-human-experience

Ankit, Kumar, A., Jain, V. *et al.* (2021). Environmental impact of COVID-19 pandemic: more negatives than positives. Environmental Sustainability. https://doi.org/10.1007/s42398-021-00159-9

Bhuyan, Anoo (2021). The Lancet. Experts criticise India's complacency over COVID-19. Retrieved on 02 May 2021. https://www.thelancet.com / journals/lancet / article / PIIS0140-6736(21)00993-4/fulltext

Business Line (2021, April, 21). Covid-19: Public healthcare expert recommends new vaccine strategy for India. Retrieved on 30 April 2021. https://www.thehindubusinessline.com/news/national/covid-19-public-healthcare-expert-recommends-new-vaccine - strategy-for-india/article34373402.ece

Chaudhary, M. Sodani, P. R. and Das, Shankar (2020, August, 11). Retrieved on 11 April 2021. Effect of COVID-19 on Economy in India: Some Reflections for Policy and Programme. https://doi.org/10.1177/0972063420935541

Dizikes, Peter (2021, March 10). 3 Questions: Vaccines and the power of positive reinforcement MIT News Office. Retrieved on 03 May 2021. https://news.mit.edu/2021/vaccines-positive-reinforcement-0310

Health.mil (2020). Confronting the Coronavirus and Countering Complacency. Retrieved on 30 April 2021. https://health.mil/News/Articles/2020/07/02 / Confronting-the-Coronavirus-and-Countering-Complacency

Kaila, H. L. (2020). BBS towards Mission of Bharat Bane- Surkshit for Corporate India: Is it possible, how? Industrial Safety Chronicle, October-December-2020, 63-70.

Ilan Fischer, Shacked Avrashi, Tomer Oz, Rabab Fadul, Koral Gutman, Daniel Rubenstein, Gregory Kroliczak, Sebastian Goerg and Andreas Glöckner (2020, August, 26). The behavioural challenge of the COVID-19 pandemic: indirect measurements and personalized attitude changing treatments (IMPACT). https://doi.org/10.1098/rsos.201131

Mulraj J. (2018 May 05). Dump 'chalta hai' attitude, usher in better governance. Retrieved on 03 May 2021. https://www.thehindubusinessline.com/markets/dump-chalta-hai-attitude-usher-in-better-governance/article23776203.ece

McKınsey & Company (2021 April 21). COVID-19: Implications for business, COVID-19: Briefing note #50. https://www.mckinsey.com/business-functions/risk/our-insights/covid-19-implications-for-business#

National Portal of India (2021). Building Atmanirbhar Bharat & Overcoming COVID-19. Retrieved on 14 April 2021. https://www.india.gov.in / spotlight / building-atmanirbhar-bharat-overcoming-covid-19

Nature (2021, April 21). India's massive COVID surge puzzles. Retrieved on 01 May 2021. https://www.nature.com/articles/d41586-021-01059-y

Nelson, Alondra (2020, April 23). Society after Pandemic. Social Science Research Council. Retrieved on 15 April 2021. https://items.ssrc.org / covid-19-and-the-social-sciences / society-after-pandemic/

Nzherald.co.nz (2021, April, 29). India tops 200,000 dead as virus surge breaks health system Retrieved on 29 April 2021. https://www.nzherald.co.nz/world/covid-19-coronavirus-india-tops-200000-dead-as-virus-surge-breaks-health-system / OATJ2PVO YUAVZG7UKPSDHE4T2A/

OECD (2020, July, 30). OECD Policy Responses to Coronavirus (COVID-19): Social economy and the COVID-19 crisis: current and future roles. Retrieved on 17 April 2021. https://www.oecd.org/ coronavirus/policy-responses / social-economy-and-the-covid-19-crisis-current-and-future-roles-f904b89f/

ORF (2020, April, 08). A new human being will emerge in the post-Covid-19 world. Retrieved on 18 April 2021. https://www. orfonline.org/expert-speak/a-new-human-being-will-emege-in-the-post-covid-19-world-64275/

Parashar V.D. and Singh, Rita Devi. (2021, February). Relevence of Morality in Gandhian Philosophy, IJCRT, 9(2), 1-6.

Praveen SV, Ittamalla R, Deepak G. Analyzing the attitude of Indian citizens towards COVID-19 vaccine - A text analytics study. Diabetes Metab Syndr. 2021 Mar-Apr;15(2):595-599. doi: 10.1016/j.dsx.2021.02.031. Epub 2021 Feb 27. PMID: 33714134; PMCID: PMC7910132.

Shukla Raghwendra (2020, Dec 24). Budget 2021: Covid-19 brings back focus on Yoga, industry puts these demands. https://www. financialexpress.com/budget / budget-2021-covid-19-brings-back-focus-on-yoga-industry-puts-these-demands/2156744/

Srikanth S.N. (2020, May, 16). The pandemic and the challenge of behaviour change. Retrieved on 14 April 2021. https://www. thehindu.com/opinion / op-ed / the-pandemic-and-the-challenge-of-behaviour-change/article31596370.ece

Sonis Jonathan D., Kennedy Maura, Aaronson Emily L., Baugh Joshua J., Raja Ali S., Yun Bryan J., White Benjamin A. (2020 Apr 24). Humanism in the Age of COVID-19: Renewing Focus on Communication and Compassion, West J Emerg Med, 21(3):499-502. doi: 10.5811/westjem.2020.4.47596.

The Hindu (2021 April, 10) Adopting COVID-19 appropriate behaviour best way to stop transmission of coronavirus, its variants: WHO. Retrieved on 01 May 2021.

https://www.thehindu.com / news / national / adopting-covid-19-appropriate-behaviour-best-way-to-stop-transmission - of - corona virus-its-variants-who/article34288177.ece

United Nations (2020, March). SHARED RESPONSIBILITY, GLOBAL SOLIDARITY: Responding to the socio-economic impacts of COVID-19. Retrieved on 28 April 2021. https://unsdg.un.org/sites/default/files/2020-03/SG-Report-Socio-Economic-Impact-of-COVID-19.pdf

WHO (2021, March, 1). The effects of virus variants on COVID-19 vaccines. Retrieved on 16 April 2021. https://www.who.int/news-room/feature-stories / detail/the-effects-of-virus-variants-on-covid-19-vaccines?

Xiaowen Hu, Hongmin Yan, Tristan Casey, Chia-Huei Wu (2021). Creating a safe haven during the crisis: How organizations can achieve deep compliance with COVID-19 safety measures in the hospitality industry. Int J Hosp Manag. 2021 Jan; 92: 102662.. doi: 10.1016/j.ijhm.2020.102662 PMCID: PMC7456279

Yuval Noah Harari (2020, MARCH, 15). In the Battle Against Coronavirus, Humanity Lacks Leadership. Retrieved on 30 April 2021. https://time.com/5803225/yuval-noah-harari-coronavirus-humanity-leadership/

Our daily safe behaviours together will make a long-term culture for future businesses. For a best change, we need to address the culture of our organisations again and again.

CHAPTER 7

Managing the Difference between Safety Documentations and At-risk Behaviours in Industry

Introduction

Safety documentations in industry are carried out practically more for fulfilling the purpose of audits, awards and business profits, and less for an intention towards implementation of safety culture. If people feel safe and secure, they could perform better in higher standards for their companies. In developed countries, all places of work: industries, offices, universities, medical institutions, government and social organisations adhere to environment, health and safety (EHS) standards. But in India, an estimated 82 per cent of workplaces do not comply with EHS norms, according to a cross-sector survey by research and consulting firm Kaybase. There is, however, a growing consciousness of the need to comply with such safety requirements (Rao, 2019).

The purpose of the Indian National Policy on Safety, Health and Environment at Workplace is to establish a preventive safety and health culture in the country through elimination of the incidents of work related injuries, diseases, fatalities, disasters and to enhance the well being of employees in all the sectors of economic activity in the country (DGFASLI, 2021). But it is noticed that workplace safety managements remain fractured without the end-user involvement which is a serious gap between theory and practice at workplace orientations (Kristen and Alicia, 2020).

It is well said that if you have a will for safety culture, there is a way. If you think, safety is a cost, incidents and fatalities are on your way. International Labour Organization (ILO), each year 2.78 million workers die from occupational accidents and work-related diseases, and it is estimated that lost work days globally represent almost 4 per cent of the world's GDP (International Labour Office, 2019).

OSH Code 2020 prescribed duties of employees as follows, every employee at the workplace shall take reasonable care for the health and safety of themselves and other persons who may be affected by their acts or omissions at the workplace (India Briefing, 2021). Everyone deserves safety for life at work or otherwise, not necessarily by safety rules, regulations or systems, but with care and kindness of everyone around by adopting behavioural safety approaches to give an injury-free and zero-harm work life. The importance of leading occupational safety and health (OSH) indicators in complementing lagging indicators is an emerging topic for the promotion of a prevention culture in organizations (Zwetsloot, 2020).

An unsafe behaviour brings incidents, and also brings down business and economy of the country. The absolute safety of people, society and business lies in behaviour, not the documents of safety. The documents are on the basis of one-time safety training which is 100 percent but behaviours on ground remain unsafe as much as 30 percent (Kaila, 2020).

The safety professionals expressed that the difference between safety documentation and ground behaviour of employees is because they are trained for safety but not for behavioural safety implementation. Also because the the safety culture leadership for human values such as active care, concern, affection, humility, humanity, equality, compassion are not being exercised for safety of colleagues as envisaged in ISO45001 for managing internal risk control. This gap is not being addressed urgently by top leaders of the companies (Forum of Behavioural Safety, 2021).

Research Objectives

1. To study the factors as to why the safety documentations and ground realities differ in behaviours among Indian organisations.

2. To discuss its implications and provide conclusions to improve safety culture, to save people from injuries and fatalities.

Methodology

A total of 243 HSE professionals across Indian locations reflected their viewpoint on the difference between safety documentations and ground behaviours among organisations. Both primary and secondary data were collected from the study participants with diverse backgrounds of age, experience, designation and education. Open-ended questions based interviews and personal in-depth discussions with HSE professionals were conducted through remote data collection techniques over 6-months (October 2020 - March 2021). Thematic analysis were performed.

Research Findings

The study participants were asked as to why safety documentations and ground realities differ in behaviours among Indian organisations, and how this difference can be managed? Their responses were categorised on the eight themes below.

1. Missing safety message down the levels

Surprisingly, 90% of the study participants perceived that there is a lack of penetration of safety message down stream. There prevails a Sab Chalta Hai (all is safe here) Attitude by Management and Shop Floor People along with Enforcement authority. In this cultural conext, the Prime Minister emphasised that we need to set moving from "chalta hai" to "badal sakta hai" means a cultural change. It needs a people's movement; the government can at most be a catalyst (The Indian Express, 2017). Safety is not seen as value, may witness all around people roaming around with adequate precautions as if COVID-19 is over now. Management must invest in frequent safety training and orientations to improve safety knowledge among workers (Suxia *et al.*, 2020). Missing safety message down the levels among all employees can be very risky as it is a major lagging indicator.

2. Safety documentation to make authorities happy

Almost 75% of the study participants expressed that to make regulators and statutory authorities happy, sometimes managements deceive themselves. This is salted Ahamkar tatva (ego-centric behaviours) of the company. Also, to fulfil statutory compliances, adequate resources are not provided by Indian organisations. That is why the ground reality, safety documentation and behaviour are different. This is one of the prime reasons for lack of safety culture at workplaces. The accuracy of data documentation is still a major concern (El-Menyar, *et al.*, 2016). If Safety documentation is done to make authorities happy, then the process of building safety culture is surely hampered which can be very contrary to the business sustainablity.

3. Poor adherence to documentation requirements

As many as 80% of the study participants believed that the lack of awareness regarding documentation requirements is a reason for why the safety documentation differs from the ground reality. Also they shared that an accountability for adherence to documentation requirements is very poor. This research finding is a critical lagging factor for poor safety culture at Indian sites demonstrating unsafe mindset. Documentation is one of the key areas to determine the standard of care that employees would receive for their health and safety (Mohd Aihatram Khan *et al.*, 2020).

4. Compromising risk is a regular practice

As large as 76% of the study participants stated that compromising risk is an established practice for many Indian organizations. This is a very serious finding of the study indicating that at-risk behaviours are a regular affair at sites which would lead to incidents and accidents. A new study finds 73% of employees fear return to workplace will compromise personal health and safety (Business wire, 2020). Compromising risk as a regular practice indicates a pathological and reactive safety culture which is extremely risky for the workforce as well as the businesses.

5. No review of unsafe behaviours and corrective action

About 85% of the study participants considered that there is a lack of review of individual unsafe behaviours and suitable CAPA. Corrective and preventive action (CAPA or simply corrective action) consists of improvements to an organization's processes taken to eliminate causes of non-conformities or other undesirable situations. This demonstrates a passive outlook towards safety of the manpower at worksites. In companies with strong safety cultures, safety is embedded in daily management; it is part of the fabric of daily activity. It infuses every interaction, every decision and every behavior (EHS Today, 2013).

6. Fast businesses deliver incidents

Nearly 85% of the study participants felt that fast businesses would not sustain with incidents. They further stated that the business leaders are more competitors which boils down to less leadership for sustainability of business. Competition is good only if it is not at the cost of safety, and killing people for profits. Almost 30 percent of our industries and systems are non-compliant due to profit and production. Safety behaviour survey was indicated as part of the safety performance measurements to identify at-risk behaviours for industry (Government of Western Australia, 2021).

7. Only Behavioural awareness program, not planned intervention

About 78% of the study participants are of the view that many organisations are misguided by false thinking that BBS is just an awareness program, they fail to understand that it is a planned intervention. They wish to control incidents by just an awareness program, they fail to do so, and incidents continue to take toll on the human life and business of the company. Safety is a matter of time of spot-correction, human side of safety takes backseat over the business targets and profits. All at-risk behaviours existed almost all the times, but they were not not corrected, or they were delayed in spot-correction. As per Santosh Srivastava, chief safety officer of Cairn India, "thirty percent of global fatalities are from India, as safety is enforced most of the times, lacks management commitment, and not managed in the manner like production, cost, quality. Every cultural shift takes minimum 2 year from reactive to interdependent safety culture". Hence,

BBS focused on spot-correction of all barriers and at-risk behaviours. BBS motto is to increase number of observers along with increased quality of observations. On the spot correction together by all is a live energy for organisations to excel. Behavioural safety program has limitations for its effectiveness if it is not conducted as a planned intervention on regular basis.

8. Not focusing on the antecedents of safe/unsafe behaviours

Important focused group responses of the experienced HSE professionals are described below:

- Factory occupier has to take responsibility for change of the safety culture, which is missing.
- 100% safe behaviours only ensure no incident, not 90% as 10% probability of incident remains.
- Sense of vulnerability should remain for not losing on safety actions.
- Managing heightened risk perception through ears, eyes during COVID-19 circumstances.
- Future of safety lies in how we are going to buy-in people into the humanistic process like empathising intentions among employees to be framed as organisational planned intervention.
- Discussing/sharing what factors influence employees to do at-risk behaviours at site or anywhere.
- National framework on behavioural safety in industries would greatly impact safety cultures.
- Benchmarking behavioural safety by national institutions to balance lagging/leading indicators.

These above stated responses necessitate to focus on the antecedents of safe/unsafe behaviours.

Conclusion and Recommendations

The major conclusions for the underlying difference between safety documentation and behavioural reality include the seven lagging factors for the safety cultures such as missing safety message down the levels, safety documentation to make authorities happy, poor adherence to documentation requirements, compromising risk is a regular practice, no review of unsafe behaviours and corrective action, fast businesses deliver incidents, and only behavioural awareness program, not planned intervention. These are sufficient reasons to indicate that safety culture is lagging at many sites in Indian locations. This reveals that incidents might happen and consequences can be catastrophic, which will cause potential loss of lives or severe injury, stop operation and non-productive time, undesirable cost and expenses, destruction of equipment and defame of company reputation (Mohammed Gehad *et al.*, 2020).

The visible gaps between safety documentations and behaviours (**Box 1**) need to be addressed urgently by top leaders of companies described below as recommended by the study participants.

BOX 1: Factors responsible for the difference between safety documentation and ground reality

1. Missing safety message down the levels,
2. Safety documentation to make authorities happy,
3. Poor adherence to documentation requirements,
4. Compromising risk is a regular practice,
5. No review of unsafe behaviours for corrective action,
6. Fast businesses deliver incidents,
7. Only behavioural awareness program, not planned intervention
8. Poor focus on the antecedents of safe and unsafe behaviours

1. Behavioural Safety shall be the mandatory subject on every industrial safety curriculum. At least one hour of BBS training per month shall be given to all the employees of the company including contractors. BBS implementation shall be the agenda at board level discussion and mandatory for HSE committee. COVID-19 outbreak has changed the approach towards workplace safety. Although, robust plant design, engineering controls, SOPs and OSH organisation are essential, but they will be ineffective if behavioural safety aspects are not considered (Gabhane, 2020). Any small incident even a first aid injury would call for a review of the entire BBS management system, to locate and correct what is missing.

2. Indian experiences and best practices need to be documented. There is lot of enthusiasm to adopt BBS for injury prevention amongst industrial fraternity, to name a few i.e. DCM Shriram, Sembcorp, GAIL, SAIL, Tata Projects, IOCL, HPCL Academia is searching for ways and means to introduce BBS. Statutory Authorities are looking for private partnership who has capability to implement BBS. Government institutions like DGFASLI, NSC are keen to find how to take it to industry and encourage incident reduction. Huge potential available in the market to mentor/coach/train and to deliver BBS. Industry and academia have recognised BBS as an effective tool for intervention in the safety management. Online sessions can be conducted for promoting BBS to increase networking and outreach to various industries and educational institutions.

3. Though we are successful in promoting BBS in various industries but real need is to address this at schools and colleges if we really wish to see the change we want. That's part of CSR in various villages, most of the companies are doing awareness on environment, road safety and good health. BBS must be taken to community, as Road Safety and

Social distancing and personal hygiene are already being tracked in our BBS checklist.

- We cannot be safe unless community around us is safe
- BBS plays vital role in building positive safety culture
- BBS can be integrated from work place to any place
- Reward safe behaviours
- Promote safety learning from the childhood
- Make safety a compulsory subject in all curriculum
- All-out support for BBS expressed by DGFASLI, NSC and Director NITIE
- BBS from workplace to any place is possible. BBS can be applied anywhere.

4. Measurement matrix and maturity ladder of BBS program are very important to exercise. For implementing BBS, sufficient time minimum 2-3 years should be given to achieve the good result, normally managements think that it should happen in few months. Top management's involvement and support are crucial for program success.

5. India has very vague safety culture. Negative reenforcement is required in unorganised sector to make it a habit leading to positive reinforcement. Zero Accident Vision is possible and it can be achieved by Behaviour Based Safety. Companies have realised the importance of BBS, which is not industry specific and applicable to all sectors. BBS along with traditional safety systems, industries can dream of the vision Zero Incidents/accidents. Behavioural intervention or BBS are most successful at the time when all employees in the organisation are thinking together about the concept of BBS, starting with the leadership and the last person at sites. Top leadership and all the rest thinking together about implementing BBS to save human life from an injury. At-risk

behaviour is an emergency for its spot-correction and a possible safe behaviour for a safety culture. BBS should not rest in conversation rather get implemented. Total behavioural safety implementation for sites would require professional mentoring as well as doubt clarifying sessions. Progressive companies who have passion and innovation for safety are ready to enable their manpower for BBS approach. If there is a will, it is possible to implement in big and wide spread organisation also.

6. Indian Industry lags in following safety protocols, and betterment can be achieved only if the people at work start understanding that their life is precious and it's them individually who will lose if they don't remain safe. Understanding the importance of "Learning to Unlearn". There is a need to understand the importance of saying "no" to whoever if they feel that the work they have been assigned is not being carried out safely. A safety professional shared, "as a 4th Engineer, I have seen a Cadet dying in the Container because he wasn't properly equipped with PPE and was asked by his senior to go down, all he had to say was "No". Understanding that an accident doesn't ask if you are highly experienced or if you have a training certificate. It's you who have to take a call".

7. There is a need to use the leading and lagging indicators for rating BBS while implementing. It is well said by a safety officer,"being as a shop floor person (manufacturing/process unit) if the shop floor people are safe, then organization is safe". To make them understand about their safety, daily interaction/training/feedback is must and make BBS a humanistic movement and emotionally connect people at site in order to succeed it fully.

8. Post-Covid the work place concept is changing. New concerns in safety, health and psychosocial relations arise.

BBS has to transform to address such concerns. e. g. ergonomics, workaholic culture. There is plenty of scope for MSME and service sector to adopt BBS. The challenge would be to offer BBS to smaller groups or to even individuals. Post COVID-19, Behaviour-Based-Safety (BBS) became more popular approach to safety management, which sees the main cause of accident in unsafe behaviour or act (Gabhane, 2020). How much value is being delivered by the BBS implementation is measured by the percentage of participation of observers. That is how many people are being observed and spot-corrected by each observer, divided by what was the goal of participation for observers in each department. BBS means an instant spot-correction of at-risk behaviour by everyone at site, therefore an observer is trained for a moment of correcting, and an organisation is trained to sustain it. A leadership of dream and determination can do it.

9. What is lacking in sites at department level, is as follows;

- Appreciation of BBS observers
- Observers positive approach of correction as big brother
- Developing more observers
- Making observation round daily
- Goal setting by departments for number of observations by each observer to calculate % of observers participation
- Alternatively, you may decide at the steering team for inclusion of observee name in the BBS checklist, for those who do at-risk behaviours repeatedly.

10. What is lacking organisationally somewhere is the Humanistic Behaviourism and Mindfulness (Safety with Human touch & actively caring). We need to refresh people with these basics aspects of behavioural safety periodically. In

this regard, a 10-point an organisational BBS implementation commitment test for zero-harm actions (Kaila, 2020) is recommended:

- Has your CEO issued circular to all employees for BBS implementation?
- Have your organization displayed BBS banners across all work areas?
- Has your organization formed BBS steering team?
- Is the BBS steering team meeting every month and reviewing progress?
- Are all employees and workmen aware of BBS concept of observations-cum-spot-correction?
- Is organization calculating and displaying BBS score board each month?
- Has organization issued BBS identity sticker to all observers to fix on helmet?
- Do all HOD's make BBS rounds each day?
- Has BBS implementation effected in reduced incidents at sites?
- Has BBS implementation effected in reduced barriers in safety?

11. Risk perception is important especially when we have low safety consciousness in majority of the contract associates. Timely observation by employees is precious for someone to be saved from injuries. So BBS is to be a part of Risk Assessment and HAZOP study as an integral OHS management system. BBS means Better Business Sense.

12. To conclude, it is imperative that the safety documentations are in tandem with ground realities. Mismatch of HSE documentations with that of ground behaviours would raise many serious doubts about the compliances of safety rules and regulations on part of everyone concerned such as

the company management, factory owner, auditors, safety department, factory inspectorates etc. Finally, this hampers business sustainability, and exposes manpower to risks as threat to life. Hence, safety is to be implemented with an outlook of humanity and to be managed with humanistic philosophy more actively, it would save human beings from fatalities and business from losses. Needless to mention that the insurance as well as enforcement agencies take cognisance of this research and its implications for reinforcement of safety culture in workplace establishments.

References

Business Wire (2020, October 14). New Study Finds 73% of Employees Fear Return to Workplace Will Compromise Personal Health & Safety. Retrieved on 26 March 2021. https://www.businesswire.com/news/home/20201014005131/en / New-Study-Finds-73-of-Employees-Fear-Return-to-Workplace-Will-Compromise-Personal-Health-Safety

DGFASLI (2021). National Occupational Safety and Health (OSH) Profile. Retrieved on 26 March 2021. https://dgfasli.gov.in/sites/default/files/service_file/Nat-OSH-India-Draft%281%29.pdf

EHS Today, (2013, Feb 07). Building the Foundation for a Sustainable Safety Culture. Retrieved on 28 March 2021. https://www.ehstoday.com/safety/article/21915559/building-the-foundation-for-a-sustainable-safety-culture

El-Menyar, A., Mekkodathil, A., & Al-Thani, H. (2016). Occupational injuries: Global and local perspectives. *Nepal Journal of Epidemiology*, 6(2): 560-562. https://doi.org/10.3126/nje.v6i2.15161

Forum of Behavioural Safety (2021). 5th Annual National Conference (virtual), New Challenges of Behaviour Based Safety (BBS), 24 January, 2021.

Gabhane, Lalit R. (2020). Editorial, Industrial Safety Chronicle, July-September and October- Decemebr, 2020, 5. https://nsc.org.in/wp-content / uploads / 2020 / 12 / July-September-2020-E-Chronicle.pdf

Government of Western Australia (2021). Safety performance measurements for industry. Retrieved on 26 March 2021. https:// www.dmp.wa.gov.au / Safety / Safety-performance-measurements-7939.aspx

India Briefing (2021, January 22). India's Occupational Safety, Health and Working Conditions Code, 2020: What is it and How Should Companies Prepare? Retrieved on 28 March 2021. https://www. india-briefing.com / news / indias-occupational-safety-health-and-working-conditions - code - 2020 - what - is - it - and - how-should-companies-prepare-21545.html/

Mohammed Gehad, Naji Gehad, Isha, Ahmad, Isha Nizam, & Al-Baraa Abdulrahman, Al-Mekhlafi Al-Baraa, Sharafaddin Osama & Ajmal Muhammad (2020). Implementation of Leading and Lagging Indicators to Improve Safety Performance In The Upstream Oil and Gas Industry. 7. 265-269. 10.31838/ jcr.07.14.45.

Mohd Aihatram Khan, Nilima Nilima, Jackline Prathibha, Bhaskar Tiwary & Monika Singh (2020, March 17). Documentation compliance of in-patient files: A cross sectional study from an east India state. *Clinical Epidemiology and Global Health*, Volume 8, Issue 4, P994-997, December 01, 2020. DOI:https://doi.org/ 10.1016/j.cegh.2020.03.010

International Labour Office (2019). Safety and Health at the Heart of the Future of Work: Building on 100 years of experience. Retrieved on 21 March 2021. https://www.ilo.org/wcmsp5/ groups/public/---dgreports/---dcomm/documents/publication/wcms _686645.pdf

Kaila Harbans Lal (2020). Critical Questions on COVID-19 and Management of Behavioural Safety Interventions: India Case Study. Industrial Safety Chronicle, July-September, 2020, 43-54. https://nsc.org.in/wp-content / uploads/2020 / 12/July-September-2020-E-Chronicle.pdf

Kristen A. Rost & Alicia M. Alvero (2020) Participatory approaches to workplace safety management: bridging the gap between behavioral safety and participatory ergonomics, International Journal of Occupational Safety and Ergonomics, 26:1, 194-203, DOI: 10.1080/10803548.2018.1438221

Rao, Parimala S. (2019, June 05). Corporate budget allocation for health, safety on the rise: Study. Retrieved on 29 March 2021. https://www.thehindubusinessline.com / companies / corporate-budget-allocation-for-health-safety-on-the-rise-says-study / article 27526538.ece

Suxia Liu, Edmund Nana Kwame Nkrumah, Linda Serwah Akoto, Emmanuel Gyabeng, Erasmus Nkrumah, "The State of Occupational Health and Safety Management Frameworks (OHSMF) and Occupational Injuries and Accidents in the Ghanaian Oil and Gas Industry: Assessing the Mediating Role of Safety Knowledge", *BioMed Research International*, Vol. 2020, Article ID 6354895, 14 pages, 2020. https://doi.org/10.1155/2020/6354895

The Indian Express (2017). Changing chalta hai. Retrieved on 23 March 2021. https://indianexpress.com/article/opinion/columns/pm-modi-ias-india-changing-chalta-hai-5004287/

Zwetsloot, Gerard & Leka, Stavroula & Kines, Pete & Jain, Aditya. (2020). Vision zero: Developing proactive leading indicators for safety, health and wellbeing at work. Safety Science. 130. 104890. 10.1016/j.ssci.2020.104890.

Integrating our employees and associates workmen together as brothers of safety brings a change of culture in the future. Those who lead the change will see the change, so make safety leaders out of your workforce. Safety leadership would sustain safe business.

CHAPTER 8

Behavioural Benchmarking as a Robust Tool of Total Safety Culture in Industries

Introduction, Rationale and Context

Tata companies emphasised behavioural change in Robust People Practices. The organisational journey in safety has evolved from 'compliance-driven' standards and guidelines to a 'behaviour-centric' safety culture to help achieve the 'zero harm' goal (TATA METALIKS, 2020). A longitudinal employee-driven behaviour based accident prevention initiative implemented in industrial settings of 229 companies were examined. Comparisons of pre- to post-initiative incident levels across groups revealed a significant decrease in incidents following the BBS implementation. The effect sizes were estimated from the average percentage reduction from baseline. The average reduction from baseline amounted to 26% in the first year increasing to 69% by the fifth (Krause *et al.*, 1999).

BBS FRAMEWORK (**Box 1**) reveals that safety cultural change is an essence of managing all incidents at the workplace. Hence, the BBS benchmarking ought to focus on the significant change in incidents rate as an outcome for comparing organisations.

Safety culture was consistently and independently associated with safety performance. In addition, employees' perceptions of safety were consistently and independently associated with individual safety performance, health and wellbeing. These associations were not limited to particular sectors of industry, suggesting that they are robust and generally applicable (Smith and Wadsworth, 2009).

Most benchmarking studies have historically not taken the state of operation into account. This can create distorted comparisons. Considering these, three variables are allowed: industry type, company size, and the incident frequency (Dyne and Tolbert, 2017).

Benchmarking concept is likely to achieve the best work related safety outcomes. Comparison has been done to show the different understanding of benchmarking approach and how safety performance can be benchmarked. The safety quality can be improved by doing the right benchmarking process on it to seek what are the best practices to be applied (Ishak and Azizan 2018).

Research Objective

The present article is focused to explore BBS as a robust tool for benchmarking of industries in improving safety cultural change (SCC).

BOX 1: BBS Framework (Kaila, 2020)

1. BBS premise is that near-misses, injuries, fatalities etc. are behaviour-based
2. Behaviour is the root cause of all incidents
3. BBS helps build safety cultural change to achieve zero incidents
4. Culture is the summation of behaviours and culture drives all behavioural change.

Methodology

Since the BBS programmes are implemented in many Industries, it will be good idea to share the data, learnings and good practices. It will also be a good tool for Benchmarking present data of Peer Industries/Plants. A total of 171 HSE professionals were requested to reflect their viewpoint on the comparison of BBS data of peer industries for considering BBS as a robust tool for benchmarking. Both primary and secondary data were collected from organisations across India. The BBS method, being a generic one, can be adopted by the managers to assess present safety performance and find a suitable peer to which, it should follow to improve own technical efficiency followed by in what respect it has to improve for benchmarking based on safety performance in Indian industries (Beriha, Patnaik and Mahapatra, 2011).

Results and Findings

The findings of the study are presented in following points for evolving conclusive recommendations for benchmarking BBS as a tool towards establishing total safety culture at sites.

1. The workmen must be vocal in spot-correction of the safety risks at workplace and anyplace. That's the basis of BBS implementation i.e. empowerment up to the lowest person of the pyramid. But critically, according to Mrs. Angela Vaz, a senior manager, in a large aluminium company, "only staff will correct and fill BBS observations in dashboard/4 per month. Each week schedule is fixed by BBS committee members. IT has prepared the dashboard. Total flop show designed by Safety corporate office. They talk only to make their plant safe, not family and society. But who will make the management understand that they want only work

without good results towards development of an independent/interdependent safety culture" (Personal Communications, 2020).

2. Benchmarking is a larger issue that needs a re-definition in terms of behavioural practices in safety management in a plant or site, as being depicted in this research article. Total safety culture demands a clear fundamental clarity/difference between what is safe and what is unsafe to one and all. A line between compliance and non-compliance is very thin visible safety culture that can be seen and not seen by many as culture drives the behaviours. Safety awakening by each of us is the key to creating safety culture. We need to transform the safety culture in many organisations and finally at community level for mankind. Human bonding saves people from injury not merely the safety manuals or procedures. Mere standards are not enough to achieve safety of employees.

3. Benchmarking for peer classification to develop a robust program to help industry for better BBS practice by involving everyone in risk correction would finally lead to business excellence. According a safety professional, basic concept of BBS implementation is same for all industries. We can compare performance/rating industry-wise such as Chemical, Oil & Gas, construction.

4. The following themes emerged for understanding the scenario of comparison of BBS data of peer industries for developing BBS Benchmarking as a robust/right tool for safety cultural change.

(*a*) Benchmarking BBS as best practice helps identify opportunities for change to fully optimise our return on investment (ROI) by comparing data of peer industry on a behavioural safety measures that can be developed accessed and scrutinised for a robust tool. The data can also help to find out the gap which can be helpful for strengthening for development of such a tool (BSMS, 2020).

(*b*) The comparison were done between similar industries having similar types of management controls. For example, data of an Oil and Gas Industry can not be compared with engineering industry or cement industry etc. Once the working conditions change, type of management change, workers involvement in field activities change, comparison of data will be misleading. Secondly, even within the same Industry data of a public sector organisation can not be compared with that of a private MNC. Considering above limitations similar type of industries and management controls be identified, and thereafter comparison could be done which would be beneficial.

(*c*) Parameters/Data comparison were done Apple to Apple meanings:

1. Years since implementation
2. No. of Employees
3. No. of Associates
4. Who all are Drivers of BBS Programme
5. Monitoring Mechanism
6. Hot Spots
7. Action Plan to address the Hot Spots.

An example:

1. Years since implementation: 2 Years 3 Months
2. No. of Employees: 650 Employees [O&M-450 Employees]
3. No. of contractors workmen: 2 X 1000 Nos.
4. Who all are Drivers of BBS Programme: Business Head & HODs
5. Monitoring Mechanism: Weekly by BU Head, Monthly by Group

6. Hot Spots: 1st Social Distancing & Personal Hygiene, 2nd Material Handling

In order to make BBS a benchmark, we will have to work out some parameters basis which the industry-wise comparison could be made and ranking could be done. If we really compare with same or similar industries. Risk profile (high risk, medium and low risks), and workers profile (skilled, semiskilled and unskilled) varies from industry to industry and so is behaviour. The safe behaviour of people is always better in private MNCs than most of the Indian public sector companies. So this factor also needs to be considered while comparing. According to Mr. Pavan K. Rao, EHS Head of a MNC, "any benchmarking will need parameters, to know where we excel and to know where we need to improve" (Personal Communications, 2020). We can also have following considerations:

(*i*) National Safety Rating

(*ii*) Risk Rating of Industry

(*iii*) Duration since implementation

(*iv*) Number of Employees and Contract Workers [Associates]

(*v*) Work Area of Industry [More the work area of facilities, supervision is a challenge]

(*vi*) Training Records [% of Workforce trained]

(*vii*) No. of Audits, Safety Index [Safe Observations/Safe + Unsafe Observations] and Unsafe Observations/hour

Also there are challenges in comparing as it also depends on many factors apple to apple such as:

- Type of industry
- Process steps involved
- Operations-manual/auto

- Manpower employed (skilled/unskilled)
- Age of equipment/plant/machinery
- Type of industry : private/govt/multinational etc.

(*d*) Though, competitive feeling is good if looked at in the right spirit for achieving excellence and not just showcasing. Certainly not downgrading others which is experienced in many awards by putting numbers to get the awards. In reality, the competition should be raising one's performance bar to the next level. According to Mr. Sivaramakrishna Rao, a HSE general manager of a large construction company, "there is a saying 'Measure to Improve' and measurement needs statistics. Their ups and downs are the indicators of improvement. We already have SR/FR/IR. for the Safety Department. But Near-miss and potential near-miss (At-Risk behaviours) numbers are for the BBS and for the whole company. Safety department is the custodian of the statistics. I was in tremendous pressure by the management for comparison. with peers and superiors. But my stand was to let the competition come from within the company, not from outside. I am only sharing my experiences as ultimately BBS should be there in every company and every employee shall be benefitted" (Personal Communications, 2020). BBS helps to develop culture of care in organisation and leads to create positive safety culture. It empower each employee including each working hands to become safety officer for his team. Preventing accident is like saving someone's life and pain and it gives peace and humbleness. It would be a wonderful and ultimate idea. It will immediately strike to everyone mind and become easy to implement. It is must, otherwise purpose of BBS wouldn't be served (Kaila, 2020).

(*e*) Due to high attrition rate of contractual employees, it is much challenging to get on the result. It is a good insight that we added 'spot-correction' a psychological approach in the history of Indian Safety. 'Spot-correction' (with cool mindset) in the hands of 'everyone at site' changed the safety culture. This clarified the 'process of achieving behavioural reinforcements in safety'. 'Continuing this safety culture' would save generations! Be a Mentor of BBS to make more!! Be a Proud human! According to a veteran safety expert, Shankar Rajagopalan, "Spot Correction, erstwhile BBS went into analysis paralysis after recording observations and creating a nightmare of data" (Personal Communications, 2020).

Conclusion

This article have raised a thought provoking question, comparing two persons/children in a family or two of the friends on a scale! This initiative should be useful for many industries for benchmarking and to know where they stand. We may invite industries to present their BBS performance/ learnings with whatever metrics they are using currently. However, when we go for comparison, we lose track, as every company/industry is led by human beings. In oil and gas itself if you compare companies like ONGC and SHELL, there is a huge difference because of their origin. So every company has its own characteristics what we call behaviours and attitudes. Our benchmarking shall be, whoever is guided, REDUCTION in INJURY (RIN) whatever may be the percentage. As it takes years for the parents to see prosperity/happiness to nurture the children. We shall also take care of the organisations to achieve excellence in their respective fields.

Reducing accidents and incidents shall be the primary responsibilities of any management. In that there is no cast, creed, religion or region (chemical, oil and gas, metros, manufacturing etc etc.). It's a humanitarian effort. It's also in the CSR category. Our aim is to reduce injury/pain and make a human being happy. again not only at work at home also. Hence, being elite and gaining a lot of experience, we shall encourage any industry to achieve excellence in reducing injuries. As parents want the prosperity of their children, we shall guide everybody on the principles of BBS to reduce injuries in turn create a happy and enjoyable atmosphere which will contribute to more production/progress resulting in profits. As it is felt, BBS is Physical (injury), Psychological (behaviours/Attitudes) and Philosophical (happiness/contentment) effort. Any one P suffers, then BBS is lost. This needs Shraddha & Saburi (Commitment - Patience) as we are the missionaries of happiness.

ILO focused upon safety for all economic activities. National Safety Council emphasised safety from workplace to anyplace. World Safety Forum themed for safety as a way of life. Forum of Behavioural Safety pushed the concept of safety in the behaviour of all as emphasised in the ISO45001 to empowering the workforce in the internal risk control and management. There is a transformation in the leadership behaviour as well as safety cultures of the corporates. But achieving an interdependent safety culture is a journey of continuous struggle and patience, as the corporate values fumble between business profits and caring for safety of people at the lower levels. Mr. Rajam Krishnamurthy who headed the Dubai Burj Khalifa project for safety said, "never compromise with less than the best as it comes to safety of people and the project" (ANI, 2019).

Recommendations

1. It is imperative for companies to benchmark their BBS process against the parameters of zero at-risk behaviours to realise a sustainable zero injury rate. Parameters for BBS

Benchmarking are: the behaviour categories that are defined as observable, measurable, spot-correctable, and an organisation-wide planned intervention was launched in every site among Indian organisations. How do we know where we need to improve: an organisation needs to check how far an organisation has reached towards zero at-risk behaviours, and continue this organisational planned intervention. The research and practice trends reveal that BBS Benchmarking can be done on the generic 11 behaviour categories across an organisation, across peer industry, across the zone, as our measurement index remains the same for every site i.e. reaching zero at-risk behaviours, by involving everyone till last person for achieving an interdependent safety culture. These behaviour categories are: PPE, Housekeeping, Using tools, Body positioning, Material handling, Communication, Following procedures, Visual focusing, Using mobile at work, Road Safety, COVID-19 Behaviours (Kaila, 2020). Almost, every organisation has been benefitted for significant improvement in safety performance with BBS implementation. Some organisations took longer time to reach zero at-risk behaviours, depending upon management continuous engagement with BBS progress, frequency of observations for spot-correction, size of organisation, etc.

2. According to Mr. K. K. Sharma a director EHS of DCM Shriram, "the concept of benchmarking like any other performance excelling is an excellent idea for BBS program implementation to get the maximum value and achieve zero accident goal. However, the competitive feeling is good if looked at in the right spirit for achieving excellence. The objective of the competition should be raising one's performance bar to the next level" (Personal Communications, 2020). Also the organisations have experienced challenges in

comparing two sectors/sites as it also depends on many factors to compare apple to apple such as:

- Type of industry
- Process steps involved
- Operations: Manual/auto
- Manpower employed (skilled/unskilled)
- Age of equipment/plant/machinery
- Type of industry : Private/govt/multinational etc.

Certainly, benchmarking on BBS will help us in moving ahead following principles of inclusiveness and healthy competition. Challenge is to put a framework addressing all the criteria for a uniform assessment giving due weightage to all the 10 aspects as described below.

In order to review quantitative and qualitative analysis of your BBS Project Rating, the following are a list of 10 BBS measurable practice and criteria for peer benchmarking.

I. Safety cultural shift from reactive, dependent culture to independent, interdependent culture

II. Increase in Leadership involvement

III. Regularity of Monthly BBS meetings

IV. Continual Incidents reduction

V. Monthly Behavioural trends improvement

VI. Sharing of at-risk behaviours during Tool Box Talk daily

VII. Motivational reward, recognition for observers, units, HODs

VIII. Top Managements' regular observation rounds

IX. Repeat BBS awareness sessions for spot-correction

X. Quarterly reviews across units/sites

These 10 indices of BBS Benchmarking are tested and proven as a robust tool of total safety culture of Industries. Over the past 30 years, the implementation of BBS programs have resulted in dramatic reductions in the number of lost time/minor injuries that companies have experienced across the globe (Byrd, 2007). However, the high management commitment led to the success of the BBS intervention resulting towards higher safety performance (Choudhry, 2012). Focusing on the prevention of losses of life and business (in the context of daily incidents like fires and fatalities at sites), this article based on the industrial settings of Indian corporates, is an endeavour to address on the possibilities, approach and vision of how an ambitious corporate safety movement through BBS is achievable, by an understanding of a variety of key benchmarking aspects such as positive outcomes of BBS implementation, BBS culture rating, quality of observations and spot-correction of at-risk behaviours, criteria for selection of BBS observers, the BBS organisational procedure to behaviouralize ISO 45001, focusing on the margins of BBS implementation to optimise it, BBS content design for HODs adopting site BBS policy etc. (Kaila, 2020).

3. Some of the critical factors that affect achieving BBS benchmarking criteria, need company's special attention, are: (*a*) the dynamic sync between safety versus business excellence among top leaders, (*b*) change in company leadership and priorities, (*c*) integrating safety culture with the changing manpower requirements, d) addressing the socio-environmental conditions like COVID-19. Beside this, as long as the focus of the organisations is, like safety function is being treated as daughter-in-law, and the company business as daughter, it would be difficult to achieve total safety culture. Both safety and business are to be

treated at par, which is lacking in company's behaviours. The following reflection describes this organisational behaviour.

Q. Do you think, in our Indian companies, SAFETY is being treated as daughter-in-law, and BUSINESS as daughter, which is why, total safety culture lacks due focus?

Ans. Surprisingly, 90% of the senior HSE professionals agreed to this logic and their responses were as follows: Safety gets STEP MOTHERLY. TREATMENT. It's Indian industrial culture that drives our action. Production or profits is the mother-in-Law. Most of the company's Top management have business on top priority. Only 10% responses are positive like: this type of culture is not so much in good companies. Safety and ethics (human values as a whole) generate profits for organisation.

The behavioural scientists who mentor the BBS planned intervention must consider these mindsets, that impede the progress of BBS program planning and action, while implementing a robust technique like BBS. Broadly, the national safety rating as well as the backdrop of non-compliance in a cultural context need attention of the managements for balancing safety and business scenario.

References

ANI (2019, January 30). BESAFE's 3rd Annual Conference on "Measurable Impacts of Behavioural Based Safety Implementation in Indian Industry. Retrieved on 29 Nov 2020. https://www.business-standard.com/article/news-ani/besafe-s-3rd-annual-conference-on-measurable-impacts-of-behavioural-based-safety-implementation-in-indian-industry-119013000572_1.html

Beriha, G.S., Patnaik, B. and Mahapatra, S.S. (2011), "Safety performance evaluation of Indian organizations using data envelopment analysis", Benchmarking: An International Journal, Vol. 18 No. 2, pp. 197-220. Retrieved on 25 Nov 2020. https://doi.org/10.1108/14635771111121676

Byrd, Herbert (2007). A Comparison of Three Well Known Behavior Based Safety Programs: DuPont STOP Program, Safety Performance Solutions and Behavioral Science Technology. Thesis/Dissertation Collections. Rochester Institute of Technology. Retrieved on 27 Nov 2020. https://scholarworks.rit.edu/ cgi/viewcontent.cgi?article = 1689&context = theses

BSMS (2020, September, 28). Benchmarking Best Practice. Retrieved on 29 Sept. 2020. http://www.behavioral-safety.com/behavior-based-safety-solution-center/behavior-based-safety-assessments/bbs-benchmarking-with-the-behavioral-safety-maturity-ladder

Choudhry, Rafiq (2012). Implementation of BBS and the Impact of Site-Level Commitment. *Journal of Professional Issues in Engineering Education and Practice*. 138. 296-304. Retrieved on 26 Nov 2020. 10.1061/(ASCE)EI.1943-5541.0000111.

Dyne Peter Van and Tolbert Don (2017). Crash Frequency Benchmarking and Behavioral Approaches to Fleet Safety. American Society of Safety Engineers. Retrieved on 24 Nov 2020. https://www.onepetro.org/conference-paper/ASSE-17-746

Ishak Nurfadzillah and Azizan Muhammad Azizi (2018). A review on the benchmarking concept in Malaysian construction safety performance. AIP Conference Proceedings 1930. Retrieved on 21 Nov 2020. https://doi.org/10.1063/1.5022918

Kaila, Harbans Lal (2020). Planned Intervention of Behaviour-Based Safety (BBS) Helps Organisations Improve their Safety Time Arithmetic, *World Safety Journal*, Vol. XXIXNo. 3 34–41.

Kaila, Harbans (2020). Behaviour Based Safety for Corporates: a shift towards an interdependent safety culture. *Industrial Engineering Journal.* 13. 10.26488/IEJ.13.1.1208.

Krause T.R., Seymour, K.J. and Sloat. K C.M. (1999). Long-term evaluation of a behavior-based method for improving safety performance: a meta-analysis of 73 interrupted time-series replications. *Safety Science,* 32, 1-18.

Personal Communications (2020, Oct, 25). Benchmarking of behaviour based safety.

Smith Andy P. and Wadsworth Emma J.K. (2009). Safety culture, advice and performance. Centre for Occupational and Health Psychology Cardiff University. Retrieved on 29 Sept. 2020. http://www.behavioral-safety.com / articles/cardiff_safety_culture_report.pdf

Tata Metaliks (2020). Robust People Practices. Retrieved on 28 Nov 2020. https://www.tatametaliks.com/tata-metalik-ir-19-20/robust-people-practices.html

Make sure that you turn unsafe to safe immediately before it becomes risk.

CHAPTER 9

Planned Intervention of Behaviour-based Safety Helps Organizations Improve their Safety Time Arithmetic

Introduction

Like a health risk such as the Coronavirus, a single person, if not controlled, can shake a country badly. Similarly a single safety at-risk behaviour, like a procedural violation, can destroy a business organization. Indian industry with a large diversified workforce and work cultures, has on an average 30 percent of at-risk/harm behaviours, resulting in daily work related fatalities and disabilities. Unsafe acts have been identified as a major factor of incidents and accidents (Xu, Zou & Luo, 2018). In behaviour-based safety (BBS), it is believed/practiced that 5 minutes observation-cum-spot-correction of unsafe/at-risk behaviours daily by the company employees is considered as:

5 minutes used in saving a life;

5 minutes of sharing goodness;

5 minutes practice in humanity;

5 minutes of brotherhood;

5 minutes of affection;

5 minutes of caring;

5 minutes of safety dialogue;

5 minutes of empathy;

5 minutes safety involvement;

5 minutes of zero incident;

5 minutes of zero-harm culture

BBS is an approach to save employees from the traumas of injuries and incidents in industry. Like a child feels safe with their mother, the person observed feels safe with the big brother safety (BBS) observers at sites/plants. True BBS observers don't differentiate amongst people while saving their life from at-risk behaviours. They don't differentiate in observing people due to their education, income, designation or age. True observers save people equally. Equality in saving people from even smallest injuries is valued by a true and active observer. BBS is a worldwide application of behavioural science to save life and business from incidents.

Methodology

This paper is an interdisciplinary intervention of behavioral science, management and industrial safety disciplines that are part of an ongoing national longitudinal action survey in India. Thematic data analysis was used to reflect the findings. The BBS program as part of this action survey was implemented in diverse locations in India for employees of multinational companies that were trained as BBS mentors and observers during the years 2018-20. This program included the concept and process of BBS, plant visits for observation and correction of at-risk behaviors, developing road map for implementation of BBS, developing training module for imparting training to all employees, formation and functions of BBS steering team. More than 5000 training participants included managers, heads of departments, contractors, safety officers and contractors' staff belonging to the public and private industrial sectors such as chemicals, construction, gas, power, and steel across geographic locations (See figure 1).

Results and Findings

The following findings and themes emerged from the data collected as described in the methodology.

1. Safety behaviours can be defined, observed, corrected on the spot, measured, implemented, and sustained (Kaila, 2018). BBS implementation is likely to collapse if these aspects are missed.
2. Lack of understanding the BBS concept/process is adversely proportional to its implementation by people at sites. Those who understand implement it and vice versa. Hence, it becomes crucial for each Head of Department to ensure this repeatedly for creating a true interdependent safety culture. In a Malaysian Oil and Gas Companies' case study (Ismail *et al.*, 2011), it was found that lack of leadership was the primary cause of ineffective implementation of BBS. The role of top management is important to make safety programs successful and sustainable. Possibly, the government safety rules and industry bodies should make BBS implementation mandatory for every organization in the interest of people's life and company business.
3. A reactive/blame/punishment safety culture will not allow BBS culture to survive, as a reactive culture is inherently negative and a BBS culture is positive and supportive.
4. It would be very important and helpful to fix and follow the strict timelines strategically to control the existing at-risk behaviours identified with immediate effect by one and all.

5. BBS is essentially a planned/Informed organizational intervention initiated by the company top management along with a behavioural scientist for its implementation.
6. The level of informed behavioural risk increased after BBS was rolled out at sites, because the behavioural risk monitoring increased, not only by the safety department, but also by the BBS observers of each department and work area.
7. Safety Time. It is important that the heads of departments ensure their colleagues are giving safety time of 5 minutes every day. The Chief Executive Officer (CEO) has to announce this message on the BBS launch day. Being a safety caretaker, empathizing concern for life without injury is what is called *suraksha seva parmo dharam* which means safety service is superb religiousness. Safety time gets increased multifold when everyone gives 5 minutes. It is of paramount importance that organizations improve their safety time arithmetic by increasing BBS trained observers. More safety time leads to less unwanted incidents at site. More parameters can be identified in order to improve and sustain organizational safety time arithmetic, such as reward and recognition to observers. Great safety leaders spend time out where their employees are. It's where the real work gets done, the shop floor (Mark, 2019).

Clarifications on BBS

Q: *What is BBS implementation?*

Ans. Involving everyone in actively correction of behaviour is BBS implementation. An employee who does an at-risk behaviour is convinced subconsciously that it is safe as he or she has been engaged in working this way for a long time. When everyone around observes and convinces him/her to correct it, the correction power serves as a group influence and dynamic force for him/her to get corrected. Finally he/she becomes conscious of this behaviour and keeps doing correction on his/her own.

Q: ***We started this exercise in the month of June, every month tracking is done. The graph is showing uneven trend. Seniors are asking why it is not in decreasing trend. Please give your comment on it.***

Ans. People need to be communicated about *daily observation of at-risk behaviours and their spot-correction* through mass-communications. public address system (PAS) as well as tool box talk (TBT) by their heads of departments. This is part of the BBS action plan. You will see the trend changes on implementing this aspect.

Q: How to implement BBS in a company?

Ans. Behaviour-based Safety commences with the safety professional and others performing observations on the CEO to check that the company CEO is ensuring that the workplace, all work processes, all equipment and products used by employees is fit for purpose and safe. The employer/CEO controls the finances and makes the decisions on how this money is spent. Without a safe workplace and work processes provided by the employer or CEO, employees will be unable to work safely and work related injuries, ill health and deaths will continue to occur, no matter how much employees are trained to work in unsafe situations or with unsafe equipment or products. Handholding companies to reduce injuries through series of systematic training in BBS implementation plan spanning a year or two, and get them BBS certified is also recommended.

Q: ***How to collect BBS data? How to approach observee for correcting at risk behaviour for your group?***

Ans. Refer to the following two tables, A and B.

A. How to approach an observee for correcting at risk behaviour for your group

Sl.	11Ps	Description
1 .	Parikarma: observation round	Take an observation round of your unit/plant and observe your own group at any one site for 5- 10 Minutes on daily basis.
2.	Prashan: question	If you find any one at risk, Put a question to an observe whether he is safe.
3.	Prashansa: praise	If you find someone always demonstrating safe behaviour, please praise for his safe behaviours to reinforce.
4.	Parivartan: change	If you find someone at risk behaviour, try to correct him by positive feedback and convert his unsafe behaviours to safe.
5.	Prashiksan: educate	If you feel someone at risk behaviour due to lack of training, then please educate/re-train him for his unsafe behaviours.
6.	Pratigya: oath	After counselling, please take an oath/promise from him that he will not repeat unsafe behaviours in future.
7.	Prachar: spread	Ask an observee to observe another co-worker and do spot correction. This will help in involving 100% employee and strengthen internal implementation.
8 .	Prarthana: request	Behave Like big brother not like Boss, than only observee will be in acceptance mode.
9 .	Purushkar: reward	Develop a system of Spot-reward and recognition to observee to motivate them.
10.	Promise	Take a promise from observee that, observee would also observe the observer, so that he will feel empowered.
11.	Pursue	It need continuous effort for make BBS success, so inform observee that others will also observe you if you repeat at-risk behaviours.

B. **Suppose you have 10 persons in one group and want to observe that group while working on the 10 parameters below.**

Sl. No.	Behaviour	How to collect data	Safe Behaviour	At-Risk Behaviour	Spot Correction
1.	Use of PPE's	Suppose 8 person are perfect but one is not using a chin belt + one found without safety shoe. Spot correction done to belt person, but unable to correct person not wearing safety shoes.	8	2	1
2.	Housekeeping	If you are observing two spots and find one good housekeeping but one unsafe condition and not able to correct immediately	1	1	0
3.	Using tools/ Equipment	If only 4 out of 10 are used while you were observing+ found two person using correct tools, but other two were either using wrong tools or defective tools and you are able to correct both of them	2	2	2
4.	Body positioning	Out of 10 workers during 10 minute of observation, found 7 with perfect position, but three of them with at-risky behaviour and corrected all of them	7	3	3

Sl. No.	Behaviour	How to collect data	Safe Behaviour	At-Risk Behaviour	Spot Correction
5.	Material handling	If a material is being handled by three person in a wrong manner then it will be three if not able to correct them	0	3	0
6.	Communication	If two persons communicating regarding job and if it is correct	2	0	0
7.	Following procedures	If SOP is followed, but work permit was not taken. You are able to stop the job and convince them to take a work permit	1	1	1
8.	Visual focusing	If out of 10, three are found not alert while working, but you are able to do spot correction	7	3	3
9.	Using mobile while working	During 10 minute of observation, you found 5 persons used mobile. Three of them moved out of workplace and used mobile, but two of them started speaking while working, but you could correct one of them	3	2	1
10.	Road Safety behaviours	While coming to duty or while going home, check if all of them taking care of road safety. If three found at-risk, but able to correct one of them	7	3	1

FIG. 1. Example picture of a BBS training workshop of employees

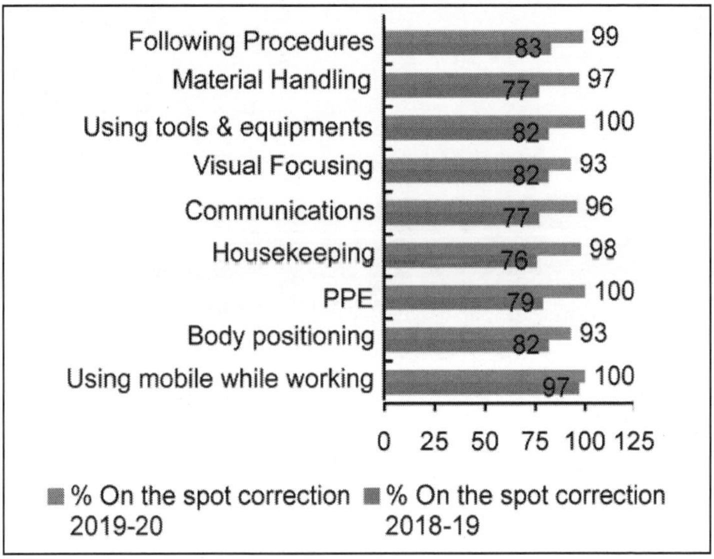

FIG. 2. Uflex Chemicals BBS Performance 2018-19 v/s 2019-20

All behaviours are spot-correctable, so let all observers emphasize on the spot-correction of all at-risk behaviours. They need to be trained during mass-communications and to be told regularly for observation/spot-correction daily.

Experiences and outcomes of BBS

Indian Multinationals Jindal Steel Plant

Behaviour Based Safety programs are currently being used as an effective techniques in safety programs. Behaviour Based Safety programs use positive reinforcement to prevent work related injuries and illness. Behaviour Based Safety program directly involves the employer and employees in accident prevention by their involvement and participation in workplace safety. Implementation of BBS changes the approach of individual, as *I am responsible for my own safety as- I follow the rules because I want to be safe.*

Bhilai Steel Plant

At the Bhilai Steel plant for sustaining the BBS culture, daily monitoring, weekly reporting, monthly review, conducting regular training on BBS by trained faculty, display banners for maximum awareness, empowering observee and observer, display BBS achievement at prominent locations. (i.e. Best observer, Best BBS implemented site, project BBS performance data.) and quarterly review for continual improvement are being done.

ONGC

For ONGC safety and safe behaviour has been included in the Performance Appraisal Report of individual employees. These measures helped management to sustain the BBS program even after 2 years of its launch.

Tata Projects

The simplest and most effective way to implement a BBS is to coach a set of employees on keeping an eye out for Unsafe Actions and stop by doing their bit to coach, counsel & correct their behaviours through a positive interaction.

Essentially, if every one of the observers ensures they never walk past anyone working unsafely - this sets the tone for an acceptable culture that does not tolerate deviations.

AFCONS

At AFCONS BBS has been a long-drawn out approach and necessitated patience and perseverance, so, there was carefully manoeuvring for the entire process of observation and analysis. Giving-up is never a solution to the process of BBS. It needs a careful and periodic boost in the form of re-inventing the process or re-viewing for improvement.

DCM Shriram

For DCM Shriram the safety performance is continued to be assessed by tracking both leading and lagging indicators and accordingly identifying areas for building a strong safety culture at this work place. With this approach of reinforcing positive behaviour through the BBS program, it was anticipated that a *Zero Accident* goal should be achieved in the near future making safety a way of life.

Uflex Chemicals

At Uflex Chemicals though it is initial stages of BBS implementation significant improvements have been observed in the last 2 years (See figure 2). The company is in the process of eliminating the unsafe behaviour by 100% and promoting proactive reporting as much as possible for making this workplace site one of the safest.

Conclusion and Implications

Constant disregard for dignity to life and having a safe environment by the industry leadership led to incidents resulting in a loss of life as well as company business. Achieving and sustaining an injury-free workplace demanded strong leadership (Jim Spigener, 2019). BBS concept and approach, as implemented by many organizations, has resulted in positive outcomes in safety culture management. BBS has been successfully implemented in India by organisations that include Bilag, GAIL, HPCL, IOCL, L&T, AFCONS, Vedanta, Tata Projects, Sterlite, Privi, HCC, DCM Shriram, Dorf Ketal, Sembcorp, Galaxy Surfactants, SAIL, Jindal, Uflex, TRL, IGL, Agrocel, Torrent, Aarti, Solaris, CFCL, Bayer's Crop Science, Oil India, Greentech, Sanofi-Aventis, Sabic, Piramal, Bajaj Auto, Volkswagen, etc. As a result of the ISO 45001: Occupational Health and Safety (2020), organizations are increasingly implementing behavioural safety approach at sites. It is much easier to increase the safety time out by employees and workmen following BBS concepts (Forum of Behavioural Safety, 2020).

The safety time arithmetic of an organization depends upon the following calculation of the lead indicators numbers 1 to 8 and 10 as follows and the number 9 lag indicator.

1. Number/sufficiency/quality of BBS trainings conducted by expert.
2. Number/percentage of observers developed amongst employees for each work area.
3. Number/percentage of HODs involved.
4. Number/percentage of contractors staff involved in observation and spot-correction.
5. Number of Mass-communications held in each month.
6. Number of TBTs (Tool Box Talk) being conducted each month.
7. Number/percentage of seniors involved in observation and spot-corrections.

8. Number of monthly BBS review meetings held by departments.
9. Number/percentage of incidents reduced.
10. Whether the last person at the workplace received training in BBS and participated in observation and spot-correction of at-risk behaviours at site.

Mark each of the above aspects out of 10. Then calculate your organizational safety time score? Total score 10 x 10 = 100. This basic, practical and rapid method of calculation would decide which aspects need more focus to improve safety time score of the site. If this score is increasingly higher each month, positive outcomes of safety culture can be reaped. This overall safety time arithmetic, in turn, would affect the frequency of incidents at work sites. Some organizations are slow, whereas others are fast in obtaining this score depending upon the focus, emphasis and regular monitoring of leaders at all levels: top to bottom. Applied behavioural science is a science of actions of which BBS is an application and a planned intervention of the company management to save both life and business from incidents. People in organizations value safety when everyone engages in safety for a couple of minutes, and then it becomes an organizational value. The above 10 lead and lag indicators are mechanisms to actionize safety time.

Since the role of top managements is significant, it is important to design a BBS sensitization-training workshop for them including the components such as hazard identification, risk assessment, risk management, safety and risk control evaluation, effective communication, clarity on scientific concepts of BBS, what is BBS and what it is not. How to measure behavioural safety in organizations. Which behaviours to observe and how to interact during risk-based conversation. BBS as a well-planned and informed organizational intervention. Display of BBS banners and monthly scoreboard. How to conduct BBS steering team meeting every month, including BBS in weekly mass-communications and daily, digitally enabled BBS checklist. Understanding risk management and behavioural analysis of their own site for spot-correction. Case analysis of other organizations. How to continue and sustain this intervention. How to develop an interdependent safety culture. Monitoring of BBS outcomes and risk control measures implemented. Reward and recognition for motivation to observers. Roadmap for further implementation of BBS. Impact of at-risk behaviours on business of the company etc. This training module needs to be given to MD, CEO, all VPs, GMs, HODs including business, finance, operations etc. This approach was used in all organizations mentioned above (Kaila, 2019).

As seen at Uflex Chemicals, and at other companies, behaviour-based safety can contribute to making safety a way for life for everyone at the workplace. A motto of behaviour-based safety is to *save others, save yourself as big brother of safety*.

References

Forum of Behavioural Safety (2020). Souvenir of 4th National BBS Conference held at Scope complex, New Delhi on 17th January 2020. Besafe.org.in

Ismail, F., Hashim, A. E., Zuriea, W., Ismail, W., Kamarudin, H., & Baharom, Z. A. (2011). Behaviour based approach for quality and safety environment improvement: Malaysian experience in the oil and gas industry. *Procedia-Social and Behavioural Sciences*, 35, 586-594.

ISO 45001: Occupational Health and Safety (2020). https://www.iso.org/iso-45001-occupational-health-and-safety.html

Kaila, H. (2018). Behavioural Intervention in Safety Management of Indian Corporates. *Journal of Psychosocial Research*. 13(1): 165-188.

Kaila H. (2019). Behaviour based safety: simple and scientific approach for corporates. *Industrial Safety Chronicle*, Vol. 50 (3): 69-72, Oct-Dec. 2019.

Middlesworth, M. (2019). 25 Signs You Have An Awesome Safety Culture. https://ergo-plus.com/25-signs-you-have-an-awesome-safety-culture/

Spigener, J. (2019). Safety Leadership: Why system-focused behaviour-based safety is the real deal. https://www.safetyandhealthmagazine.com/authors/7-jim-spigener.

Xu, S., Zou, P., & Luo, H. (2018). Impact of attitudinal ambivalence on safety behaviour in construction. Advances in Civil Engineering, hindawi.com

Without practicing safe behaviours, safety culture can not be cultivated.

CHAPTER 10

Possibilities and Challenges of Making Safety a 'Way of Life' in Indian Society

Introduction: Context and Rationale

Without access to any kind of formal training in Occupational Safety and Health (OSH), the overall awareness levels in India are low (Hart, 2018). The ILO Global Commission on the Future of Work report that in all countries, under reporting, particularly of non-fatal occupational accidents and especially work-related diseases, is common. The governments/employers/workers, and all stakeholders must seize opportunities to create a safe and healthy future workplace and sustainable businesses (Walter, 2019). Countries have to take a new stand on safety-and-health.

"Safety is not a slogan, it is a way of life" is a poster which is seen by, or heard of, by almost everyone who can read or hear. Then why safety is not a way of life. It is bypassed in almost every country. How much "safety is a way of life", differs between countries depending upon the population size, respect for the laws of the land, discipline in individual behaviours, etc. In today's scenario, an average Indian mindset does not consider safety as an essential element that needs to be incorporated in the daily activities and this mindset manifests at various levels of social, commercial and professional hierarchy. Safety policies and practices need to merge. Sehgal (2016, *p6*) wrote let us strive to move ahead on the "Path to Safety" and build Safety Consciousness in every citizen of the country.

What is the role of Indian heritage, culture and philosophy for human safety and health? Bhagavad Gita, a great Indian epic, includes that human Karma (actions, behaviors) lead to consequences. Safe Karma leads to safe consequences and vice versa. Here in Madhya Pradesh (MP) State of India, people are getting married in the month of June, in spite of lockdown and all awareness on COVID-19. It is not known how to explain the importance of social distancing to them. They don't listen. They say, our ancestors want the children to get married creating a horrible situation. The traditional thinking has overruled safety practices. Behavioural patterns are predominantly driven by values/needs of the culture and traditions of the land. If a person values going for job and not losing it, they are focused on that, and bypass safety measures to achieve whatever it takes. The person has to follow certain traditions, maybe, at the cost of safety, and this is being practiced by many at the same time. In other words, the health/safety needs of people are based on their socioeconomic status. The poor people are less inclined to meet health/safety needs than those whose socioeconomic status is better. In the Mumbai city's dense low-income settlements, safety measures to prevent coronavirus infections are an unachievable privilege (Johari, 2020). Culturally unsafe practices are those that "diminish, demean or disempower the cultural identity and well-being of an individual" (Nursing Council of New Zealand, 2002, p628). Williams (1999) defined cultural safety as an environment that is spiritually, socially and emotionally safe, as well as physically safe for people.

The government of India is committed to regulate all economic activities for the management of safety and health risks at workplaces and to provide measures so as to ensure safe and healthy working conditions for every working man and woman in the nation as per National policy on safety, health and environment at the workplace. But, the citizens need adequate infrastructure and life support systems to conduct themselves in safe and healthy ways. Also, it would not be possible to achieve 'safety as a way of life' without the corporate social responsibility (CSR) and social change initiatives at community levels. Indian cities rank low according to Safe Cities Index. Mumbai ranks 45th and Delhi 52nd on the Economist Intelligence Unit's Safe Cities Index, which ranks 60 countries worldwide across indicators including digital, infrastructure, health and personal security (Khanna, 2019).

The safety topic was discussed as hundreds of thousands of fatalities occurred across countries due to coronavirus risk exposure, in spite of rigorous awareness campaigns by governments to wear masks, maintain physical distancing etc. On the 14th July, 2020, the John Hopkins University COVID-19 Dashboard showed that there were 878,254 cases and 23,174 COVID-19 related deaths from March in 2020 in India. Normally, we say "safety as a way of life". We want to know, what do we mean by this. Secondly, have we done any activity to promote 'safety as a way of life' beyond our cites. Safety awareness should extend beyond the workplace (Van Oord, 2020).

A safety professional provides an anecdote, "can enforcement bring behavioural safety culture in the community at this stage? Yes, if the residential building management puts the rules in writing and enforcing done through housing society security, the discipline is well maintained. But practically, does it get sustained? There are one, two violations that happened in the past and a warning notice was put in the WhatsApp group to conduct safe behaviours and inform others of the same" (Maheshwaran, 2020).

Research Objectives

Despite emphasis by Indian culture and laws, there are problems in seeing safety culture as a way of life among Indian society, the implications of which are seen in terms of hundred thousands of fatalities due to COVID-19. Hence this research leads to find out ways for the same.

Research objective one: To identify ways to make safety a way of life in the Indian Society.

Behavioural safety culture in industry has been successfully practiced but how it can be followed as a way of life among sociocultural settings, is a difficult research question which was approached for this article? This question became increasingly relevant during COVID-19 scenario among all countries.

Research objective two: To identify how a behavioural safety culture can be included in socio-cultural settings.

Methodology

Participants, measures, procedure, analysis

Focused group discussions (FGD)/interviews/webinars with 540 Health, Safety and Environment (HSE) professionals/trainers were conducted through remote data collection techniques over 2-months (May-June 2020) in India from diverse locations and organizations. FGDs are used to understand an issue at a deeper level than can be achieved with a survey (Monishankar & Garcia, 2017). Broad themes were identified for data interpretations. Behavioural safety training methodology for planned interventions were followed at sites (see figures 1 and 2).

Results and Findings

1. *Enablers and Barriers in making safety and health a way of life in India*

Jansz *et al.* (2020) presented an exhaustive list of enablers and barriers of 12 countries for workplace safety and health. In India, the safety professionals during the FGDs envisaged positive and negative correlates of establishing a safety culture in terms of the enablers and barriers as stated here below.

Enablers or Leading Indicators are: the education right from school days, efforts by non-government organisations (NGO) and the Government on health, motivation by Institutions and industries, promotion of safety by elders at home after current COVID-19 education was provided. Other enablers are:

- Improvement trend in community awareness,
- Increase in community engagement programs in health and safety,
- Improvement in infrastructures,
- New technologies,
- Building of cultures including people getting sensitized and management control,
- Belief in Omni-energy (God), respect to mythology,
- Respect for Elders,
- Belief in "Vasudheiva Kutumbakam" (world as one family)
- Market requirements,
- Goodwill

Barriers or Lagging Indicators are poverty, behaviour of educated people, Indian tradition and customs, lack of safety leadership by top management of industries, non-stringent enforcement of law, corruption among law enforcers and government spending on health and safety. Some more barriers are:

- Negative example setting by leaders,
- Low literacy,
- Risk taking nature,
- Lack of risk assessment ability,
- Tendency to act safe only under supervision,
- Lack of systematic approach,
- Believing in quick wins (shortcuts),
- Priorities of management towards production and quality,
- Low and loose involvement of governments' body towards standards,
- Do not take Hygiene related issues seriously,
- Do not get safety education since childhood,
- Education system as a whole does not speak about basic Safety Standards and Precautions,
- Insurance,
- Human cost,
- Failure of Enforcement agency (Corruption).

One needs to ponder over an upward trend of incidents and fatalities over the past decades. It needs to be understood that the above set of barriers are responsible for deteriorating safety and health environment as well as hundred thousand fatalities every year that can be averted provided there are focused efforts to contain these barriers and at the same time, the enablers of safety and health are taken forward by all concerned.

2. *Examples and Experiences of HSE professionals on 'safety as a way of life'*

From the 540 Health, Safety and Environment Professionals that took part in focus group discussions, the following are the seven main theme experiences to emerge, in addition to the above-said enablers and barriers in making safety and health a way of life in India.

Theme 1

In my building, all delivery is done at gate. No delivery personnel are allowed to enter the building. If plumber or service provider to come in to the building, mask is a must and his hands are sanitized by the security personnel. If he is coming from a containment zone, he is not allowed. Any residents coming back to the building after visiting worst affected places such as Chennai or Ahmedabad, 14 days quarantine is mandatory. No visitors are allowed inside the building. All residents shall wear masks when they go out of the building.

Theme 2

I have done programs for behavioural aspect of road safety. This program was conducted in school, colleges and some of residential societies. This was done as a service to the nation to improve safety perceptions.

Theme 3

The COVID-19 itself has taught us the many examples as lessons of societal behaviour. Like people are keeping away from others. Using mask and reminding others who are not using. Most of the people are keeping mask with them all times. People started cleaning hand with sanitizers. Many more such examples are there.

Theme 4

Raising concerns and real life story sharing and learnings. Some still don't relate as they feel, this will not happen to me. Many have worked without domestic help for last 3 months and now are desperate. But still, few senior citizen still manage without maids as they think it is high risk and can reduce one of the chance of infection.

Theme 5

Enforcement is key to the successful implementation of any initiative in India due to our mind set which is different from the world. Inherited from our predecessors but is changing now and a time consuming process.

Theme 6

Coronavirus numbers in India are rising. Why? We are in community transmission phase, though Government is not agreeing. Government is trying to open the market, on basis of building back the lost economy. But people think that COVID-19 has come down and that's why Government has opened up the market. So communication is not clear. Myth is that COVID-19 cannot affect me. People are in stress due to this lockdown. When someone is in prolonged stress, their body immunity becomes weak. So even a minor infection could result in major.

Theme 7

Hiranandani Fortune City (HFC) has imbibed all COVID-19 related safe behaviours for its residents and staff (See Figure 1) to make it as a way of life.

In spite of the HSE professionals' efforts, it is relevant to note that as per recent estimates released by the ILO, each year 2.78 million workers die from occupational accidents.

FIG. 1: COVID-19 related safe behaviours

Source: *Shared by a FGD respondent from a construction site of Tata Projects*

and work-related diseases (of which 2.4 million are disease-related) and an additional 374 million workers suffer from non-fatal occupational accidents (ILO, 2019). 'Safety as a way of life' objective seems far away. Nevertheless, 'Safety to be a way of life' is to be in the syllabus for all education levels as a reinforcement constantly from school to university to employment, etc. Life-long learning helps to achieve such global perspective to save human lives. Education is the great equalizer, wrote the American educational reformer Horace Mann (1848). A motherly-motivational observer who would use social-media to reflect observations/spot-correction of self and others daily is all what is needed everywhere in society to make safety a way of life.

3. HSE Professionals Question Behaviour Based Safety Management

Behaviour based safety (BBS) can spread from industry to community through awareness webinars, sessions by trained BBS Mentors and experts for developing observers in communities for observation and spot-correction to make safety and health a way of life (Kaila, 2019). In this regard, the HSE professionals clarified the below questions and answers that arose as the result of the focus group discussions.

- **Do you think behaviour based safety management (BBSM) is the future of safety culture?**

  HSE professionals' answer:

  Yes, as behaviour is the root cause of all incidents, as also emphasized in ISO45001. Also culture drives the behaviours, hence BBS implementation focuses on developing safety culture.

- **How can an organization successfully implement BBSM?**

  HSE professionals' answer:

  In three phases.

  Introduction of behavioural safety to top management and development of roadmap. Rolling out BBS in entire workforce.

  Sustain it by monitoring and rewarding employees every month.

- **What are the challenges faced during the implementation of BBSM?**

  HSE professionals' answer:

  Challenges were passive involvement of Head of Departments (HODs) not letting behaviour based safety management be known till the last person at site shows appreciation of observations by seniors.

- **What are the advantages of successful implementing BBSM?**

  HSE professionals' answer:

  Advantages are incidents control, saving from injuries, increased productivity without loss. As long as, there is a focus on BBSM, that would bring business outcomes and positive implications. Further, link BBS with CSR and its community application especially in COVID-19 scenario.

- **Who benefits through BBSM?**

  HSE professionals' answer:

  Employees, management, contractors, even casual visitors and all stakeholders benefit.

- **What type of environment requires a change in its safety culture?**

  HSE professionals' answer:

  A reactive and dependent safety culture/environment.

- **What are the important aspects of BBSM?:**

  HSE professionals' answer:

  The important aspects are observation, observers and spot-correction of at-risk behaviours. Forming BBS steering team, and sensitivity and communication of leaders for implementation. Overall, behavioural safety and health approach is a 'caring' way of life and an art of positive living. It is an intense conversation and counselling for getting rid of any risks around.

- **Who should take the first step in implementing BBSM?**

  HSE professionals' answer:

  Top management by involving all HODs and stakeholders.

- **Do you think BBSM implementation has improved over the past decade?**

  HSE professionals' answer:

  Yes, almost 10,000 units in India have implemented and frequency and severity of incidents have significantly reduced at sites.

- **Why do you think BBSM must be an integral part of safety systems?**

  HSE professionals' answer:

  BBS focus is on behavioural issues of safety, no other systems do that. Moreover, BBS alone can't bring total safety culture so BBS is to be integrated with safety systems. Question remains whether safe conditions prevail to live safely or are we privileged for conditions to live safely? Essentially, safe behaviours plus safe conditions would rebuild safe-societies.

Conclusion and Recommendations for Social Policy and Planning

The deliberations in this section should help to identify ways to make safety a way of life in the Indian Society, and to identify how a behavioural safety culture can be included in sociocultural settings.

Managing safety culture is a big challenge, as it is hard for people to perceive the safety and health risks, for those who belong to communities that do not emphasize an inter-dependent safety culture. It is personal behavioural safety pattern of individuals that is influenced by social cognition and culture. Social cognition perspectives shape social milieu and social response. Most behavioural applications use social cognition frameworks for social change management, like establishing behavioural safety culture as a way of life in societies (Vinney, 2020). Department of Science and Technology, Govt. of India (2020) emphasized that safety should evolve as a habit of every person, and needs to be propagated as the culture. Safety should be of prime concern as it plays an important role in the socio-economic sectors in a significant way that will affect the growth of the institutions and have an impact on a national level. Thus, safety implementation and financial performances are correlated vertically and horizontally.

Difference between safety cultures of Indian and other countries needs to be understood. Yet, to date, the relationship between national culture and safety culture has received relatively little attention. The researchers have examined the relationship between organizational culture and the dimensions of national culture (Mark *et al.*, 2015). Organizational culture and behaviour in multinational organizations vary according to the national cultural norms of the countries. Associations exist between safety culture and Hofstede's (2001) five critical dimensions of national culture namely Power Distance, Individualism - Collectivism, Masculinity, Uncertainty Avoidance, Long-term Orientation. Moreover, the management of occupational safety and health in a culturally diverse working environment demands an approach that includes multiple voices, and one in which it is possible to considerably broaden the knowledge base for alternative decisions and to increase the number of possible paths leading to solutions to problems (European Agency for Safety and Health at Work, 2020).

Research findings and conclusions are that 'safety-culture-as-a-way-of-life' mission is possible to prevail among societies when it is not reactive, least dependent on others, its independent and also interdependent. The distancing between these cultures is crucial to manage. This mission is possible when it begins with family, school and social values and a long-term orientation and uncertainty situations are not avoided. It is a planned intervention. When this is achieved the societies are believed to be safe for their futures. The unplanned would not be safe. 'Safety as a way of life' is a conscious effort of everyone.

The findings of this research could raise certain questions as to whether the Indian way-to-life itself is on right path. 148,000 people were killed in traffic accidents in India during 2019. By 2030, traffic deaths are expected to account 1.25 million deaths across the world each year according to the World Health Organization (2020). Fortunately, a planned intervention called the Swedish Indian Transport Innovation and Safety Partnership (SITIS), comprised of companies that include Volvo Group, Autoliv, SAAB, Manipal Hospitals, and Altair; research institutes such as Chalmers, RISE, IIT-TRIPP and IISC and authorities such as VTI, ARAI, Swedish Administration Authority, and Niti Aayog, could help put a stop to these unnecessary suffering (Hogman, 2020) and make road safety a way of life.

Though there are efforts being put in the direction that would ensure "safety to be a part of our daily lives", it is a long time multi-pronged journey for countries. It is increasingly recognised that the ambitious initiatives such as safety-as-a-way-of-life is complexly determined by socio-cultural factors at many different levels of scale (Lomas, 2015). Toward this, some specific suggestions are described below that could help consolidate our deeds and increase the probability to make safety a way of life.

"Safety and health - a way of life" needs to be definable, observable, correctable on-the-spot, measurable, implementable and sustainable. The difference between a planned/long-term and unplanned/short-term behavioural safety and health culture intervention, is to be made for effective social change program as a way of life (New Brunswick Department of Education Instructional Resources Branch, 2000). For an example, Health & Safety - Choices for Life: An activity-based resource was developed for New Brunswick schools, grades K to 12 to make it as a way of life for children. This is the right time to introduce safety and health in schools syllabus in India.

There is a need to work with people down the levels in their language to make safety culture as a way of life (Jansz *et al.* 2020). India witnesses a life casualty every 4 minutes in a road accident. Mother India Care is working as a pressure group to educate and encourage the people in general, and drivers in particulars, for safe driving (Mother India Care, 2020).

There are a hundred thousand or more community groups across the globe that organize people towards social goals and indirectly contribute to providing safe mind sets and behaviours. On the other hand, certain sections of society that are not organized, or part of any planned group, and remain at higher risk whenever any health or safety disaster occurs. (WHO, 2020). CSR projects in India focused on community development, skill development as well as road safety (Mitra, 2018).

Several companies organized behavioural safety programs for organisational transformation and emphasised need to involve everyone empowering them to bring a change. Many companies' sites initiated behavioural safety culture programs for communities under CSR and BBS Project activities like road/home safety/employee families/ villages/school/college etc.

FIG. 2: Empowering employees to be the change catalysts

Dorf Ketal, under CSR, adopted certain schools, and prepared a manual for them that covered precautions to be taken by all students/teachers, staff and parents with regard to COVID-19. Precautions included what they should do at home, during travel, in school and after returning back to home. It focused on how to maintain social distancing, sanitization, use of mask, hand wash, disinfection of vehicles, school premises etc. the objective was to see behavioural safety as way of life. Dorf Ketal's quality, health, safety, security and environmental systems are purposely designed to maintain corporate and community resiliency for the long-haul in every country where they operate (Dorf Ketal, 2020).

In order to make safety and health a way of life, the change leaders/catalysts need to monitor regularly, monitor personally, monitor frequently, monitor numbers of change, interact with change observers team, make site visits, be an inclusive catalyst with vision and mission (Hariton, 2020). Leaders need to review whether empowerment is going down, core incompetence of organizations need to be managed, evaluate to develop, and check whether most human abilities are being wasted rather than being used.

Strong leaders drive culture of safety and health. They influence to make it a way of life through their programs and actions. Organisational cultures and community expectations are powerful drivers of change and collectively influence the nation's health and safety culture (Safe Work Australia, 2020). Organizations, through their CSR activities, need to raise community's awareness levels on safety and health. Frequency and clarity of communication of safety behaviours among communities improve safety culture.

Critically speaking, the enablers and barriers would keep interplaying and safety and health at-risk behaviours would continue as it is, depending upon the cultural values and compliances of the country's population, and so would be implications in terms of incidents, injuries and fatalities, as being witnessed. Developing and maintaining HSE culture remains a continual journey for all. However, a collective mind set of the world leaders might help move India out of an array of the multiple crises (HSE crisis, natural and political disasters) that have gathered the humanity. The losses are certain and immense whether they are of human lives or economic ones. It would obviously be a long term affairs and testing times ahead across the globe. An elevated mind is a solution toward the united goals with myriad wisdoms, that would prevail with a practice of education, meditation and continuation of persuasion, for safe life of everyone with a sense of equality and quality of caring, and making it a way of life (Long, 2015). For example, the UN-Volunteers supported the COVID-19 response efforts through the network of Indian District Youth Volunteer Coordinators (UNV, 2020) as a social reform.

Thus, the safety/health culture is to be elevated to a symbolic level of solar energy for an immense power, so as to make safety-a-way-of-life in communities with support of government/non-government bodies. A new thinking, focus and energy are needed to meet this goal in question, which would involve many factors like change concept and process, leaders, educational tools, timeframes, coordinators and volunteers, monitoring and tracking procedures, government controls, projects management strategies etc. In this regard, an exemplary services of India needs a mention of the hundred thousands of Accredited Social Health Activists who are large scale grass root community health workers (CHWs like ASHA/AWW/ANMs) across the nation to combat the health disaster (Government of India, 2020). Similar multilevel national safety initiatives would help and are a need of the times. It is crucial to unite more such initiatives, and the national budget must support considerably to make 'safety and health a way of life'.

References

Department of Science & Technology, Govt. of India (2020, March, 9). *Need to evolve safety as a habit highlighted in celebration of National Safety Day 2020 at ARCI.* https://dst.gov.in/pressrelease/need-evolve-safety-habit-highlighted-celebration-national-safety-day-2020-arci

Dorf Ketal. (2020). *Sustainability is Smart Business.* https://www.dorfketal.com/about-dorf-ketal/sustainability

European Agency for Safety and Health at Work (2013). *Diverse cultures at work: ensuring safety and health through leadership and participation.* Luxembourg: Publications Office of the European Union. (http://europa.eu).

Government of India (2020). *National Health Mission.* https://nhm.gov.in/index1.php?lang = 1&level = 1&sublinkid = 150&lid = 226

Hariton, L. (2020). *Why Inclusive Workplaces Matter in a Time of Crisis.* https://www.catalyst.org/2020/03/24/inclusion-in-crisis/

Hart I. (2018). *Health & safety culture in India.* https://www.shponline.co.uk/occupational-health/health-safety-culture-in-india/amp/

Hofstede, G. (2001). *Culture's consequences: Comparing values, behaviors, institutions and organizations across nations.* Beverly Hills, CA: Sage.

Hogman, Rowan (2020, February, 24). *Can tens of thousands of lives be saved every year in India?* https://www.ericsson.com/en/blog/2020/2/sitis-technology-traffic-safety-india

Horace, M. (1848). *Twelfth Annual Report to the Secretary of the Massachusetts State Board of Education.* Retrieved on 2 July 2020. https://genius.com / Horace-mann-twelfth-annual-report-to-the-secretary - of - the - massachusetts-state-board-of-education-1848-annotated

ILO (2019). *Safety and health at the heart of the future of work. Building on 100 years of experience.* https://www.ilo.org/safework/events/safeday/WCMS_686645/lang--en/index.htm

Jansz, J., Ulomka, U., Shadgett, A., Brown, M., Sarmiento, E., Logan, M., Choueiri, E., Zakaria, R., Hsu, Y., De La Rosa, A., Gilkey, D., Perryman, D., Ramli, S. & Kimeu, J. (2020). Workplace Safety, Enablers and Barriers. *World Safety Journal,* 24(2): 1-23.

Johari, A. (2020, April, 1). *'Not much we can do to keep ourselves safe': Fear grips Mumbai's slums as Covid-19 cases rise.* https://scroll.in/topic/56256/coronavirus-crisis.

Kaila H. (2019). Behaviouralizing Safety Implementation among Indian Corporates: A Research Review. *University News, 57* (20), May 20-26, 2019: 14-16.

Khanna, P. (2019). *Indian cities rank low according to Safe Cities Index.* https://www.livemint.com/news/india/indian-cities-rank-low-according-to-safe-cities-index-1567061693906.html

Lomas, T. (2015). Positive Social Psychology: A Multilevel Inquiry Into Sociocultural Well-Being Initiatives. *Psychology Public Policy and Law.* 21: 338-347. 10.1037/law0000051.

Long, R. (2015). *A Philosophy of Safety.* https://safetyrisk.net/a-philosophy-of-safety/

Mark, C. Noort, T., Reader, S. & Shorrock, B. (2015, December 12). The relationship between national culture and safety culture:

Implications for international safety culture assessments. *Journal of Occupational and Organizational Psychology.* https://doi.org/10.1111/joop.12139

Mitra, M. (2018). *India's Best Companies For CSR 2014: Community development and road safety propel Maruti in the fast lane.* https://m.economictimes.com / indias-best-companies-for-csr-2014-community-development-and-road-safety-propel-maruti-in-the-fast-lane/articleshow/45296152.cms

Mother India Care (2020). *Mother India Care - Road Safety is Life.* Safetyhttps://www.motherindiacare.com/road_safety_is_life_safety

New Brunswick Department of Education Instructional Resources Branch. (2000). Health & Safety - Choices for Life. Audio Visual, 2000 Media Catalogue. Fredericton, New Brunswick.

Nursing Council of New Zealand. (2002). Guidelines for cultural safety, the treaty of Waitangi, and Maori health in nursing and midwifery education and practice. Wellington: Nursing Council of New Zealand.

Maheshwaran, V. (2020, May, 20). Personal communication on HSE culture in India.

Prasad, M. & Garcia, C. (2017, September, 11). *How to Conduct a Successful Focus Group Discussion.* https://humansofdata.atlan.com/2017/09/conduct-successful-focus-group-discussion/

Safe Work Australia (2020). *Leadership and culture.* https://www.safeworkaustralia.gov.au/leadership-culture

Sehgal, S. (2016, May, 26). *Concept of safety in India - a perspective.* https://indianlawwatch.com/concept-of-safety-in-india-a-perspective/

UNV. (2020). *The fight against COVID-19: keeping communities safe in India.* https://www.unv.org / Multimedia / fight-against-COVID-19-keeping-communities-safe-India

Van Oord (2020). *Safety is a way of life.* https://www.vanoord.com/safety/safety-is-a-way-of-life.

Vinney, C. (2020 February, 11). "Social Cognitive Theory: How We Learn From the Behavior of Others." Thought Co, thoughtco.com/social-cognitive-theory-4174567

Walter, D. (2019, May, 20). India must seize the opportunity to create safe and healthy workplace. https://www.hindustantimes.com/analysis/india-must-seize-the-opportunity-to-create-safe-and-healthy-workplace/story-6MNrICCxTNcc4N3azhWZaO.html

WHO (2020). High-risk groups. https://www.who.int/malaria/areas/high_risk_groups/en/

Williams, R. (1999). Cultural safety – what does it mean for our work practice? *Australian and New Zealand Journal of Public Health,* 23(2): 213-214.

The comforts of safety culture is within your reach and it is observers based completely at your site.

CHAPTER 11

Mission Bharat Bane Surkshit: Safer Corporate India by Behavioural Science Approach

Introduction and Context

People in industry think that if they have received awards in quality, they are obviously best in environment and safety as well, which is an unsafe mindset, as because all these areas viz. quality, safety and environment, are integrated, yet independent functions of the organization. If not given due attention, would result into incidents leading to manpower and business loss.

BBS is a mechanism to remove unsafe behaviour from our sites and demonstrate to the neighbourhood industry that we can manage our unsafe behaviours and we can also support you do the same. Sudhir Kumar, Head EHS, Jindal Stainless expressed, "over a number of years, safety systems' efforts tend to produce dramatic reductions in accident rates but still accident happens due to human failure. As per critical disaster happened globally, investigation report reveals, unsafe risk behaviours of workmen was also a major cause of disaster".

Industry safety leaders must stick to the behavioural safety goals of zero at-risk behaviour and prepare their corporate managers and sites/plants observers accordingly. Industry has realized that the BBS implementation is a journey, and undoubtedly the impact and success of BBS has been felt, but the corporate has to involve a little more to put a thrust on observation and spot-correction procedure that can save from incidents, not only the human life but business as well. Corporate need to push behavioural safety in policies, practices and mind-sets.

Behaviour-Based-Safety means safety in action in terms of spot-correction of at-risk behaviors by one and all at site. In BBS culture, not only EHS but everyone connects and implements safety (Geller, 2004). An adoption of an interdependent safety culture by organizations will pave the way towards the safer India or Bharat Bane Surkshit.

Objective of this Research

To initiate, reach and fulfil the mission of BBS - Bharat Bane Surkshit for corporate India towards achieving zero-harm, zero tolerance for zero unsafe behaviours to prevent losses of life and business.

Methodology

This paper is an interdisciplinary intervention of behavioural science, management and industrial safety disciplines which is part of an ongoing national longitudinal action survey in India. Thematic data analysis was used to reflect the findings as mentioned here below. Steps used in analysis were: become familiar with the data, generate themes, review themes, define themes, write-up. reading and re-reading the transcripts is most important in the thematic analysis.

The BBS programme as part of this action survey was implemented in diverse locations in India for employees of multinational companies that were trained as BBS mentors and observers during the years 2018-20. This programme included the concept and process of BBS, plant visits for observation and correction of at-risk behaviours, developing road map for implementation of BBS, developing training module for imparting training to all employees, formation and functions of BBS steering team. More than 3000 training participants included managers, heads of departments, contractors, safety officers and contractors' staff belonging to the public and private industrial sectors such as chemicals, construction, gas, power, and steel across Indian locations.

Results and Findings

This research article covered the following salient aspects of the BBS implementation for developing an interdependent safety culture at sites.

1. Recommendations of the 4th BBS National Conference
2. Positive Outcomes of BBS implementation
3. Rating BBS Culture
4. Bharat Bane Surkshit (BBS) for Corporate India
5. Key persons behind Some Companies who implemented BBS
6. Conclusions and Implications

1. Recommendations of the 4th BBS National Conference

A national conference (Figure 1) was organized by the Forum of Behavioural Safety at SCOPE Complex, New Delhi (Forum of Behavioural Safety, 2020). Keynote speakers for the program were Dr. S P Garg-Executive Director (GAIL India Ltd.), Mr. Sushil Agrawal, CEO (Sterlite India Ltd.), Mr. S. K Awasthi, Executive Director (IOCL) and Mr. Kishwer Jawed (Tata Projects). some of the main learning points elaborated by the keynote speakers are as given below:

It was voiced that Behaviours Based Safety should be measurement based, planned on continual basis and it should be countable for making it success in any organization. Companies today are moving towards a common goal to focus on behavior and digitalize BBS.

Mr. S P Garg: He explained any that organisation has to pass from four phases namely Reactive to Dependent to Independent and to finally Interdependent. GAIL started BBS movement in 2013 with only 65% safe behaviour and now they are at 90% safe behaviour.

Mr. S K Awasthi: Emphasize on Samskara as it comes in the children from parents, how children are groomed. Similarly, once, if safety culture is developed and maintained then frequent change in contractor worker will not affect our culture rather their behaviour will get change within no time. He also compared how human behaviour changes within no time once he lands on any European countries. Public sectors are having sufficient infrastructure, but all incident reports are remaining on paper only. it has to be engraved in the heart and mind of each and every employee.

Mr. Sushil Agrawal: He has highlighted on some of the important points which are as given below:

- Top management are focusing only on profitability and financial aspects but not paying much attention on safety aspects. According to Poncelet *et al.* (2017). when cost-cutting/profit prevails, safety suffers, people lose their lives.
- Investing in safety will pay in long run and help in improving financial aspects also.
- Reaching a level is simple but sustaining at that position is very difficult. Top Management must spend some time on safety aspect also. he also said quality and safety move together.

Kishwer jawed: He said that a true leader should demonstrate (Monkey See, Monkey Do), he also gave stress on making strong system so that the repeated violation can be addressed differently, like ICU case. He also informed that how better safety data helped Tata Projects while bidding. He proudly said that Pryagraj Airport developed by Tata projects in record time of 11 month without any causality.

FIG. 1: 4th BBS National Conference at Delhi

Speakers from oil and steel sector, construction and gas, chemical and energy segment spoke on how BBS has been implemented in their organizations and what are difficulties faced by them and what innovative steps taken by them to overcome those constraints.

This 4th BBS National Conference at Delhi (Forum of Behavioural Safety, 2020) on 17th January 2020 brought out and concluded the following facts of BBS:

1. There are several positive outcomes of BBS implementation like frequency and severity of

incidents are significantly reduced from first aid to fatalities.

2. BBS is a Cultural transformation from reactive/ dependent to independent/interdependent safety culture.
3. BBS is Measurement of at-risk behaviours at site which indicates directions and goal setting.
4. It's a planned Organizational intervention procedure involving one and all at work areas.
5. Increase in the number of organizations implementing BBS across all sectors in the country.
6. This is the only national conference happening on BBS in the country every year.
7. BBS is one application of behavioural science to safety, there are many applications.
8. BBS is counting behaviors (safe & unsafe) like count of RBC, WBC. If these are reduced or increased significantly, effect is adverse. Similar impact is of unsafe behaviours which is almost 30% at Indian sites (Kaila, 2020).
9. Raise slogan Bharat Bane Surkshit (BBS) every time, a BBS workshop is held at site in order to create a general BBS mindset and the felt culture amongst people.
10. BBS is an ISO-45001 Compliance. Involvement of all top to bottom for daily observation and spot-correction for 5 minutes.

2. *Positive Outcomes of BBS implementation*

Positive results of BBS are reported below by prestigious organisations (that implemented BBS across India) such as

Bilag, GAIL, HPCL, IOCL, L&T, AFCONS, Vedanta, Tata Projects, Sterlite, Privi, HCC, DCM Shriram, Dorf Ketal, Sembcorp, Galaxy Surfactants, SAIL, Jindal, Uflex, TRL, IGL, Agrocel, Torrent, Aarti, Solaris, CFCL, Bayer's CropScience, Oil India, Greentech, Sanofi-Aventis, Sabic, Piramal, Bajaj Auto, Volkswagen, Toyota, etc.

- The lead trainers are now involved in training in addition to HSE staff.
- The frequency of safety meetings has increased.
- The safety awareness and compliances have gone up.
- People are working more safely (safe behaviors increased).
- There is an increased focus on behaviour, and a structured approach is being used.
- There is a distribution of safety ownership. Interdependent Safety culture has evolved.
- Contractor involvement in safety has boosted.
- There is a shift in safety culture from reactive/ dependent to independent/interdependent.
- The frequency and severity of incidents have significantly decreased.
- Behavioural trends on an average across companies is 72% of safe behaviours; at-risk behaviour of 28%% and at-risk behaviours corrected is 2% by each observer.
- The number of safe behaviours increased from 60% to 96% in 6 months of BBS launch.
- The number of observers has also increased every month.
- The number of unsafe conditions and unsafe behaviours has drastically gone down.

- BBS has been recommended to other locations of the company with an introduction of BBS in one location.
- The management commitment for safety has gone up due to involvement.
- Safety has become a real line function due to BBS approach.
- The incident reporting is not there from locations where BBS is implemented.
- There is a significant decline in Near miss and injuries.
- There is an increased reporting of unsafe behaviours.
- Leadership involvement has increased.
- 50% reduction in incidents as depicted by AFCONS (Figure 2).

Ramakrishna Rao GMS, Corporate HSE Strategist at AFCONS emphasized that companies are continuously working striving to find new ways to improve their safety culture and reduce injuries and fatalities. One of such ways is observation-based safety programs which have been utilized for several years in the industries. This form of safety program generally aims to shift organizational safety practices from a traditional reactive, failure-oriented approach (e.g., chastising employees for making mistakes or sustaining injuries) to a proactive, achievement-oriented approach. Behaviour Based Safety is a tool to create strong safety motivation in employees, improve culture of safety, and ultimately reduce incidents and fatalities. "The very words of wisdom from our gurus SHRADHA(Determination) & SABURI (Patience) plays a great role in the sustenance of BBS - holistic approach of injury prevention program".

3. *Rating BBS Culture*

It is essential to rate and rank the company's ongoing BBS project activities to sustain the safety culture. Make your own review of the BBS processes for your site as per checklist below. An Example is stated here.

Changes in Safety Parameters after BBS Implementation

	Particulars	Before BBS Training (June 2019)	After BBS Training (December 2019)
1.	Safety Violations	Approx. 60 Nos per month	Approx. 40 Nos per month
2.	Environmental Incidents	Approx. 10 Nos per month	Approx. 4 Nos per month
3.	Health and Hygiene	Approx. 30 Nos per month	Approx. 20 Nos per month
4.	PPE's Compliance	Approx. 100 Nos per month	Approx. 20 Nos per month
5.	First Aid Cases	Approx. 15 Nos per month	Approx. 7 Nos per month
6.	Non Conformances by client	Approx. 4 Nos per month	Approx. 2 Nos per month
Reduction on an average by 50% after implementation of Behavior Based Safety			

Mark each process below out of 10. Check, what's lacking.

1. Safety cultural shift from reactive/dependent culture to independent/interdependent culture (8)
2. Leadership increased involvement (7)
3. Monthly BBS meetings (8)
4. Incidents reduction (9)
5. Behavioral trends improvement (8)
6. Sharing of at-risk behaviours during TBT (7)
7. Motivational reward, recognition for observers, units (7)

8. Managements regular observation rounds (8)
9. Regular repeat BBS awareness sessions for spot-correction (7)
10. Quarterly reviews across units/sites (8)

    Total: 10 × 10 = 100

    Average Indian Site BBS Rating Score: 79

BBS Culture Rating Score of 79 means there is a large scope to focus on above areas where score is less. S K Srivastava, Chief Health & Safety Officer- Rajasthan Gas, Cairn Oil & Gas, Vedanta Limited, clarifies, "to sustain the BBS culture - the Safety culture of any organization has to be aligned with zero tolerance behavior towards unsafe acts, however correcting the unsafe behaviours by regular and persistent counselling instead of punishing and exercising consequence management at the incipient stage of unsafe behaviours by workers. To me, Safety is always a Top down approach which in the long run transforms the safety culture of an organization and finally changed to bottom up approach; wherein every employee/worker leads the safe behaviours by their own, without being monitored; thereby emphasizing buddy system and strengthening the concept of Brother to Brother Safety (BBS)".

4. Bharat Bane Surkshit (BBS) for Corporate India

For large multiple-unit organizations, the company needs a strong BBS team for regular training, monitoring and reviewing. This team in principle is a group of lead BBS trainers themselves. And fundamentally, BBS is not a consultant driven or safety department driven process.

The following considerations suggested by the industry experts for the possibility, approach and vision of Bharat Bane Surkshit are as follows:

- Involvement of people and organizations in BBS implementation philosophy
- Demonstrating case studies of successful implementations
- Spread of BBS by leaders from industry
- Making every Indian aware of the Benefits of BBS.
- By training, awareness, motivate safe behaviour and Top management involvement.
- That is the aim of BBS. We all need to add efforts towards the goal.
- Some hard steps are required such as consequences management. It is good to clarify that the BBS implementation does not replace other safety systems. hard step may be taken after a year of BBS implementation until 90% of safe behaviours have been achieved, ensuring people that the company provided enough of positive reinforcement through soft peddling of BBS approach for an year or more.
- Making spot-correction a reality with strategic approach of Top management policy that all we are doing really BBS.
- With PPP model: Public Private Partnerships: Govt institutions shall authorize Private entities in achieving the results.
- Improvement of beliefs and perceptions of BBS at sites: Change in numbers of safe behaviours by observation and spot-correction daily by trained BBS observers help organizations strengthen their understanding and beliefs that safety culture can be transformed so quickly and effectively.

5. *Key persons behind Some Companies who implemented BBS*

Demonstrating case studies of successful implementations, it is best to interact directly with people who implemented BBS at sites for first-hand information. Here below is a list of persons who achieved positive results of BBS implementation. They served as continuing BBS mentors for contributing to the mission of Bharat Bane Surkshit. The details of corporate Safety Heads are given below for immediate support.

- SP Garg, ED GAIL India, sp.garg7826@gmail.com 09958933556
- Vikas Gupta, DGM (Safety), SAIL/Bokaro Steel Plant, Mobile:8986872784, dgmsafetybsl1@gmail.com
- Subhamoy Maitra, Chennai Cluster EHS Head, L&T Construction, TIIC, smsft@lntecc.com +919840452709
- Dr. R K Sharma | Head-Sustainability | India Glycols Limited r.k.sharma@indiaglycols.com 09837056451
- Kaushlendra Singh, GM EHS, DCM SHRIRAM, kaushlendrasingh@dcmshriram.com, 7518604695
- Avinash Shinde, Galaxy Surfactants Ltd. Mobile-09867965021
- Prabha Mishra, AFCONS INFRA +91 7666350515, pmishra@afcons.com
- Pavan K Rao, Head - HSE, SGPC, pavan1965@gmail.com +917032967480
- Shankar Rajagopalan - ESG Head, Granules, shankarrajag@gmail.com +918754426685
- Md. Quaisar Imam, Head - Environment, Health and Safety (EHS)- O&M, Sterlite Power Grid Ventures Limited md.imam@sterlite.com +917571908671
- Sudhir Kumar, HEAD-EHS, sudhir.kumar@jshl.in +918851854438

- Krishan Kumar Sharma (Delhi), Director, DCM Shriram, kksharma@dcmshriram.com +919968660606
- Sanjay Khare, Vice President, Volkswagen, sanjay.khare@volkswagen.co.in +919971090105
- Sunil Sanas, HPCL, sunilsanas@hpcl.in 09820945801
- M Ravikumar, Tata Projects Limited. Mob: +91-9676602507
- Surender Singh, CGM, Bhilai Steel plant, +919407981087
- Srinivas Salunke, EHS Head, Bajaj Auto, 9890500594
- Santosh Srivastava sksrivastava1981@yahoo.com Cairn India, 07894406115
- Niranjan Dash, Tata Krosaki Refractories, +918455867895
- P.K. Singh, Tata Projects Limited, Noida. +917300740317, pradeepkumars@tataprojects.com

6. *Conclusion and Implications*

According to KK Sharma, a Director, "We at DCM Shriram, believe that a safe and healthy work environment is a prerequisite for ensuring employee well-being, and adopting best EHS practices bears a direct impact on the Company's overall performance. An Implementation of behavior based safety program has provided positive rewards to change unsafe behavior at workplace, reduce job-related injuries, minimize lost production hours, and improve workplace morale - essential ingredients for creating a strong safety culture. Over the year, we have achieved more than 95% reduction in at-risk behaviours which has resulted in reduced injury incidents and impacted positively on employee behavior with visible change in their actions".

In order to move ahead towards a mission of Bharat Bane Surkshit, companies need to address and adopt the following aspects (Forum of Behavioural Safety, 2018).

(a) Margins of implementation of BBS

Sandeep Sharma, Sr. Manager stated, "though it is initial stages of BBS implementation for Uflex Chemicals, but significant improvement was observed in last two years. We are in process of eliminating the unsafe behavior by 100% and promoting proactive reporting as much as possible for making our site one of the safest". Dr. U K Chakrabarty, General Manager, Oil & Natural Gas Corporation Ltd. Institute of Petroleum Safety Health and Environment Management narrated his experience, "the Behaviour Based Safety (BBS) movement in industry saw quite encouraging results in terms of management commitment and increasing workers involvement in the process. However, initial euphoria of implementation of BBS programs needs to be maintained and it is a challenging task to sustain such BBS movements so far of achieving desired results of injury reduction in industries".

Organizations need to think on the margins of implementation of BBS to optimize it, and here below are certain points to consider in this direction (Lal, 2020).

- Make a news that zero-harm is achievable, and we together will make it possible;
- Promise that we will make safe working culture in and around my place;
- Encourage safe behaviour each day;
- Assure that I will create observers for spot-correction of at-risk behaviors in my work areas;
- See that BBS award is a guiding force for future reference and development of BBS at other sites

- Ensure that BBS system evolves through continued training, motivation, monitoring and reviewing the BBS implementation at sites.
- Confirm that BBS implementation continues at sites as you reflect in BBS documents.
- Organizational approach is improved to achieve the zero unsafe behaviour
- BBS observers are regularly increasing
- Implementation of BBS observers in the corporate office
- Improve the quality of selection process of observers
- Increase BBS workshops for management
- Implement reward system for observers to appreciate their observations
- Corporates shouldn't increase production with a drop of blood or injury to anyone, rather by increasing significant participation in safe behaviours mobilizing people.

(b) Criteria for selection of BBS observers (as practised at Torrent Power)

Chief Observers: Steering Team; comprising Senior Management and HODs; they must act as chief observers at site level and must support area observers/coordinators.

Lead Observers: Line management; Engineers, Managers from all the departments are lead observers to support and encourage key observers and take feedback from them regularly.

Key Observers: Ground level personnel; From O&M (Plant Operation and Maintenance) and non-O&M area, covering all type of activities including Horticulture, Housekeeping, Canteen, Transportation/Drivers, Security etc. for BBS observations, spot correction and communicating feedback including that of observations of at risk activities/behaviours.

Along with above defined roles, we have encouraged all employees to be observers for a 360 effectiveness in BBS. Since BBS calls for changes in one's behavior pattern itself, there may be difficulty in convincing individuals the need for change as people in general tend to have 'resistance to change'. However, training with case studies and examples do bring in acceptance. This has been our experience. Once people get convinced that the changes, in turn, is to their advantage, the acceptance is quite fast.

(c) Quality of observations/Spot-correction important, that element is missing now. May be because all are forced to do, so dedicated team for daily observation and correction is missing, all are only filling their targets set by corporate and each unit. All are fulfilling targets, no one is serious about it. That's most hurting and painful.

(d) BBS organizational procedure is to behaviouralize ISO 45001

"Everyone will give 5 minutes Daily Round as a Big Brother of Safety (BBS) to achieve zero-harm targets at every site" Please display this across the board. Observation and spot-correction is the mantra. In words of a CGM (Safety & FS) Bhilai Steel Plant, "considering the present safety environment in the plant, where occurrence of accidents/ incidents has increased significantly and can be reduced only by cultural breakthrough. This is only possible, if and only if, 100% employee is involved in developing safety culture, by changing human behavior, toward safety in the plant. BBS helps comply with ISO 45001 for everyone to manage risk.

(e) Dependent safety culture is a huge risk in corporate safety management as HODs don't take ownership of safety implementation and it is left to the safety department.

Ismail *et al.*, (2011) reported that behavioural safety needed effective leadership if it was to be a successful part of the organization's safety management system. Shankar Rajagopalan - Sterling Wilson Solar Head QSHE & PI, who is Driving Change across 3 decades said, "true safety leadership is all about being safe oneself and walking the talk - but also talking the walk by way of being aware that calling out on deviations followed by on the spot corrections is what goes a long way in fixing the foundation and helps shaping the interdependent safety culture".

(f) BBS Content Design for HODs (as practised at SEIL for interdependent safety culture)

According to Head HSE - SEIL, "BBS is our flagship programme and we are determined to excel in it". From our safety culture perception survey, we need to work on those 20% employee who still feel that we are in independent safety culture. If we convert them to demonstrate and believe that we are in interdependent safety culture than our major work will be done. Thereafter we must sustain it. BBS hotspots also match with hotspots of near-miss and first-aid. Last year we reduced first aid cases by 45%. This year further 50%.

The Content Design for HODs at SEIL is as below:

- Brief scientific background of BBS to scoring of behaviour checklist
- They should not question the BBS score card as it is being followed at all Oil, steel companies, Tata projects, L&T etc
- HOD to lead to take to next level

- Analysis of the BBS scores and Hot Spots
- Prepare action plan to address top 3 hot spots
- Have a monthly meeting with engineers and contractors
- Make daily visit to site, do one observation, talk to workers
- Address concerns of all HODs
- Share success stories of corporates
- How to move rest of 20% employees from independent to Interdependent Safety Culture
- Why zero harm culture is possible?
- Pledge for involvement and sustaining it
- Daily 10 mins quality BBS round by HODs
- Daily 10 mins round by everyone in the department
- Weekly Mass Communication with the department to increase BBS awareness down the level (mentoring of observers)
- 1st week of every month BBS data analysis, HOT SPOT identification and action plan along with HSE representative

(g) Each Company Adopts a BBS Policy

BBS is highly interactive, proven and positive model of safety cultural transformation in organizations. Whereas a small unsafe behaviour has high stakes for the company.

The BBS policy signed by the Managing Director has positive implications and would involve business heads and departments heads to move in jumps and leaps for achieving spot-correction of every at-risk behaviours down the levels at sites.

BBS Policy like below was unveiled at Sembcorp Energy India Limited as well as DCM Shriram.

SITE BBS POLICY

BBS (behavior-based safety) is a modern safety tool of behavioural science. our site has launched and adopted BBS policy & procedure to ensure zero unsafe behaviours to result into "zero incident, zero harm".

I am pleased to empower and give right to every employee as well as each vendor in our premises to involve and be an active BBS observer for "spot-correction of every small at-risk behaviors of your colleagues around on daily basis and value human life". Spot-correction is your quickest response to any smallest at-risk behavior being done by anyone.

I expect everyone to go back to his/her family without even a small injury. site performance and well-being of individuals are closely connected. Everyone at site will observe for less than 5 minutes daily and spot-correct more than one at-risk behavior of their peers.

BBS is an integral part of our business, performance and EHS policies. Hence, with an immediate effect, Each HOD will take role and responsibility as site BBS implementer for training, implementing, reporting, reviewing, rewarding all employees, workmen till the last person in BBS mission for development of an interdependent safety culture.

All HOD shall sign and display this policy in respective departments.

Signed by the Managing Director & Circulated by the Site Head
Dated:

To conclude: The guidelines, narratives, data reports indicate that this mission is possible to achieve, it requires continued efforts of all. The Forum of Behavioural Safety has about 170 life members to support this objective and mission. Moreover, the Forum already conducted 4 national BBS conferences to involve the corporate India towards this goal. This BBS mission has been initiated in Indian industry and getting rooted. The approach is clearer and hence the possibility of Bharat Bane Surkshit is achievable by focusing on the actions recommended in this paper. The latest researches (EHS Today, 2020) indicate that the major reason Behavior Based or Behavioral Safety is so effective, is its scientific base, and it further quotes Professor E. Scott Geller who asked audience members if they had been injured in a workplace incident and then asked, "How many [incidents] were caused by another person? An equipment failure? Your behavior?" When the majority raised their hands when he asked if their behavior caused the incident, he said, 'I rest my case,'" Geller, alumni distinguished professor at Virginia Tech and director of the Center for Applied Behaviour Systems in the Department of Psychology, remembers: 'What influences behaviour?' It all happens as part of the culture." And the safety culture is transformable with BBS.

To sum up, an unfailing aim of a BBS observer at the site is to keep his/her eyes open around to observe at-risk behaviour, connect as a big brother/sister and conveying the risk and its consequences to the person and helping the person to do the correction on-the-spot in his presence before he moves on. And broadly, every corporates' aim in full BBS implementation is to orient and train everyone as an active BBS observer at their sites in order to achieve a larger objective of Bharat Bane Surkshit which is zero-harm culture to save life and business for our nation to grow and benefit our country's citizens health and safety. BBS culture also needs to be connected with safety rewards and punishment, to reward all employees who contribute BBS observations and identify and discourage the ones who don't, as safe employees would sustain business of the company and unsafe ones are a huge risk and threat to the company business. The company in the long run would get away with such unsafe employees, the ones who don't behave safe and not contribute BBS observations and spot-correction of at-risk behaviors at site for saving human life. Each employee's observation matrix would need to be linked to reward and penalty every month to achieve safer corporate India.

References

EHS Today (2020). Behavior-Based Safety: Myth or Magic? https://www.ehstoday.com/safety/article/21908747/behaviorbased-safety-myth-or-magic retrieved on 6th February 2020.

Forum of Behavioural Safety (2018). Souvenir of National BBS Conference on Best Experiences, Practices and Challenges of Behavioural Based Safety Implementation in Indian Industry at Mumbai 0n 19th January 2018.

Forum of Behavioural Safety (2020). 4th Annual National Conference, Theme: Sustainable Behavior Based Safety (BBS) in industry For Interdependent Safety Culture. 17th JANUARY 2020.

Geller, E.S. (2004). Behavior-based safety: A solution to injury prevention. Behavior based safety empowers employees and addresses the dynamics of injury prevention. Risk & Insurance, 15(12, 01 Oct), 66.

Ismail, F., Hashim, A. E., Zuriea, W., Ismail, W., Kamarudin, H., & Baharom, Z. A. (2011). Behaviour based approach for quality and safety environment improvement: Malaysian experience in the oil and gas industry. *Procedia-Social and Behavioural Sciences*, 35, 586-594.

Kaila Harbans Lal (2019). Behaviour Based Safety for Corporates: A Shift toward an Interdependent Safety Culture. *World Safety Journal,* Vol. XXVIII No. 4, 5-8.

Lal K. H. (2020). Behaviour Based Safety for Corporates: A Shift Towards an Interdependent Safety Culture. *Industrial Engineering Journal,* Volume 13 Issue 1 * January 2020, 1-8.

Poncelet, E., Anderson J., Chirkov, V. (2017). Observation-based safety programs. In Chirkov, V., Anonson, J., Anderson, J., Press, M., Gerrard, A., & Ha, C. (Eds.). Enhancing cultures of safety and safety engagement in the Saskatchewan mining industry: A collaborative and multidisciplinary inquiry (pp. 200 - 213). Saskatoon, SK Canada: International Minerals Innovation Institute.

HSE culture development depends upon an involved emotional response of everyone around there at site.

CHAPTER 12

Exploring and Managing Psychosocial Risks in Organisations as per ISO45003

Introduction

These are causes of workmen anxiety that result from multiple factors including the ways the work is organized (hours of work, consecutive days to work), ways the tasks or the work environment are structured, or not being included in decision-making for their safety (Velocity EHS, 2020).

The National Statistics reports in UK revealed that 19% of adults are affected with some kind of depression, up from 9.7 per cent pre-pandemic. In Europe as a whole, 62% of the staff reported higher levels of stress, with 81% having a poor state of mind. The big corporates have implemented video-conferencing platforms, wellness programmes and resilience trainings in an attempt to tackle this, but majority of the global employees, working for small and medium-sized enterprises (SMEs), are missing out. And it's starting to show as 30 per cent of businesses with 250 to 499 employees' mental health being negatively affected (Laboris, 2021).

The first International Standard ISO45003 is a new standard that addresses an important gap in health and safety systems, that is psychological health and safety. This addition to the ISO 45000 family is a proactive effort to make mental wellbeing a core part of the organisational culture. Mental health is on business agenda now (Hurndall, 2021). Employers have a responsibility to protect both the physical and psychosocial health of their staff (Naden, 2021). The rises in mental health absenteeism have come from increased workload and poor managerial support, which apply to companies of all sizes (CRUSH, 2021).

Organisations have many different workplace risks to assess and control, but they don't adequately identify and address psychosocial risks. Mental distress is found to increase the risk for workplace incidents, adversely affecting risks for workers both on and off the job. Some employees may experience fatigue as a symptom of mental distress, or substance abuse, increasing the risk for impairment at the workplace (Molé, 2021).

Study Objective

The present article is focused on exploring and managing the psychosocial risks in organisations as per ISO45003 in multiple industrial sectors, and recommend solutions thereof.

Research Methodology

A total of 180 HSE professionals across Indian locations in multiple industrial sectors, reflected their viewpoint on what are the organisational psychosocial risks in organisations and recommended solutions. Multiple industrial sectors such as chemical, oil, petroleum and gas, engineering, manufacturing, power, energy, and construction industries were included in this study. Both primary and secondary data were collected from the study participants with diverse backgrounds of age, experience, designation and education. Open-ended questions based interviews and personal in-depth discussions with HSE professionals were conducted through remote data collection techniques over 2-months

(June to July 2021). Qualitative content and thematic analysis were performed.

Results and Discussion

What are the psychosocial risks (as described in ISO45003), we should address at sites and how? According to HSE professionals, there are a combination of factors that trigger these risks, which are mentioned here below.

1. Power and energy plants: Nearly 90 percent of HSE professionals who participated in this study expressed that there are a specific set of psychosocial risks in the power and energy plants such as boredom, mental fatigue environment to feel free to speak with concerns, admit mistakes, feel free to say I don't feel safe, let's stop and re-access, behaviour of senior, mentorship, always ready for guidance rather than scold on his/her understanding. People should first respect each other, they will automatically respect work and safety also and will enjoy it, will overall definitely reduce all type of risk including psychosocial. Addressing mental distress among the workforce can help reduce workplace incidents (Molé, 2021).

2. Construction sites: HSE professionals (89% of the construction sites) stated the psychosocial risks as follows: the lack of family benefits, personal incentives, future promotions, are the best psychosocial stresses. Production/ company, innovation, environment are the after-thoughts in the minds of employees, and the high stress individuals who should be covered under high risk group. Job dissatisfaction is found as a big psychosocial hazard in construction sites (Shrestha, 2021).

3. Chemical units: According to a EHS Director of a chemical group of companies, "honestly, the managers are not aware of the psychosocial risks except anxiety and stress while work from home (WFH) which is being addressed through regular health talks, yoga sessions and confidential counselling for our employees". A study indicated huge deficiencies in the implementation of psychosocial risk assessments, especially for small companies (Beck and Lenhardt, (2019).

The HSE professionals (87% of the chemical plants) listed a host of psychosocial risks:

- Family stress,
- Social stress,
- Supervisor work Instructions and continued follow up,
- Fatigue (Corona Thoughts),
- Leave issue,
- Holiday works,
- Targets of Check and assurance,
- Team work issue,
- Tobacco habit,
- Duty timing punctuality,
- Work stress,
- PPEs not receiving timely,
- Salary increment,
- Job promotions problems,
- Workplace hygienic conditions

Conclusion

The findings suggest that the psychosocial risks across industries are similar irrespective of the sectors or locations, which are mainly in three categories: aspects of how work is organised, social factors at work, and work environment, equipment and hazardous tasks. Research from the University of South Australia (2021) finds that the companies who pay inadequate attention to workers' psychological health keep employees at higher risk of depression. Interventions to control psychosocial risks are the key challenges for occupational health specialists and the managers at sites. There are barriers that are responsible for the gap between recommendations and occupational health and safety (OSH) practices in psychosocial risk evaluation (Weigl, 2017). UAE has been recently recognized by the British Classification Foundation, as the world's first to obtain the ISO Certification for the management of psychological health and safety at work. 'The ISO 45003 is a new standard that begun this year with the aim of helping the institutions using the ISO 45001 for occupational health and safety management. It's the first global benchmark that provides practical guidance on managing mental health in the workplace (Dubai PR Network, 2021).

Recommendations

The psychosocial risks management needs to be a part of the business strategy to develop leaders who will take it to the entire organisation for complete implementation of these recommendations. Following are some recommendations to consider.

1. There is a need to develop sensitivity towards psychosocial risks all across industry, community as well as educational and medical institutions. The development and enhancement of occupational health services (OHS) at the national level is central to ensuring the sustainable health, well-being and work engagement of the working population (Jain, 2021). Psychosocial counselling for COVID-19 positive persons and their family members is recommended (ICMR, 2021). There is a huge number of affected employees who would require this service.

2. A training module for all employees to manage psychosocial risks (Table 1) need to be developed on the

TABLE 1: Training module for all employees to assess and manage psychosocial risks

Characteristics of negative psycho-social environment in Indian workplaces (subjectively assess these factors below out of 100)	**Characteristics of positive psychosocial environment** (subjectively assess these factors below out of 100)
• Fault-finding, Bullying, Blaming, • Supervisor work Instructions/ continued follow up, • Fatigue (Corona Thoughts), Mental fatigue • Leave issue, Working on Holiday, • Team-work issues, Work stress, Targets, • Tobacco habit of employees/ workmen, • Duty timing punctuality pressure, job boredom, • Interpersonal social stress, • PPEs not receiving timely/safety issues • Salary increment/Job promotions problems, • Workplace hygienic conditions, • Anxiety and stress while Work From Home. • (Write here your overall score of psychosocial risks and an action plan to minimise these factors):	• Appreciation of each other daily, Supporting staff, • Build Positive culture: Spirituality/ Yoga/Meditation, • Connect between people as brother/sister, • Corporate values of caring not scaring employees, Employee assistance support program, • Festivities at workplace (birthdays, festivals) Regular mental health talks by experts and HODs, • Role of psychologist, psychiatrist, social worker • Programs for employees families, • Psychological safety: Feel free/safe to speak up, • Mentoring program: seniors' guidance not scolding, • Rewards and Recognition program for employees. • (Write here your overall score of positive psychosocial environment and an action plan to maximise these factors):
Consequences of negative psychosocial environment is reactive business culture, high stress risk groups leading to increased psychosocial risks and downward business trends.	**Consequences of positive psychosocial environment** is business excellence with healthy culture. People enjoy work and safety and it will definitely reduce the overall psychosocial risks.

following two areas: the factors that trigger negative psychosocial environment and the factors that facilitate positive psychosocial environment are as follows below. These factors do not immediately carry a negative or positive connotation. However, when reference is made to psychosocial hazards then it is implied that these aspects of work organisation, design and management have the potential to cause harm to individual health and safety (e.g., poor mental health, burnout, heart disease, musculoskeletal disorders) as well as other adverse organisational outcomes such as sickness absence, reduced productivity or human error (ILO, 2016; WHO, 2010). Effective management of psychosocial risks can lead to benefits such as improved worker engagement, enhanced productivity, increased innovation, and organizational sustainability (Continuity Central, 2021).

The psychosocial risk assessments identify and assess the organisational psychosocial risk factors that negatively impacts the employee health and wellbeing. There is a significant return on investment from building a mentally healthy workplace (Finbarrstapleton, 2021). The standard provides guidelines for psychosocial risk assessment in Clause 6.1.2 hazard identification and assessment of risks and opportunities, of ISO 45003. Organisations are required to maintain processes for hazard identification that are ongoing and proactive.

3. Risk management in an organization represents a decisive function in seizing opportunities and managing the risks that can affect a business's reputation, prosperity, growth, value creation, stakeholder engagement, longterm survival, and a firm's contribution to sustainable development (Gomez *et al.*, 2021). Shankar Rajgopalan, a HSE expert underlined (ASSOCHAM, 2021) that all three bottom lines

has it's own challenges. For a decision to be sustainable, it has to pass through all the three sieves, each of these has a weightage relevant to the industry, defining the Economic Prosperity (as against profitability), the Social Equity and the Environmental Performance. The ROI would therefore need all three levers to be factored, for the decision to be Equitable: fair and impartial. Bearable : able to be endured and Viable : capable of working successfully. But, safety behaviour gets a back seat on the Triple Bottom Line focus. All ESG (Environmental, Social and Governance) parameters end up in beliefs and behaviours standards (BBS) for ensuring safety and wellbeing of citizens starting from schools through communities, industry, and so on.

ESG is to be a part of life cycle of each one to make it relatively easy. ESG is a social ethics responsibility, ESG funds are being created. Non-ESG companies are not being favoured by stake-holders. It has moved to a centre stage. It is a must for business sustainability. ESG compliance and rating is a must for investors. It is gaining momentum in education as well as corporates, though the notion is prevalent that spending on ESG is not worth it. Involve workers, community, employees is a long way for sustaining businesses. It is not a philanthropy. If you are not prepared, it can hit us, if prepared, it can raise business opportunities. Skill building on the subject is needed for people in corporates and so on. Time horizon has to be longish say, 3-5 years. The customers and clients would drive the businesses. Nevertheless, companies need to be behaviourally active, more on actions, not social lectures. Intellectually, we are on same page about the topic of ESG, but behaviourally, our corporates have not even achieved the safety culture for saving lives and businesses from the incidents and accidents. The ground realities have to change and be initiated by leaders. In fact, largely, the clarity of focus of industry in not on ESG. A research suggested that enhancing companies' utilisation of OSH experts, and strengthening the advisory and control capacities of the OSH inspection authorities in the observation of psychosocial risks would be beneficial for improving the existing scenario at workplaces [Beck and Lenhardt, (2019)].

4. Develop Behavioural safety, psychosocial support, EAP groups in each department as a planned intervention to meet every month. Use affection instead of hardiness to your colleagues, they would listen to you with respect These are simple interventions for organisational practices (such as don't be reactive but responsive, don't scare but care) which increase human affection among people at work of for positive synergies between teams and groups at work sites. Be careful: your actions, your body language that you demonstrate to others, have an effect on their behaviour. Hence demonstrate appropriate safe behaviours so that it becomes a part of others memory and behaviour which becomes an overall safety culture.

Connect between people at site as brother or sister, develop skill of observation and approach for spot-correction of any at-risk behaviours, and an overall sensitivity to risk perception and prevention. In behaviour based safety (BBS), sincere observers having sensitivity to safety risk perception and prevention of unsafe behaviours play a great role in building positive safety culture. BBS is a pipeline connected between people on BBS concepts and actions. Any disconnect is potentially an incident creating antecedent.

Proper planning and involvement of workers in the assessment of psychosocial risks can optimise working conditions through preventive measures, for creating benefits for workmen and employers (EFBWW, 2019). Employee assistance support program need to be developed for all employees top to bottom as a planned intervention. Every employee must be trained on making a compliments round daily just for 5 minutes for observing and complimenting their colleagues for their best or safe behaviours which is observable. Then they can continue extending conversation to talking about their own physical or mental health, any issues that they are comfortable to talk about. This employee round would bring in lots of material for a positive psychosocial environment. The employees find a platform to talk about their anxieties, fears, stresses with their peers or mentors. Five minutes round daily per employee multiplied by a total number of employees makes it an organisational positive experience. A steering team of HODs can be formed to handhold this program to sustain it longer.

References

Assocham (2021, June 25). Webinar: Environmental, Social & Governance (ESG) Resilience. Retrieved on 04 July 2021. https://www.youtube.com/watch?v = PBMcTCvlt5w

Beck, D., Lenhardt, U. Consideration of psychosocial factors in workplace risk assessments: findings from a company survey in Germany. *Int Arch Occup Environ Health* 92: 435–451 (2019). https://doi.org/10.1007/s00420-019-01416-5

Continuity Central (2021, June, 08). New ISO standard on managing psychosocial risks in a work environment published. Retrieved on 29 June 2021. https://www.continuitycentral.com/index.php/news/erm-news/6339-new-iso-standard-on-managing-psychosocial-risks-in-a-work-environment-published

Crush, Peter (2021 January 20). Delving deeper into ISO 45003. Retrieved on 27 June 2021. https://www.ioshmagazine.com/2021/01/06/delving-deeper-iso-45003

Dubai PR Network (2021, June, 22). UAE First Country in the World to Obtain ISO Certification for Psychological Health and Safety at Work. Retrieved on 01 July 2021. http://www.dubaiprnetwork.com/pr.asp?pr = 153233

EFBWW (2019, March, 1). Psychosocial Risks in Construction. Retrieved on 02 July 2021. https://www.efbww.eu/publications-and-downloads / reports-and-studies/psychosocial-risks-in-construction / 227-a

Finbarrstapleton (2021, April 21). ISO 45003 – Risk Assessment for Psychological Hazards in the Workplace. Retrieved on 26 June 2021. https://antarisconsulting.com/iso-45003-risk-assessment-for-psychological-hazards-in-the-workplace/

Gomez-Valencia, Manuela & Gonzalez-Perez, Maria Alejandra & Gomez-Trujillo, Ana. (2021). The "Six Ws" of sustainable development risks. Business Strategy and the Environment. 10.1002/bse.2794.

Hurndall, Suzanne (2021, April, 29). A new standard for managing psychosocial risk. Retrieved on 27 June 2021. https:www. personneltoday.com / hr/a-new-standard-for-managing-psychosocial -risk/

ICMR (2021). Guidance Document for Psychosocial Counselling for COVID-19 Positive Patients and their Family Members. ICMR, New Delhi. Retrieved on 05 July 2021. https://www.icmr.gov.in/pdf/covid/ techdoc/PSC_COVID_patients_v1_30042021.pdf

ILO (2016). Work Related Stress: A Collective Challenge; International Labour Office: Geneva, Switzerland.

Jain, A.; Hassard, J.; Leka, S.; Di Tecco, C.; Iavicoli, S. The Role of Occupational Health Services in Psychosocial Risk Management and the Promotion of Mental Health and Well-Being at Work. *Int. J. Environ. Res. Public Health* 2021, 18: 3632. https://doi.org/10.3390/ ijerph18073632

Laboris Ius (2021, March, 2). Is mental health stressing out small and medium size enterprises? Retrieved on 01 July 2021. https://www.lexology.com/library/detail.aspx?g = 81d77a00-f6a3-494e-8d08-4b6c932b3b09

Mcd Phil (2021, May 24). Employers Face Urgent Need to Address Psychosocial Risks: ISO 45001 can help manage psychosocial risks in the workplace. Retrieved on 01 July 2021. https://www. nsc.org / safety-first / employers-face-urgent-need-to-address-psychosocial

Naden, Clare (2021, June, 8). Mental Health in the Workplace. Retrieved on 27 June 2021. https://www.iso.org/news/ref2677.html

Shrestha, Sunil. (2021). Occupational Hazards in Building Construction. SCITECH Nepal. 15. 16-21.

University of South Australia. (2021, June, 24). Companies who pay scant attention to workers' psychological health leave employees at higher risk of depression, research finds. Science Daily. Retrieved on 30 June 2021. https://www.sciencedaily.com/releases/2021/06/210623100300.htm

Weigl M., Müller A., Paramythelli A., Angerer P., Petru R, Checklist for psychosocial risk evaluation: a prospective evaluation study, *Occupational Medicine*, Volume 67, Issue 1, 1 January 2017, Pages 7–12, https://doi.org/10.1093/occmed/kqw151

Velocity EHS (2020, Oct, 13). How ISO 45001 Can Help Manage Psychosocial Risks in the Workplace. Retrieved on 30 June 2021. https://www.ehs.com / 2020 / 10 / how-iso-45001-can-help-manage-psychosocial-risks-in-the-workplace/

WHO (2010). Health Impact of Psychosocial Hazards at Work: An Overview; World Health Organization: Geneva, Switzerland.

Switch to a BBS culture for sustainable future of our businesses caring employees' safety right. Let's change the OSH scene together, as there's no retake for life lost at site.

CHAPTER 13

Behavioural Economics of Safety Culture Management in Companies

Introduction

Profits should not come at the cost of employees health and safety. Paul O'Neill knew that safety is not an expense but an opportunity to increase profit and productivity, reduce medical and compensation costs and improve the bottom line (Berthold, 2016). Benefits accruing from a safe work environment include reduction in lost employee hour, decrease in hospital costs, reduced sick leave, down-trend in pollution costs, low property damages, and significant reduction in insurance premiums which ultimately result in higher productivity (Ekenedo, 2013).

It is debated over the decades that the wilful violations of systems rules and procedures can be explained as non-adherence of some propositions of behavioural economics by the system designers and managers: first, unclear rules; second, the delayed or ambiguous feedback; and third, is the conflicts between high and low level safety commitments (Battmann and Klumb, 1993).

The theoretical framework of the safety culture is that it reflects the way people think and behave in relation to safety and a proactive mechanism to improving occupational safety by targeting the safety issues which is best achieved by focusing on the company's safety systems and their people's safe behaviours. There are multiple definitions on the safety culture (Vu & De Cieri, 2014). The American Petroleum Institute (2015) adopted that the existing safety culture is reflected in terms of the employees' perceptions, their attitudes toward organisational safety goals, their' daily safe behaviour; and the company's safety systems to support the safe behaviours (Cooper, 2018).

The Journal of Accounting and Economics found that U.S. companies managers facing market pressures to meet earnings expectations may risk the health and safety of workers to please investors (Smith, 2017). The ILO has adopted more than forty standards dealing with occupational safety and health, that provide tools for governments, employers and workers to establish practices to ensure maximum safety at work. Yet for millions of workers the reality is very different (ILO. 2021).

Behavioural economics is the study of how psychological, social, and emotional factors override economic value when companies or employers make decisions. Behavioural economics can help us reveal ways to control the organizational biases and cognitive limitations or ethically influence them to help drive the enterprise value (Deloitte, 2021).

According to a Chief General Manager of ONGC, the benefits of behavioural safety culture implementation in any company, small or big, would definitely outweigh the monetary gains of not implementing it. There is an increase in productivity and monetary gains of managing safe behaviour, and opposite is also true in case of occurrence of disasters due to unsafe way of working such as fire incidents, rail or road accident, family suffering, gas leak (Personal Communication).

The author provides insights to achieve an organisational safety culture excellence based on the research evidence and his field experience gathered over the past 36 years in different industrial sectors and countries. This paper explores the role of behavioural economics in safety management to make decisions more profitable by discussing possible issues on perception of at-risk behaviours.

Literature Review

Did you know that the International Labor Organization regards a safe working environment as a human right? Providing decent working conditions is also amongst one of the 17 Sustainable Development Goals (SDG). Economic benefits of health and safety management are huge, so much so that for every Euro invested in OSH, there is a return of €2.2 Euros (Tanya, 2021).

Does safety culture create a base to an economic value for an organisation? Researches over the past years indicate that it is 'money' of the behavioural economics that provide the answer, along with actionable insights for employers and policymakers as they negotiate between the safety management and profits (Jaggi, 2021). Insights from behavioural science helps understand how companies make financial decisions for health, safety and environment (HSE). Hence, behavioural economics is central to a firm's actions for implementation of long term safety culture (Dash, 2020).

Behavioural economics relates to the economic decision-making processes of individuals and institutions (Academy 4SC, 2021). Safety culture is about an organisation's values, beliefs, norms, practices, competencies and behaviours related to HSE. You can influence organisations via the people within them through organisational procedures (Drummond and Pietikainen 2021).

International research on the return on investments in prevention proves that every unit invested in safety and health generates a potential benefit of more than two units in positive economic effects. Improving safety and health in the enterprise does not necessarily mean to increase spending (DGUV, 2021).

The COVID-19 situation highlights the significance of balancing the economy with safety and health, considering the interdependencies between safety and micro-economics, for supporting this kind of decision-making in terms of cost-benefit analysis and cost-effectiveness analysis in safety culture management, and a little attention has been paid to these fundamental issues and the methodologies in behavioural safety economics (Chao, et al., 2021).

The COVID-19 pandemic has shown how vital occupational health and safety is for protecting employees' health, for the smooth functioning of our societies, and for the economic and social activities. The European Commission is renewing its commitment to update occupational safety and health rules by adopting the EU strategic framework on health and safety at work 2021-2027. It sets out the actions required to improve the workers' health and safety over the next few years (European Commission, 2021).

Objective of the research is to explore whether safety culture creates a base to an economic value for an organisation or why do companies fail to decide to spend basic expenditures for establishing safety culture? The present article is focused to explore various aspects of behavioural economics of safety culture management of companies, and formulate recommendations.

Research Methodology

Review of literature revealed that the behavioural economics of safety culture management is a relevant, critical and major concern for companies. In this direction, it is good idea to explore various learnings of field professionals especially during COVID-19 scenario when economic spending on safety is a real concern. Both primary data (interviews, discussions) and secondary data (incident and accident rates) were collected. Interviews based on open-ended questions and personal in-depth discussions with 309 HSE, medical, education, management, mental health professionals were conducted through remote data collection techniques over 2-month (during June-July 2021) from diverse locations and organisations in India. The sampling method used was a non-random convenience sampling. Participants were selected from the researcher's contact list, invited by WhatsApp, and email to complete the online survey. This is a concept building, innovative and exploratory paper at the behest and involvement of field professionals as being study participants.

Data Analysis

This study is part of an ongoing interdisciplinary intervention of behavioural science, management and industrial safety disciplines, and part of a national longitudinal action survey in India. Crucial element in this research was data collection conducted by means of controlled interviews and questionnaire surveys in these organizations. For this research a total of 500 people were approached out of which 309 completed an action field survey with the researcher. These research participants had been implementing behavioural safety culture at their work sites. The research participants included, the CEO, Directors, Managers, Heads of Departments, Safety Professionals belonging to the public and private industrial sectors, including chemicals, construction, gas, power and steel, across Indian locations. Their responses to questions related to behavioural economics and safety cultural aspects were collated and thematic data analysis was used to reflect on the findings. Ten themes were identified and discussed as the survey results. a list of themes.

List of ten themes that emerged from the qualitative data are discussed below:

- Perspective of safety culture management in industries
- Bleak future of businesses if they are not establishing longterm supportive safety culture
- It doesn't support zero-harm policy, if you don't measure at-risk behaviours
- Basic reasons that the Indian companies are not ready to spend on safety
- Increase in participation at bottom line can be linked to a good safety culture
- Prime challenge in implementation of behavioural safety culture program
- Positive safety culture management ensures that the businesses are making sustainable profits
- BBS culture is a business standard.
- Organisations who embrace behaviour safety approach, can ensure that no-one is injured
- Economics of behavioural safety culture implementation

Discussion

In order to avoid the expensive issues of incidents and accidents, it's time for a culture change. A safety-first culture is an emerging trend in several industries. It's critical decision-making on this unique moment in business (Brown, 2020). This paper provided below the myriad researched information on why to decide and how to implement a long term workplace safety culture that begins with employer health and safety education and the provision of safe, healthy work practices in the community, government and private industry workplaces.

The NATIONAL SAFETY DAY INDIA 2021 Campaign emphasised at renewing the commitment of employees and general public to work safely throughout the year (safetyrisk.net, 2021). The basic query remains for HSE professionals that the risks are everywhere, so how much safety is safe? Towards this, **Box 1** reveals the multi-pronged perspective of safety culture management in industries as described by the study participants.

BOX 1: Risks are everywhere. So how much safety is safe? 92% of study participants find that:

1. It's like for prosperity how much money is enough, It's relative.
2. It's an awareness of individual towards his life.
3. 100% as long as assurance of not causing any harm to any living creature.
4. How much safe is the existing safety system?
5. Safety to be adhered "as low as reasonably practicable" or as per the standards of specific requirement.
6. There is no limit for the betterment, so go with basic first.
7. Nothing less than 100 percent, it has to be always 100 percent.
8. More safety still falls short, No one should get injured.
9. If a person feel himself safe in all aspects and in all conditions, that will be optimal safety.
10. Sustainability and climate risk is way forward for safety which is achievable only through BBS which makes safe considering recent code Red for Humanity by UN
11. We can't be restricted with measurements. Safety is always alive and It should be 100%.

If companies or their HSE teams are not establishing longterm supportive safety culture at their sites, they seem to have a bleak future of businesses. Though a large number of companies believe in this, yet they do not appear to be acting accordingly. In this regard, it is interesting to understand that the features of companies that do not empower their workforce for performing safety implementation. These organisations are those that were low on the concept of psychological safety for their workforce. That were low on the values of human compassion and empathy. That were low on corporate social responsibility. That were low on corporate care as a core value. That were low on international business operations. That were low on leading indicators but high on lagging indicators. That were high on reactive, and dependent safety culture. That were low on independent and interdependent safety culture. That were low on their leadership safety consciousness. That were low on safety implications on business and employees. These findings provide us a framework for facilitating organisations on performing safety implementation by their workforce. According to ILO (2021b), managing safety and health is an integral part of managing a business to ensure that hazards and risks cannot cause harm to workers.

Further, nearly 84% of this study participants expressed that it doesn't support zero-harm policy, if you don't measure at-risk behaviours at site work areas. If you don't measure, you don't understand it well. Beware, it may give you surprise. Then the question arises, whether a BBS intervention is useful without its measurement aspect. The answer is yes, but it is useful in a limited way, and the risk control is not covered fully, as it is not understood without measurement. Implement a simple measurement system to effectively track the frequency of both safe and at-risk actions employees do during behavioural safety observations (Alcumuse Compliance, 2021).

People should not get injured as because employers do not have safety culture in their eyes or heart. Almost 90% of the study respondents felt that the basic reasons that the Indian companies are not ready to spend on safety are: the ignorance, cost, wrong regulation, misuse of regulation, workers reluctant behaviour. The behaviour and safety both are positively correlated, if one is reduced, other will fall vis-a-vis. If everyone will demonstrate safe behaviour, at all times, probably safety will automatically be taken care including technical safety aspects. If one does the Root Cause Analysis, the underlying cause of safety implementation, is the behaviour of people. Also the companies not willing to spend on safety is due to, the feeling and the perspective of being safe every time is not in their mind and heart. Entrepreneurs haven't been given any feel of being safe. ILO urges better policies to protect workers and businesses, as digital platforms proliferate (ILO, 2021c).

The study respondents (78%) also emphasised that in quantitative terms, increase in participation at bottom line can be linked to a good safety culture. Concept to understand is that risk is part of our daily life, but accidents need not be. This is why, precisely, the behavioural implementation is recommended in all world safety standards (Kaila, 2019). The National Safety Council estimated that work-related deaths and injuries cost the nation, employers, and individuals $151 billion in 2016. Employers that implement effective OSH management systems significantly reduce injuries and illnesses and reduce the costs associated with these injuries and illnesses (OSHA, 2021).

The prime challenge in implementation of behavioural safety culture program is the involvement of all employees including contract employees which can only be possible once fear from their minds be removed for carrying out spot-correction of at-risk behaviours on the shop floor. In other words, a buy-in by each employee is paramount for successful implementation. This can be demonstrated by head of the departments and other senior leadership team through their visible actions reinforcing safe behaviours and reducing at-risk behaviours (Cooper, 2020). It is pertinent to regularly review the BBS checklist for inclusion of new risks such as road safety, COVID-19 appropriate behaviours and emotional health care. Employees should be encouraged for openly reporting of at-risk behaviours without any fear with 'No Blame, No Fault, No Name' way with prime objective of on-the-spot behaviour correction to reduce the risk of accident or incident as reported by 86% of the study respondents.

The principle of any positive safety culture management ensures that the businesses are making sustainable profits. Safety culture is sum of beliefs, attitudes and practices being followed in various activities of business. The 88% of study respondents perceived that a strong safety culture ensures everyone is empowered and feels responsible for safety and pursues it on daily basis by carrying out spot correction of at-risk behaviours without any fear with prime objective of Zero Harm to anyone. When an employee feels valued, listened to and truly cared for, his or her outlook towards the organization is different with high morale and full of positivity in all other aspects too. This puts onus on the senior management to create an environment in which employees feels comfortable speaking up when they see safety hazards or at-risk behaviours (Michie, 2020). Thus, making safety a way of life.

Management of psychosocial risks, promoting well-being at work and behaviour based safety (BBS) culture is a business standard (ISO45003, 2021). If implementing incorrectly, BBS approach can backfire negative experiences, like stopping or refreshing this program. The challenges of BBS culture have been addressed actively for gaining results as the experts feel that it really stood the test of time, almost 50 years, dealing with critical at-risk behaviours, implementing it correctly. Managing behavioural safety can directly increase productivity and can foster better employees engagement which are the indirect benefits as reported by 77% of the study respondents. Numerous case studies exist revealing the positive relationship between safety and productivity, which can be applied to any aspect of safety for justifying investments to reduce the probability and severity of accidents, and logically address questions such as: how do the managers convince the plant manager to spend money from the annual budget for safety improvements? How does the plant manager influences their corporate to prioritize safety improvements? (Swinderman, 2018).

The study participants (89%) also expressed that it has been proven that organisations who implement behaviour safety approach, ensure that no-one is injured. By taking their health and safety to a different level they are able to add a real value into the organisation. But many who start the behavioural safety journey do not complete it, due to inadequate program structure, insufficient training or as the processes becoming too routine. Implementation of a safe culture comes not only with a change in behaviour but also with a change in the mindset. Krishna Rao, a veteran safety professional stated that advertising safety has become like role modelling. For every award won for excellence in safety is only a step towards excellence in safety, but winning it just a year will not reflect good safety systems rather maintaining it throughout and improving continually shall be the Goal of Zero Harm (Forum of Behavioural Safety, 2020).

Economics of behavioural safety culture implementation in companies is expressed by 82% of the study participants in terms of:

(*a*) Unsafe way of working will lead to disaster. Any disaster is beyond economic valuation.

(*b*) Road accidents.

(*c*) Rail accidents.

(*d*) Family suffering.

(*e*) Impact on new generations.

(*f*) Most of fire incidents, gas leakage of Bhopal tragedy.

Managerial Implications

COVID-19 has deeply challenged the Occupational Safety and Health Administration adhering to the basic foundational health, safety, and environmental requirements. So far the industry prioritized the health and safety of its workers, now companies are focusing on their expectations as well (Duane, et al., 2020). Supportive Safety Culture is one of the essential pillars for building a progressive and sustainable organisation. Every individual's own behaviours as safety ambassadors, collaboration and engagement with all levels, encouragement, rewards and recognition for right safety behaviours make a big contribution towards developing and implementing a long term safety culture. To embed a sustainable safety culture, companies must overcome the mind-sets that underlie unsafe behaviours (Hortense et al., 2019).

According to the Lorraine M. Martin, the President and CEO of NSC, “Business leaders must support safety now more than ever, I appreciate your constant dedication to safety” (National Safety Council, 2021). A second of risk is sufficient for an incident, or a second of human care is sufficient for spot-correction of that risk. You may choose, or lose, be quick in deciding. A one-minute message of the MD/CEO must go to employees each month on the relevance of 5-minute daily 'at-risk behaviours' observation care for spot-correction' by each employee. It helps pushing longterm safety culture at site.

Culture is the key Driver. If a person has a positive attitude and a good culture in the organisation, then it's easy to implement any policy or new thought. We need to work a lot in this regard. There is a strong hope of establishing principles of long term behavioural safety culture by the industry leaders. Their will and sustained actions, in this regard, can surely control incidents and the related loss of lives and the business. Economics and Country Risk insights and analysis provide a clear 360 degree perspective on what concerns most to the businesses allowing to bring opportunities and risks into focus, as global economic growth rests largely on COVID-19 vaccination progress reflecting safety behaviours of all involved (Johnson, 2021).

Measuring BBS Cultural System Efficiency as Core Value of Corporates based on 25 Points: GAIL advisor S. P. Garg, stated that now "Safety" is considered as one of the core values of organisations. "Behaviour" is getting more attention, as it plays important role in developing organisations culture. Safe behaviour and attitude can help come out of the "chalta hai culture". This index score of measuring BBS system efficiency as a core value of corporates, indicate how much organisational time is spent on safety functions to build safety culture, not how much money is spent. Surprisingly, Safety time of an organisation is one of the best leading indicator in developing sustainable safety culture, not the safety budget. Hence if your score on the index below is increasing, it means clearly that safety is a core value and everyone at work cares for safety behaviour of each other around. Planned intervention of behaviour-based safety (BBS) helps organisations improve their safety time arithmetic (Kaila, 2020).

(25 points x 4 marks each = 100) (Please give your score very frankly to each item below)

Assign marks between 1 to 4 to each item below as per your own assessment.

1. What is the percentage of shop-floor people doing BBS observations daily for five minutes?
2. What is the percentage of contractors/security staff doing BBS observations daily for five minutes?
3. What is the percentage of managers doing BBS observations daily for five minutes?
4. Is Cultural change from 1st (reactive) to 4th (interdependent) level taking place?
5. Is BBS a part of your EHS policy and annual review?
6. Are observers/departments being recognised /rewarded?
7. What is the percentage of incidents reduction after implementing BBS?
8. Is BBS Goal-setting each month by HODs to down the level happening?

9. Is BBS a part of KPI for departments?
10. What is the percentage of at-risk behaviours overall at each site?
11. Has BBS been included in vendors T&C?
12. Is BBS seen as a business value by top management?
13. Are all barriers in HSE management being spot-corrected by managers?
14. Are top process hazards being corrected?
15. How far business heads involve in BBS?
16. Has BBS been extended to families/ residential colonies/ communities?
17. Has BBS been extended to surrounding schools/ industrial associations?
18. Has BBS been extended to road safety?
19. Has BBS been extended to COVID-19 observations?
20. Has BBS been extended to psychosocial risks as per ISO45003?
21. Has the culture of spot-correction become a way of work life?
22. Has BBS become a big brother safety approach by all?
23. Has HODs become role model for BBS?
24. Has reactive safety culture gone away?
25. Do juniors observe and spot-correct seniors for BBS?

Scoring:

(*a*) You total score out of 100:

(*b*) Your weak areas with less score for improvement:

(*c*) Your strong areas to sustain BBS:

Fortunately, it is still the 'total time spent on safety by each member in an organisation by way of daily observations and spot-correction of at-risk behaviours', is the "Best Leading Indicator", and not how much money is spent on safety. Hence what really matters is not merely economics but the social sciences approach of safety culture management. But the critical question is, are companies ready to organise for this safety time? Largely, no, as time is money for most companies. They think of only minimum to minimum safety implementation. Thus, economics tend to override safety as the leaders' sensitivity towards humanity remains low. Employees, employers, managements, and all need to understand that without total safety culture, there would be no enterprise's survival in future times to come. Though the safety training implementation in low and middle income enterprises is difficult, yet it is possible to facilitate it through the team-based internal mentors and coaches (Penkunas et al., 2021).

In overall, Indian companies do not seem to be realising that spending on safety is an investment not expenditure, which deserves a national level debate in public interest. Also, Nature is the mightiest teacher, the world could ever have in support of safety, health and environment, like COVID-19. The same seems true for industry, if leaders fail in their HSE duties to inculcate safety culture for their workforces and workplaces, incidents teach in a harder way. Avoiding to create a proactive workplace safety culture is sure to result in heavy costs down the road (Lombardo, 2020).

Finally, to deal more effectively with various aspects of the behavioural economics of safety culture management of companies, the summary of findings recommend to address the list of following 20 issues mentioned in **Box 2**.

BOX 2: Behavioural Economics Aspects of safety culture management in companies to consider

1. Unsafe way of working will lead to disaster. Safety culture is a business imperative.
2. Reasons that companies do not spend on safety are: ignorance, cost, and misuse of regulations.
3. Increase in participation at bottom line can be linked to a good safety culture.
4. Organisations that implement behaviour safety approach, can ensure that no one is injured or made ill through their work.
5. Applying behavioural approach, for safe business operations, industries have to decide, safety first or behaviour first, choose or lose.
6. Behavioural safety culture is a tool which can be successfully used to mitigate risks.
7. Extend behavioural safety culture program to employees families and other key stakeholders.
8. Annual Behavioural Safety Culture Reviews are must. Culture is the key Driver.
9. Continually spreading the message of behavioural safety culture to keep the industry moving.
10. Supportive Safety Culture is an essential pillar for building a progressive and sustainable organisation.
11. Business leaders must support safety now more than ever.
12. Measure behavioural safety culture System Efficiency as a Core Value of Corporates.
13. Total time spent on safety by each member in an organisation by way of daily observations and spot-correction of at-risk behaviours is the Best Leading Indicator.
14. People need to reinforce about what is hazard and consequences.
15. In India money plays first, then human life. Life has no value.
16. HSE is shown case ornaments for the corporate.
17. Top management people are not aware about safety. They are only trained to do the business.
18. There is no minister at the Centre and State to monitor the implementation.
19. Safety should be a compulsory subject in the primary school to 12th class.
20. Companies are not realising that spending on safety is an investment not expenditure.

Conclusion

In the past 15 months, we all have witnessed direct and indirect pandemic effect jeopardizing many lives with its devastating and painful impacts. It is important to note that Covid appropriate behaviour was a key in controlling the spread of pandemic. However due to lack of awareness among majority of the urban and sub-urban communities, the spread was uncontrollable beyond anyone's imagination. Unsafe behaviours could be one of the reasons for wide spread of infection even to rural areas during the second wave. This could have been avoided or the extent of damage would have been reduced if people would have behaved responsibly following various Covid appropriate behaviours to mitigate its impacts (Nature Human Behaviour, 2020). Applying behavioural approach for safe business operations, industries have to decide, safety first or behaviour first, choose or lose.

A strong safety culture begins with visible management's commitment and highly engaged and empowered employees at all levels. This results in happy stakeholders due to reduced costs, increased plant reliability, reduced maintenance and better product quality besides benefits of motivated employees and happy customers making it more sustainable and profitable business. The 81% of study participants also stated that behavioural safety culture is a tool which can be successfully used to mitigate risks arising out of occupational health and safety as well as process safety. This behavioural science approach is currently being applied successfully in numerous companies worldwide (Geller, 2001).

Furthermore, there is need to extend behavioural safety culture program to employees families and other key stakeholders of our society especially children and youngsters. This could only be achieved through intervention of educational institutions and public forums raising awareness on behavioural safety culture to make it a way of life. One could imagine huge benefits of reducing road accidents; controlling pandemic and reducing industrial accidents etc. which ultimately would help in creating a happy society. Emily, et al., (2021) cautioned that unless efforts are made to understand and change the cultural drivers and share these findings within and across industries, the similar incidents are likely to continue to occur.

Occupational health and safety (OSH) management can and should be viewed in monetary terms as part of a business system (Eastern Kentucky University, 2021). Some challenges or questions on safety culture economics are:

- Visible or lack of management support;
- Leaders don't walk their talks at the site;
- Convincing the unit level management why BBS is important for company's business;
- Too much emphasis on at-risk behaviours, not talking safe behaviours. Positive reinforcement or appreciating safe behaviours is many times more effective than merely taking unsafe behaviours towards building longterm safety cultures;
- Receptive or resistant employees
- Observations data being shown to all employees to make impact to continue observations
- Barriers to safety, resources, engineering solutions to be addressed, otherwise people understand that BBS is only about talking and not taking actions on the ground

- Focus on 3 or 4 percent of negative people also who don't cooperate as well as positive majority of employees;
- Disciplinary action is important if somebody does deliberate violations. Enforcement and reinforcement go together. BBS does not replace other safety systems, rather integrate it all.
- Focus on first positive reinforcements for majority of workforce, and enforcement on small number of employees. Reinforcement of positive behaviour pays back better than focusing on at-risk ones.
- it helps impacting cultural change quickly in 6 months, sustaining BBS culture would take 3-4 years.
- BBS tool is good, depends upon the user companies for its success, as 50% have implemented incorrectly.
- It takes time to change negative or resisting people for their involvement. Good to see the reasons why they resisted.
- Functioning of steering teams without involving CEO of the organisations;
- Making BBS an HODs function.
- Emphasising quality of BBS observations
- Linking with KRA of every employee
- Including BBS in vendor terms and conditions
- When monthly BBS review is not regular and feebly conducted by HODs without much involvement, the BBS culture weakens by itself ignoring at-risk behaviours, followed by sudden incidents impacting business and lives. "You May Need To Care"
- Behaviour change is a buzzword every where now. Even driving ESG in businesses requires behaviour change among business leaders setting ESG goals as business goals for a profitable business.

Annual Safety Culture Reviews are crucial for continuous development; these are often not addressed actively by managers. Importantly, change in hierarchy of safety controls at sites is very important; this also is not emphasized so much by HODs. Most important, 5-minutes of safety-time each day each employee, to be fixed as a SOP, plays a significant role in developing good safety culture. Performance reviews must be used as part of safety culture for maintaining a safe work environment (Hestbak, 2019).

As per President of the chemical plants, Focus on continually spreading the message of behavioural safety culture to keep the industry moving. There is nothing more precious than human life. In the industry, if we truly believe in the adage of Safety First, it has to become a daily ritual with empathy, consideration, alertness and anticipation. To ensure observations and spot-corrections for Zero unsafe behaviour, these are the crystallized learnings that has been imparting with a BBS missionary zeal, impacting all the practitioners in the industry continually raising the bar of safety. Whether a fire accident or a national disaster, behavioural safety culture has enriched lives by proactive prevention (Personal Communication, 2021). It's truly a noble initiative towards the safety of industry and people working there. Organisational antecedents are a kind of prop which works as a support route in weakening the existing safety culture. There should be only a Go or No-Go treatment in behaviour at the workplace. The No-Go gate should bear a penal action depending upon the potential of violations. Leaning on antecedents in explaining an at-risk behaviour allows build up of probabilities for a serious consequences.

Developing an interdependent safety culture is be on the agenda for forward looking organizations to ensure a long term business sustainability. An organisations' culture is best indicated by the way their workforce behaves when they're away from the workplace. A shared vision of the people of a Zero Harm future would be the bedrock of a safety culture, reflected by the safety beliefs, values, attitudes and reflecting in everyday behaviour. It is important to motivate and engage employees to pursue the behaviours that contribute toward a strong HSE culture (Scace, 2018).

Scope of Future Research

It's important to remember that poor workplace safety and health costs money. Good OSH is good for business (EU-OSHA, 2021). The industry craves for the social wellbeing. Safety is the core value in the industries of the developed nations. There has been dramatic changes in the benchmarking of the safety statistics from all the developed nations. Similarly, environmental standards are implemented as a disciplinary benchmarks. Now due to spread of pandemic COVID-19, OSH standards have been dramatically improved. but Safety is way beyond. It is still starving for the benchmarking excellence. The root cause of every injury caused by incident is behaviour. The fraternity must find metrics to measure the behavioural changes and improvements. This has a cascading effect on environmental health also (Chao, et al., 2021). It would be critical to understand the changes in the work conditions, and decide on the corporate practices for safety, health and wellbeing (Glorian, et al., 2021). Anticipate, prepare and invest now in resilient occupational safety and health systems (ILO, 2021a). Understanding the top risks in the workplace is the first step in better protecting employees and the bottom line (Liberty Mutual Insurance, 2021).

References

Academy 4SC (2021). Introduction to Behaviours al Economics: Acting Irrationally. Retrieved on 26 July 2021 from https:// academy4sc.org / video / introduction-to-behaviours al-economics-acting-irrationally/

Alcumus eCompliance (2021). 8 Steps to Building a Successful Behavior Based Safety Program. Retrieved on 12 August 2021 from https://www.ecompliance.com/blog/behavior-based-safety-success/

American Petroleum Institute (2015). Pipeline safety management systems standard (ANSI/API RP 1173).

Battmann, Wolfgang & Klumb, Petra. (1993). Behavioural economics and compliance with safety regulations. Safety Science. 16. 35-46. 10.1016/0925-7535(93)90005-X.

Berthold, Janice (2016, Nov 04). Profits Should Not Come at the Cost of Workplace Safety. Retrieved on 15 August 2021 from https://www.industryweek.com/operations/safety/article/21992214/profits-should-not-come-at-the-cost-of-workplace-safety

Brown, Alex (2020). Two Vital Elements of a Safety-First Workplace Culture. Retrieved on 12 August 2021 from https://www. supplychainbrain.com / blogs / 1-think-tank / post / 32165-safety-culture-in-the-supply-chain-getting-back-to-basics

Chao Chen, Genserik Reniers, Nima Khakzad, & Ming Yang (2021). Operational safety economics: Foundations, current approaches and paths for future research, Safety Science, Volume 141, 105326, ISSN 0925-7535. https://doi.org/10.1016/j.ssci.2021.105326.

Cooper, D. (2020). Faces of EHS: Talks Behavioral Safety and Managing COVID-19. Retrieved on 14 August 2021 from https://ehsdailyadvisor.blr.com / 2020 / 03 / faces-of-ehs-dominic-cooper-talks-behavioral-psychology-and-managing-covid-19/

Cooper, M.D. (2018). The Safety Culture Construct: Theory and Practice. In: Gilbert C., Journé B., Laroche H., Bieder C. (eds)

Safety Cultures, Safety Models. SpringerBriefs in Applied Sciences and Technology. Springer, Cham. https://doi.org/10.1007/978-3-319-95129-4_5

Dash, Sanket Sunand (2020, December 20). Behavioural Economics: A New Driver of Strategic HRM. NHRD Network Journal, Volume: 14 issue: 2, 206-215. https://doi.org/10.1177/2631454120977240

Deloitte (2021). Behaviours al economics and management. Retrieved on 29 July 2021 from https://www2.deloitte.com / us / en / insights / focus / behaviours al-economics.html

DGUV (2021). About Vision Zero. Retrieved on 29 July 2021 from https://www.vz-rsi.in/about

Drummond, James, and Pietikainen Anna (2021). How behavioural science can promote safety culture. Retrieved on 27 July 2021 from https://apolitical.co / solution-articles / en / how-behavioural-science-can-promote-safety-culture.

Duane Dickson, Noemie Tilghman, Tom Bonny, Kate Hardin, Anshu Mittal (2020, October, 05). The future of work in oil, gas and chemicals. Retrieved on 15 August 2021 from https://www2.deloitte.com/us/en/insights/industry/oil-and-gas/future-of-work-oil-and-gas-chemicals.html

Eastern Kentucky University (2021). The Economic Aspect of Health and Safety. Retrieved on 30 July 2021 from https://safetymanagement.eku.edu/blog / the-economic-aspect-of-health-and-safety/

Ekenedo, Golda (2013). Framework for developing and sustaining safety culture in a developing economy. European Journal of Applied Sciences. 1. 28 -37.

Emily J. Tetzlaff, Katie A. Goggins, Ann L. Pegoraro, Sandra C. Dorman, Vic Pakalnis, & Tammy R. Eger (2021). Safety Culture: A Retrospective Analysis of Occupational Health and Safety Mining Reports. Safety and Health at Work, Volume 12, Issue 2, 201-208, https://doi.org/10.1016/j.shaw.2020.12.001.

European Commission (2021). Occupational safety and health in a changing world of work. Retrieved on 11 August 2021 from https://ec.europa.eu/commission/presscorner/detail/en/ip_21_3170

EU-OSHA (2021). Good OSH is good for business. Retrieved on 15 August 2021 from https://osha.europa.eu/en/themes/good-osh-is-good-for-business

Forum of Behavioural Safety (2020). Souvenir of 4th National BBS Conference held at Scope complex, New Delhi on 17th January 2020. www.besafe.org.in

GELLER, E. SCOTT (2001). Behavior-based safety in industry: Realizing the large-scale potential of psychology to promote human welfare. Applied & Preventive Psychology 10:87-105 (2001). DOI: 10.1017.S0962184902010028

Glorian Sorensen, Jack T. Dennerlein, Susan E. Peters, Erika L. Sabbath, Erin L. Kelly, & Gregory R. Wagner (2021). The future of research on work, safety, health and wellbeing: A guiding conceptual framework, Social Science & Medicine, Volume 269.

ISO 45003 (2021). Occupational health and safety management - Psychological health and safety at work - Guidelines for managing psychosocial risks. Retrieved on 15 August 2021 from https://www.iso.org/obp/ui/#iso:std:iso:45003:ed-1:v1:en

Jaggi, Gautam (2021, Mar 23). How behaviours al economics can enable a safe return to work. Retrieved on 28 July 2021 from https://www.ey.com / en_in / megatrends / how-behaviours al-economics-can-enable-a-safe-return-to-work

Johnson, Sara (2021, July, 26). Global economic growth depends increasingly on COVID-19 vaccination progress. Retrieved on 29 July 2021 from https://ihsmarkit.com/research-analysis/global-economic-growth-depends-COVID19 -vaccine.html

Hestbak, Brad (2019 September 11). How can performance reviews be used as part of safety culture and maintaining a safe work environment? Retrieved on 30 July 2021 from https://www. safeopedia.com/ how-can-performance-reviews-be-used-as-part-of-safety-culture-and-maintaining-a-safe-work-environment/7/8088

Hortense de la Boutetiè re, Jean-Benoît Gré goire Rousseau, & Eion Turnbull (2019, May 21). Overcoming limiting mind-sets to improve safety. Retrieved on 25 July 2021 from https://www.mckinsey.com / business-functions / organization / our-insights/overcoming-limiting-mind-sets-to-improve-safety#

ILO (2021). International Labour Standards on Occupational Safety and Health. Retrieved on 28 July 2021 from https://www.ilo.org/global/ standards / subjects-covered-by-international-labour-standards / occupational-safety-and-health/lang--en/index.htm

ILO (2021a). World Day for Safety and Health at Work 2021. Retrieved on 11 August 2021 from https://www.ilo.org/global/topics/safety-and-health-at-work/events-training / events-meetings / safeday2021 / lang--en/index.htm

ILO (2021b). How can occupational safety and health be managed? Retrieved on 14 August 2021 from https://www.ilo.org/global/topics/ labour-administration-inspection / resources-library / publications / guide-for-labour-inspectors / how-can-osh-be-managed / lang—en / index.htm

ILO (2021c, February, 23). ILO urges better policies to protect workers, businesses, as digital platforms proliferate. Retrieved on 14 August 2021 from https://news.un.org/en/story/2021/04/1089962

Kaila, H. (2019). Behaviour Based Safety for Corporates: A Shift toward an Interdependent Safety Culture https://worldsafety.org/wso-world-safety-journal/

Kaila, Harbans Lal (2020). Planned Intervention of Behaviour-Based Safety (BBS) Helps organisations Improve their Safety Time Arithmetic. WSJ, Vol-XXIX No-3, 34–41.

Liberty Mutual Insurance (2021, July 21). 2021 Liberty Mutual Insurance Workplace Safety Index Helps Companies Better Protect Employees and Control Costs as the Economy Continues to Reopen. Retrieved on 15 August 2021 from https://www. libertymutualgroup.com/about-lm/news/articles/2021-liberty-mutual-insurance - workplace-safety-index-helps-companies-better-protect-employees-and-control-costs-economy-continues-reopen

Lombardo, Kevin (2020, Sep 24). How to Plan Your Safety Programming and Budget for 2021: Post-COVID Trends and Safety ROI. Retrieved on 15 August 2021 from https://dorncompanies.com / how-to-plan-your-safety-programming-and-budget-for-2021-post-covid-trends-and-safety-roi/

Michie, S. (2020). Behavioural strategies for reducing covid-19 transmission in the general population. Retrieved on 14 August 2021 from https://blogs.bmj.com / bmj / 2020 / 03 / 03 / behavioural-strategies - for - reducing - covid-19 - transmission - in - the - general-population/

National Safety Council (2021). Perspective: Safety Leadership. Retrieved on 28 July 2021 from https://www.nsc.org / workplace / safety-topics/coronavirus/a-letter-from-our-ceo

Nature Human Behaviour (2020, May, 19). EDITORIAL. Retrieved on 29 July 2021 from https://www.nature.com/collections/gdjdibibfg/

OSHA (2021). Business Case for Safety and Health. Retrieved on 14 August 2021 from https://www.osha.gov/businesscase

Penkunas Michael J., Chong Shiau Yun, Rhule Emma L. M., Berdou Evangelia & Allotey Pascale (2021). Designing the next generation of implementation research training for learners in low- and middle-income countries. Globalization and Health, 17:63. https://doi.org/10.1186/s12992-021-00714-3

Safetyrisk.net (2021). NATIONAL SAFETY DAY IN INDIA 2021. Retrieved on 11 August 2021 from https://safetyrisk.net/national-safety-day-in-india/

Scace, Emily (2018, Sep 17). Safety Culture 2018: Seven Life Lessons from E. Scott Geller. Retrieved on 31 July 2021 from https://ehsdailyadvisor.blr.com / 2018/09/safety-culture-2018-seven-life-lessons-from-e-scott-geller/

Smith, Sandy (2017, May, 16). Are Injuries Still the 'Cost of Doing Business' at Some Companies? https://www.ehstoday.com/safety/article/21919024/are-injuries-still-the-cost-of-doing-business-at-some-companies

Swinderman, R. Todd (2018, October, 01).The Economics of Workplace Safety. Retrieved on 30 July 2021 from https://ohsonline.com / articles / 2018 / 10/01 / the-economics-of-workplace-safety.aspx

Tanya (2021). Economic benefits of health and safety management. Retrieved on 11 August 2021 from https://www.ecoonline.com/blog/economic-benefits-health-safety-management

Vu, T., & De Cieri, H. (2014). Safety culture and safety climate definitions suitable for a regulator: A systematic literature review (Research report 0414-060-R2C). Monash University.

At-risk behaviours at site are life threatening to employees and business threatening for employers. Its preventable with BBS culture.

APPENDIX 1

Assessment of Longterm BBS Cultural Efficiency as a Core Value of Corporates

(25 points x 4 marks each = 100)

(Please give your score very frankly to each item below)

Assign marks between 1 to 4 to each item below as per your own assessment.

1. What is the percentage of shop-floor people doing BBS observations daily for five minutes?
2. What is the percentage of contractors/security staff doing BBS observations daily for five minutes?
3. What is the percentage of managers doing BBS observations daily for five minutes?
4. Is Cultural change from 1st (reactive) to 4th (interdependent) level taking place?
5. Is BBS a part of your EHS policy and annual review?
6. Are observers/departments being recognised /rewarded?
7. What is the percentage of incidents reduction after implementing BBS?
8. Is BBS Goal-setting each month by HODs to down the level happening?
9. Is BBS a part of KPI for departments?
10. What is the percentage of at-risk behaviours overall at each site?
11. Has BBS been included in vendors T&C?
12. Is BBS seen as a business value by top management?
13. Are all barriers in HSE management being spot-corrected by managers?

14. Are top process hazards being corrected?
15. How far business heads involve in BBS?
16. Has BBS been extended to families/ residential colonies/ communities?
17. Has BBS been extended to surrounding schools/ industrial associations?
18. Has BBS been extended to road safety?
19. Has BBS been extended to COVID-19 observations?
20. Has BBS been extended to psychosocial risks as per ISO45003?
21. Has the culture of spot-correction become a way of work life?
22. Has BBS become a big brother safety approach by all?
23. Has HODs become role model for BBS?
24. Has reactive safety culture gone away?
25. Do juniors observe and spot-correct seniors for BBS?

    (a) You total score out of 100
    (b) Your weak areas with less score for improvement
    (c) Your strong areas to sustain BBS

APPENDIX 2

BBS Culture: Basic Learning Self-Assessment

(40 Q & A that cover all aspects of BBS implementation)

(Marked in **Bold** is an answer)

1. What is BBS?

(a) Bar bending schedule

(b) Bulletin Board System

(c) **Behaviour based safety**

2. What is BOFP?

(a) Behaviour observation feedback process

(b) Business Object Framework Processing

(c) Bureau of Fire Protection

3. What is Do-IT?

(a) **Define, observe, intervene and test**

(b) Define, observe, interest and test

(c) Develop, observe, intervention tool

Mark the following as True or False or Unsure

4. Feedback is to be given one on one, immediate, specific behaviour to be reinforced, appreciate safe behaviour to set example.

   True or False or Unsure

5. Use checklist for observation to focus on critical behaviours.

   True or False or Unsure

6. BBS is collecting observation data on specific behaviours by date, months and time.

   True or False or Unsure

7. BBS is "Safety for self and others".

   True or False or Unsure

8. BBS is not a top-driven but bottom-up approach.

   True or False or Unsure

9. BBS begins by briefing sessions for all those work areas and depts.

   True or False or Unsure

10. BBS believes that each employee can make a difference in organisational safety.

    True or False or Unsure

11. BBS believes that what gets measured gets done.

    True or False or Unsure

12. BBS is data driven decision-making process.

    True or False or Unsure

13. BBS is teamwork, its group dynamics.

    True or False or Unsure

14. BBS purpose is not to enforce safety rules, force change, gossip about others, reporting to boss.

    True or False or Unsure

15. BBS purpose is to identify safe and at-risk behaviours, identify opportunity for injury, communicating the risk, helping to identify safer solutions.

    True or False or Unsure

16. BBS is Company Wide and People Driven.

    True or False or Unsure

17. Behaviour is objective, definable, observable and measurable.

    True or False or Unsure

18. Employees are source of expertise of behavioural change.

    True or False or Unsure

19. BBS as ISO 45001 Compliance

    True or False or Unsure

20. BBS is applicable from workplace to anyplace.

    True or False or Unsure

21. Safety comes in seconds, not minutes; HENCE SPOT-CORRECTION OF AT-RISK BEHAVIOURS IS NEEDED BY OBSERVERS.

    True or False or Unsure

22. Behaviour is either totally safe or totally unsafe, It can't be half safe or unsafe.

    True or False or Unsure

23. Business excellence comes with safety excellence;

    True or False or Unsure

24. Safety excellence is not in documents but in maximising safe behaviours across sites;

    True or False or Unsure

25. Behavioural safety is an application of behavioural science;

    True or False or Unsure

26. Behavioural safety comes with humanistic behaviourism;

    True or False or Unsure

27. Behavioural safety implementation is a planned intervention;

    True or False or Unsure

28. All employees are trained as observers;

    True or False or Unsure

29. BBS brings safety cultural change; There is a difference in safety and safe behaviours drive.

    True or False or Unsure

30. Behavioural Change is measured and monitored.

    True or False or Unsure

31. Behavioural safety implementation is an observation and communication of risk;

    True or False or Unsure

32. Behavioural safety implementation is possibly sustainable with one top leader;

    True or False or Unsure

33. Behaviour is definable, observable, correctable, measurable, impenetrable;

    True or False or Unsure

34. Behavioural safety Observers are the backbone of interdependent safety culture:

    True or False or Unsure

35. Behavioural safety is to implement caring not scaring as a corporate value;

    True or False or Unsure

36. Behavioural safety is a corporate decision making not a journey;

    True or False or Unsure

37. Behavioural safety is an approach, not a name and blame or fault finding process;

    True or False or Unsure

38. Behavioural safety is part of KPA;

    True or False or Unsure

39. Behavioural safety Steering team meeting is important every month to review and reward the sites;

    True or False or Unsure

40. Finally, its also an ISO45001 Compliance, and the incidents reduction is possible on a sustained basis to save life and business.

    True or False or Unsure

Total marks (40 items x 2.5 marks each = 100)

BBS Culture Support Group

Please call on us for a brief Zoom meeting any time for resolving realtime BBS culture issues, the available BBS experts would assist. No fee for human safety.

Bharat Bane Surkshit.

KAILAHL@HOTMAIL.COM

We are learning from You!

ABOUT THE BOOK

This book raises a critical query on the longterm safety culture in corporates and communities along with a well researched practical solution embedded in proactive safety practices across the board in terms of psychological, social and behavioural safety pursuits for saving lives and economy from incidents.

Experts' messages to industry and contribution of professionals are a value addition and have enriched this manuscript for readers. The participation of a few hundreds of experts over an year in the making of this book contents is going to give some relishing take away for everyone to learn and practice in the field of our health, safety and environments.

The 13 chapters of this manuscript is a multifold perspective that reflects on the organisational antecedents for managers' silence over At-Risk Behaviours, reviews Behavioural Safety and Health Culture in India during the Covid-19 scenario, emphasises on the Educational institutions to focus 'Health and Safety' as Covid-19 reminded, tries to understands as to Why Industry is Losing Faith in Safety Awards, apprehends the Contribution of Civil Society toward Industrial Safety Culture, frames an outline of Active Humanism in Public Safety Behaviours to Defeat Covid19 and Restoring Economy as a Long-term Solution, Not Fire-fighting Approach. Also, the book highlights toward Managing the difference between safety documentations and at-risk behaviours in industry, brings forth Behavioural Benchmarking as a robust tool of total safety culture in Industries, underlines how a Planned Intervention of Behaviour-Based Safety Helps organisations Improve their Safety Time Arithmetic, looks at the Possibilities and Challenges of Making Safety a 'Way of Life' in Indian Society, and reminds how Mission Bharat Bane Surkshit is possible for Safer Corporate India through Behavioural Science Approach, and finally explores how to manage the Psychosocial Risks in Organisations as per ISO45003 as well as the behavioural economics of safety culture management in companies.

The anticipated readers will be: broadly the Industry and corporate professionals, the government as well non-governmental research and training Institutions involved in OHS and environment, educational settings, and the like. The focus and query of this manuscript is whether longterm safety culture possible, yes, the answer lies on these pages to follow, by continuously perusing the journey of total safe behaviours approach by all concerned, keeping the implementation simple and scientific for everyone.

The book promises a well referenced and an original communication straight from the grassroots.